THE
INTRODUCTORY
DISCOURSE AND LECTURES

DELIVERED IN BOSTON,

BEFORE THE

CONVENTION OF TEACHERS,

AND OTHER

FRIENDS OF EDUCATION,

ASSEMBLED TO FORM

THE

AMERICAN INSTITUTE OF INSTRUCTION.

AUGUST 1830.

PUBLISHED UNDER THE DIRECTION OF THE BOARD OF CENSORS.

BOSTON:
HILLIARD, GRAY, LITTLE AND WILKINS.

1831.

DISTRICT OF MASSACHUSETTS....TO WIT:
District Clerk's Office.

BE IT REMEMBERED, That on the third day of November, A. D. 1830, in the fiftyfifth year of the Independence of the United States of America, Hilliard, Gray, Little and Wilkins, of the said District, have deposited in this Office the Title of a Book, the right whereof they claim as Proprietors, in the words following, *to wit:*

'The Introductory Discourse and Lectures, delivered in Boston, before the Convention of Teachers, and other Friends of Education, assembled to form the American Institute of Instruction. August, 1830. Published under the Direction of the Board of Censors.'

In conformity to the Act of the Congress of the United States, entitled An Act for the encouragement of learning, by securing the copies of Maps, Charts and Books, to the Authors and Proprietors of such copies, during the times therein mentioned:' and also to an Act entitled 'An Act supplementary to an Act, entitled, an Act for the encouragement of learning, by securing the copies of Maps, Charts and Books to the Authors and Proprietors of such copies during the times therein mentioned; and extending the benefits thereof to the arts of designing, engraving, and etching historical and other prints.'

JOHN W. DAVIS, *Clerk of the District of Massachusetts.*

PREFACE.

On the 15th of March, 1830, a meeting of teachers and other friends of education was held at the Columbian Hall in Boston. It was continued by adjournment from day to day until the 19th, and occupied with statements relative to the condition and wants of schools, in different parts of the New England States. It was thought that advantages would arise from future meetings of a similar kind, and from the formation of a society of teachers.

A committee was accordingly chosen on the 18th, to prepare a constitution for such a society, and to take measures for a future meeting. E. Bailey, B. D. Emerson, A. Andrews, G. B. Emerson, and G. F. Thayer of Boston, H. K. Oliver of Salem, and J. Wilder of Watertown, were this committee.

The work assigned them was executed at several meetings of the committee, held in April, May and June. The sketch of a constitution was formed; and, in order that the convention, which might be assembled to take it into consideration, might be usefully occupied in the intervals of business, it was determined to invite gentlemen to give lectures before the convention, upon subjects of interest to the cause of education.

Such are the origin and occasion of the discourses which form the present volume.

The committee invited the lecturers, and suggested the subjects. Everything else was left entirely to the lecturers. Their opinions are their own. Perfect uniformity could not be expected from men who came from different and distant parts of the country, and who met for the first time at this convention. This free expression of opinions, independently formed, will not, certainly, be considered unfavorable to the eliciting of truth.

Agreeably to their instructions, the committee called a meeting, by invitations extensively circulated through the country, in the newspapers. The time of the summer holidays, the season of literary anniversaries, was thought most favorable to a general attendance.

The convention met on the 19th of August, in the Representatives' Hall, at Boston. It consisted of several hundred persons, most of them actual teachers, from at least eleven different States of the Union. It was organized by the choice of Wm. B. Calhoun of Springfield, as chairman, and Geo. B. Emerson and Dr J. W. M'Kean of Boston, as secretaries of the convention. In the subsequent absence of Mr Calhoun, W. Sullivan of Boston was called to the chair.

"The convention proceeded immediately to discuss the draught of a constitution which was reported by the committee. This discussion occupied a large portion of four days, and terminated in the unanimous adoption of the constitution which follows at the end of the volume. The chief alterations from the original draught are in the preamble, which was first offered in the convention, and in articles first and fourth. A less comprehensive and assuming name, '*The New England Association of Teachers*,' had been offered by the committee. But as several of the Middle, Southern and Western States, were represented in the convention, and many persons, not teachers, were desirous of belonging to the society which was to be formed, it became obviously proper to adopt a name which should exclude none.

The intervals of discussion were spent in listening to the discourses contained in this volume. They are offered to the public as contributions to the storehouse of facts from which the science of education is to be formed. They are the fruits of observation and experiment. It probably will not lessen the interest with which they will be read, to know that they were, without exception, prepared in moments of relaxation from the most exhausting occupations, at the season of the year least of all suited to literary labor.

No country, it has often been remarked, has so great an interest in the education of its citizens, as this. Not only private welfare and happiness, and the advancement of the arts and sciences, but the institutions of public justice, the privileges of civil and religious liberty, and our very existence as a free republic, depend on a high state of moral and intellectual culture.

The formation of the Institute, it is hoped, will do something towards elevating the standard and increasing the efficiency of popular instruction.

It will furnish the means, by the co-operation of its members, of obtaining an exact knowledge of the present condition of the schools, in all parts of the country. It will tend to render universal, so that it shall pervade every district and village, a strong conviction of the paramount national importance of preserving and extending the means of popular instruction; thus securing the aid of multitudes of fellow laborers in every portion of the country. It will tend to raise the standard of the qualifications of instructers, so that the business of teaching shall not be the last resort of dulness and indolence, but shall be considered, as it was in the days of republican Greece, an occupation worthy of the highest talents and ambition. It will hardly fail to show that education is a science, to be advanced, like every other science, by experiment; whose principles are to be fixed, and its capacities determined, by experiment; which is to be entered upon by men of a philosophical mind, and pursued with a philosophical spirit. It will be likely to bring forward the modes and objects of instruction in foreign nations and ancient times, and their applicability to the state of things among ourselves. It cannot fail to enlist openly, on the side of popular education, the highest intellect and influence in the nation. If it accomplish these, or any of these objects, it will amply reward the labors of all who have acted in its formation. And that it will have this *tendency*, the feelings of the teachers who attended the convention, may be appealed to, in proof. Great numbers of these had come hundreds of miles, some more than five hundred, to be present on this occasion.

Many a teacher, on the first morning of the convention, must have ascended the steps that lead to the Hall of Representatives, and looked out upon the unequalled prospect commanded by this chosen spot in the 'city of the pilgrims,' with a sense of loneliness, and of doubt and misgiving; but when he beheld the numbers that came flocking from near and distant parts, and saw the earnestness with which they were engaged in the good cause, and the ability evinced in conducting the business of the convention, every one must have gone home to his solitary duties, strengthened and cheered by the thought, that strong hands were in the work, and that he was no longer toiling alone.

CONTENTS.

INTRODUCTORY DISCOURSE.—By President Wayland.   page 1

Introduction, p. 3—subject of the discourse. The subject of education, and the manner in which it is to be obtained, 4.——I. *Object of Education*—We are placed under a system of law, including the idea of rewards and punishments; this system universal—invariable. All our happiness, therefore, must be the result of obedience, and our misery of disobedience to these laws. Hence, our business here is to know and obey them, 5—mind the instrument by which they are to be known and obeyed, but an useless instrument without cultivation, 6—the science which renders it useful is education, 6—the object of education to render mind the fittest possible instrument to know, apply, and obey the laws of its Creator—improvement in all these respects necessary to the good of the species—its practicability illustrated in discovery, invention, and obedience, 7—hence it is evident, that the nature of man needs such a science, and that the object which it has in view may be accomplished, 8—hence, first, this is a distinct science; second, its connexions are extensive; third, all other sciences depend upon it; fourth, its importance calls for talent in instructers, 9.——II. How shall this object be accomplished? 14—By cultivating the original powers of the mind, 16—But how shall this cultivation be given without neglecting the acquisition of knowledge? Ans. The faculties are cultivated by use, and the acquisition of knowledge, to be thorough, permanent, and made in the shortest time, must be by the use of all these very faculties. Hence, good teaching requires, first, that a pupil understand everything; second, review it; third, put it in practice, 17--remarks—first, text-books—their defects, 18—second, the objection, it matters not what we teach, considered, 19—third, the utility of the study of the classics, 21—conclusion, 23.

LECTURE I.

ON PHYSICAL EDUCATION.—By John C. Warren, M. D. - 25

Introduction, 27—culture of the physical faculties effected by unassisted nature, 27—evil effects of application on the health, 28—of females, 29—effects of action on the bodily frame, 30—discouraged by the prevalent systems of education, 31—effects of inaction upon the vertebral column, 31—consequences to other parts, 33—general causes of those derangements, 35—first, want of exercise, 36—formerly females less injured by application, because more employed in domestic duties—second, too great occupation of mind in study, and feelings and passions of a depressing nature, 37—cases of the influence of the mind on the body, 37—competition, 39—is there no substitute? 39—influence of reason, 40—immediate local causes of spinal distortion—bad postures of the body and limbs, 40—modes by which physical education may be improved, 41—exercise, 42—posture, while at study, 43—carriage of the body, 43—expanded chest; walking; dancing; the triangle, 44—battledoor; relaxation; recumbent posture; gymnasia—effects—used by the ancients, 45—how do the German literati preserve their health without exercise? first, by active habits when young; second, by temperate drinking; third, by abstemiousness, 47—importance of regulating food and drink, 47—pernicious fashions of dress; exposure of the chest; use of corsets and stays, 48—effects, 49—consumption; headache; insanity; death, 50—use of the cold bath; practice of reading aloud, 50—concluding caution upon sedentary pursuits, 51.

LECTURE II.

ON THE DEVELOPEMENT OF THE INTELLECTUAL FACULTIES, AND ON TEACHING GEOGRAPHY.—By JAMES G. CARTER. - - - - - - - - - - - - 53

Introduction and plan, 57—purpose of early instruction, to call forth and exercise the various faculties, 58—accumulation of facts, not education, 59—the person is best educated whose faculties, physical, intellectual and moral, are most perfectly developed, 60—gradual nature and great importance of this process, 61—use of the organs of sensation acquired by intercourse with the material world, 61—so it is with the intellectual faculties, 62—and the moral faculties, 62—prevailing system of instruction formed upon a mistaken principle in regard to the importance of the acquisition of knowledge, 63—a knowledge of the phenomena and principles of the infant mind essential to an accomplished instructer, 64—the temerity of inexperienced persons in entering a profession for which they are totally unfit, 65—study of the youthful mind difficult, 65—education a science, *note*, 66—his moral education is most perfect, whose feelings and habits are so formed that he need not change them when his reason decides upon their fitness to the end of his being, 68—general principles in education must be established by instruction, 69—the states and faculties of the infant mind have not been sufficiently analyzed, 70—the work is begun, 71—the senses to be trained, 72—importance of cultivating the perceptive powers, 73—which depend on attention, 74—opposite qualities of which are to be differently treated, 75—how the sluggish attention is to be excited, and the volatile rendered fixed, 76—it is essential to the cultivation of attention to excite the interest of the pupil, in order to which the sunny side of every subject should be presented, 78—sensible objects best suited to the infant mind, 79—the transition usually too sudden from these to abstractions, 81—on the study of geography, 82—mode of teaching by prepared questions examined, 83—printed questions better omitted, 84—maps, 85—badly arranged, 85—we should begin with what is known, and proceed to what is unknown, 86—mode of beginning to teach geography, 87—what is to be connected with it, 88—recitation on the blackboard, 89—historical facts to be associated with places, 90—use of this study as a discipline, 92—conclusion, 93.

LECTURE III.

ON THE INFANT SCHOOL SYSTEM.—By William Russell. 95

Importance of infant schools as means of general improvement—as the occasion of beneficial changes in modes of education, 97—origin of infant schools in England, 99—extent to which the system adopted in these schools may be transferred to the management of elementary schools in the United States, 101—objections to the common mode of conducting infant schools—instruction—poetry—music—pictures, 101—points of excellence in the infant school system, 103—importance of physical accommodation and comfort to the moral and intellectual influence of education, in cities—in the country, 105—moral management of elementary schools—evils of prevailing methods—advantages of those which are adopted in infant schools, 109—defects of the intellectual instruction attempted in infant schools—natural and appropriate instruction for infancy, 112—books for infant children, 115—qualifications of an elementary teacher, 115—chief requisite for the improvement of elementary schools, 117.

LECTURE IV.

ON THE SPELLING OF WORDS, AND A RATIONAL METHOD OF TEACHING THEIR MEANING.—By Gideon F. Thayer. 125

Necessity of correct spelling—from its importance to our understanding of written language—from the consequences of incorrectness—from its influence on the mental habits—from the indication which it affords of the state of literature—from its influence on the permanency of a language—from its influence on the estimation of a language in a national point of view, 126—methods of teaching orthography, 127—objections to common practices—advantage of selecting the exercise in spelling from the reading lesson, 128—importance of distinct articulation in dictating a spelling lesson—advantage of transcribing words 'missed' in spelling, 129—selection of words for exercises in spelling—comparative advantages of prescribing exercises in spelling from reading books, 130—suggestion of particular reading books, from which spelling lessons may be advantageously selected, 131—advantage of presenting all practical exercises in a visible form, 133—the attention to be paid to usage in modes of spelling, 136—methods of defining words, 138—moral explanations—practice—paraphrasing—synonymes—embodying definitions in sentences, 139—disadvantages of indiscriminate defining, 140—uses of a dictionary, 141.

LECTURE V.

ON LYCEUMS AND SOCIETIES FOR THE DIFFUSION OF USEFUL KNOWLEDGE.—BY NEHEMIAH CLEAVELAND. - 145

Circumstances which may be expected to render efforts for the diffusion of knowledge, highly successful in this country, 145—difficulties which exist here; the enterprise commenced notwithstanding them, 146—the design of these institutions not to make new discoveries, but to disseminate widely knowledge already possessed, 147—method of establishing a lyceum—introductory address, constitution, fee, managers, 148—experiment at Glasgow—Mr Brougham's testimony, 149—political and theological controversy to be excluded from lyceums, 150—lectures as a means of communicating knowledge in lyceums, 151—familiar discussions, class meetings, associations of teachers, 152—Mr Brougham's suggestion for artisans working in the same room—books, libraries, neighbourhood associations, 153—apparatus, its present cheapness, 154—branches of knowledge which are proper objects of attention for a lyceum; the physical sciences not to receive an undue share of attention, 155—history and geography, political economy, literature, poetry, 156—illustration and proof of the advantages of a general diffusion of knowledge, 157—practicability of the plans for accomplishing these objects, 158—Judge Williams' remarks, 159—conclusion, 160.

LECTURE VI.

A PRACTICAL METHOD OF TEACHING RHETORIC.—By Samuel P. Newman. - - - - - - - - - 161

Introduction, 163—advantages to be attained by the study of rhetoric, 163—first, how to give the student some acquaintance with the philosophy of rhetoric: attention should be directed to a few practical principles,—familiar, talking lectures, 164—second, cultivation of a literary taste, and, the exercise of the imagination, 165—cultivation of literary taste depends on a familiarity with the most finished productions, 166—ornaments of style, 167—exercise of the imagination, 168—rhetoric a suitable branch of female education, 169—third, skill in the use of language, 169—faults in construction, 170—fourth, skill in literary criticism, 170—what is meant by style, 171—familiarity with the best writers necessary, 171—genuine spirit of literary criticism, 172—fifth, the formation of style, 172—planning a subject, 173—use of translation, 173—mode of correction, 173—uses of the study depend much on the mode in which it is taught, 175—false impressions in regard to rhetoric: first, that its only object is the formation of style, 175—second, that its rules are restraints upon genius, 176—the just rules founded in nature, 177—many of the ancient rules inapplicable to modern languages and habits, 178—rhetoric has not to do with mere words, 178—qualifications of an instructer in rhetoric, 179—first, knowledge of intellectual philosophy; second, familiarity with the best writers; third, aptness to teach, 179—most suitable time for the study, 180—what relates to taste and skill in language should be learnt early; what requires maturity of mind late in the course, 180—answer to the objection that this mode of teaching renders it laborious, 181—nothing valuable to be obtained without labor, 181—conclusion, 182.

LECTURE VII.

ON GEOMETRY AND ALGEBRA.—By F. J. Grund. - - 183

Introduction, 185—importance and purposes of education, 185—reformers of education, 186—common errors of education, 187—premature developement of the memory, 187—self-education of men after leaving college, 188—impossibility of atoning in manhood for the want of an early education, 188—misconstruction of the term practical knowledge, 189—text-books, cursory treatises, &c., 189—errors into which they lead, 190—method of instruction, 191—Pestalozzi's method, 191—definition of education, 191—importance of mathematics, 191—their use in early instruction, 192—they facilitate every other study, 192—necessity of beginning the study of mathematics early, 193—difficulties which present themselves, 193—geometry adapted to the capacity of children, 193—method of teaching mathematics; difference between adults and young learners, 193—reasons why the mathematical method is to be acquired in childhood, 194—mathematics are almost the only branch taught in schools, which are not matter of memory, 195—necessity of studying mathematics for the common purposes of life, 195—difference between the acquirement of mathematics and other sciences, 195—they are a preventive against frivolous reading, 195—error committed in teaching algebra before geometry, 195—objects of geometry, 196—it is easier than arithmetic, 196—geometry being more indispensable to the draftsman, architect, mason, carpenter, &c. than algebra, 196—history of mathematics, 197—geometry cultivated by the ancients, 197—the six books of Diophantes, 197—the writings of the Arabians, 197—beginning of the study of algebra in the fifteenth century, 197—Francis Vieta the inventor of algebra, 197—invention of logarithms—Newton—Leibnitz, 197—Euclid's Elements preceded the study of algebra nearly twentythree centuries, 197—reasons for this difference, 198—errors committed in studying algebra, 198—the synthetic method, is that of instruction 198—method of teaching algebra and geometry, 198—errors in the common system of instruction, 199—text-books used, 199—mechanism of instruction, exhibitions, 199—in the schools of Pestalozzi, mathematics are a favorite study, 199—mode of teaching the first principles of geometry, 200—the mind of the pupil must be the principal operator, 200—pupils ought to be allowed to ask explanations, 200—queries ought to be substituted instead of propositions; the reason why, 200—suggestion of a useful plan of teaching geometry to a class of children, 200—order in which the different principles of geometry ought to follow each other, 201—errors committed by attempting to prove rigidly the theory of parallel lines, 201—impossibility of it, 201—Lagrange followed the example of Euclid, 201—another error committed in defining the circle as a polygon of an infinite number of sides, 202—method of teaching algebra, 202—difficulties met with in the study of algebra, 202—text-books commonly destitute of problems, 202—mechanism of English writers, 202—deficiencies of the French, 202—mode of supplying the deficiencies of both, 203—the problems of Meier Hirsch eminently calculated for the purpose, 203—the study of analytic geometry and the calculus, 203—books adapted to that purpose, 203—La Place's Méchanique Céleste translated by Dr Bowditch, 203—the American translation offering greater facilities than the original, 204—conclusion, 204.

LECTURE VIII.

ON THE MONITORIAL SYSTEM.—By Henry K. Oliver. - 205

Introduction, 205—advantages of the monitorial system of instruction, 207—first, provides for the tuition of a greater number, 210—second, economy of time, 210—third, every scholar is kept constantly employed, 212—school rendered less irksome to the scholars—fourth, the business of teaching made more interesting to the instructer, 214—defects of the monitorial system, 217—is productive of great noise and confusion, 217—monitors apt to be unfaithful, and not competent to the duties expected from them, 219—the teacher cannot be sufficiently well acquainted with the pupils, 222—tendency to produce superficial and inaccurate scholars, 222—how far the monitorial system may be adopted in common schools, 225—mode of applying it in certain exercises, 226—use of black-boards, 227—Boston schools, 228—conclusion, 230.

LECTURE IX.

ON VOCAL MUSIC.—By William C. Woodbridge.   231

Manner in which vocal music has been regarded in the United States,—in Europe,—objects to be aimed at, in order to effect a change, 233—measures for accomplishing these objects here, 234—the Morning Call, 235—emotion spontaneously expressed by the voice—music neglected in this country, 236—its revival desirable—the immediate object of music, 237—its ultimate objects; devotion, recreation, health, 238—favorable effect upon health in Germany; remark of Pres. Dwight, 239—the Garden; effect of music in a Swiss village, 240—effect of music in softening and elevating the character; Luther's remarks, 241—Plato—effect of music in promoting habits of order, obedience and union—music combined with words; its effect on national character, 242—The Rising Sun; occurrence at Hofwyl, 243—supposed necessity of a natural ear and voice, for music; causes of erroneous opinions on this subject, 244—the number of those who are disqualified by nature, exceedingly small, 245—testimony of Pfeiffer, and of other teachers; argument from the nature of the case, 246—effect of musical skill upon elocution, 247—opinions of distinguished men in Germany and Switzerland; Niemeyer, Schwartz, Denzel, 248—Harnisch, Fellenberg, Vehrli, Pfeiffer, Nageli, 249—ordinance of the Prussian government, 250—experiment in Hartford, Conn.—inductive system of instruction in music, 251—principles of this method, 252—manner in which these principles are applied, 253-254—conclusion, 255.

LECTURE X.

ON LINEAR DRAWING.—By Walter R. Johnson.   257

Introduction, 259—formation of a habit of accurate observation, with a view to obtain exact perceptions of things, 260—drawing favorable to this, 260—a means of improving the perceptive powers, 261—and through them the powers of the understanding, 262—direct utility of drawing, 262—in the arts and trades, 263—fine arts, 264—as an introduction to penmanship, 265—Rousseau's scheme of teaching the art, 266—Madame de Genlis', 267—series of lessons in drawing; first, geometrical lines with slate and pencil, 268—second, linear drawing, 269—third, exercises requiring an acquaintance with perspective; maps and charts; fourth, parts of animated objects, 270—fifth, drawing from nature, 270—sketches and shades, machines, landscapes, heads, 271—uses to professors in the sciences, 272—and classics, 272—drawing materials, 274—conclusion, 275.

LECTURE XI.

ON ARITHMETIC.—By Warren Colburn. - - - - 277

Introduction, 279—arithmetic an important study, 280---its practical utility---mental discipline---advantages of the old and new modes of teaching arithmetic compared, 281---best mode of teaching the new system---each teacher's peculiar mode the best for him, 283---general principles of instruction, 284---but one thing should be taught at a time, 285---illustration and application of this fundamental principle---in what way the teacher should help the scholar, 287---abstract and practical questions, 288---association of ideas, 292---scholars should be allowed to reason in their own way, 293---scholars should be required to tell how they solve questions, 294---hint to authors of school-books---recitations, 294---should be in classes---modern facilities for teaching of doubtful utility---business of teaching should be a distinct profession, 297.

LECTURE XII.

ON CLASSICAL LEARNING.—By Cornelius C. Felton. 299

Letter to the Censors, 304—introductory remarks, 305-6—objections to classical studies stated, 306—violent spirit of one class of opponents to classical studies, 307—importance of deciding the question on classical learning, 307—defence of philological studies in general, 308---arguments against them applicable to the departments of learning, 309---defence of classical languages, 310---first, necessity of Latin and Greek to the perfect understanding of English, 310-11---second, English literature closely connected with the classics, 312---perfection of Grecian taste---circumstance that forms it, 313---ancient languages more finished than others, 314---intellectual effort necessary to settle the meaning of difficult passages, a useful and practical exercise, 314---do. that of comprehending the entire worth of an ancient author, 314-15---useful effects of such knowledge on the mind and character, 315-16---imperfect mode of studying the classics among ourselves, 316---ancient literature valuable on general principles of literary taste---particularly Greek, 316-17---Schlegel's opinion of Homer, 317---value of Greek drama, 317-18---circumstances that formed the drama, 318---characteristics of the drama, 318-19---character of Æschylus, as exhibited in several of his dramatic poems, 319---analysis of the 'Prometheus Chained,' with extracts, 319-20-21---summary of the general characteristics of this poem, 321---general study of the drama desirable, 322---Greek philosophy---hasty decisions of the moderns, 322---character of Plato's mind,---as illustrated in several of his works, 322-23---character of Aristotle's mind, 323-24---character of Socrates, 324---practical use of Grecian oratory, 324---Demosthenes and Æschines' contest for the crown, 325---careful and repeated perusal necessary to the full comprehension of the power of Demosthenes' eloquence, 326---Wyttenbach's account of the effect which the study of Demosthenes had upon himself, 326---moral effects of classical studies, 327---remarks upon the supposed dangerous character of ancient mythology, 327---remarks upon the pernicious character of the popular literature of the day, 328---patriotic character of ancient literature, 328---classics free from the enfeebling sentiment that taints much of present literature, 329---indifference with which the classics have been of late regarded, 329---imperfection of classical education among us, 329---proper mode of reading classics, 330---futile character of late schemes to shorten the labor of acquiring ancient languages, 330---necessity of a change in classical education, 330-31---sketch of a classical teacher's duties and pursuits, 331---peculiar literary advantages of America, 331-32.

LECTURE XIII.

ON THE CONSTRUCTION AND FURNISHING OF SCHOOL-ROOMS, AND ON SCHOOL APPARATUS.—By William J. Adams. - - - - - - - - - - - 333

Introduction, 335---importance of school architecture, 336---location of a school-house, 337---play-ground, 337---ventilation, 338---warming, 338---sufficient space, 339---space in different schools, 340---windows, 340---inclined floor, an evil, 340---seats and desks, 342---school apparatus, 344---time-piece, maps and globes, black-board, 345---abacus, or numeral frame, 346---conclusion.

CONSTITUTION OF THE AMERICAN INSTITUTE OF INSTRUCTION, - - - - - - - - page 347

BY-LAWS, - - - - - - - - - - 350

OFFICERS, - - - - - - - - - - 351

PRESIDENT WAYLAND'S

INTRODUCTORY DISCOURSE.

INTRODUCTORY DISCOURSE,

BY

FRANCIS WAYLAND, Jr.

PRESIDENT OF BROWN UNIVERSITY.

In the long train of her joyous anniversaries, New England has yet beheld no one more illustrious than this. We have assembled to-day, not to proclaim how well our fathers have done, but to inquire how we may enable their sons to do better. We meet, not for the purposes of empty pageant, nor yet of national rejoicing; but to deliberate upon the most successful means for cultivating, to its highest perfection, that invaluable amount of intellect, which Divine Providence has committed to our hands. We have come up here to the city of the Pilgrims, to ask how we may render their children most worthy of their ancestors and most pleasing to their God. We meet to give to each other the right hand of fellowship in carrying forward this all-important work, and here to leave our professional pledge, that, if the succeeding generation do not act worthily, the guilt shall not rest upon those who are now the Instructers of New England.

Well am I aware that the occasion is worthy of the choicest effort of the highest talent in the land. Sincerely do I wish, that upon such talent the duty of addressing you this day had devolved. Much do I regret that sudden indisposition has deprived me of the time which had been set apart to meet the demands of the present occasion, and that I am only able to offer for your consideration such reflections as have been snatched from the most contracted leisure, and gleaned amid the hurried hours of languid convalescence. But I bring, as an offering to the cause of Education, a mind deeply penetrated with a conviction of its surpassing importance, and enthusiastically ardent in anticipating the glory of its ultimate results. I know, then, that I may liberally presume upon your candor, while I rise to address those, to very many of whom it were far more beseeming that I quietly and humbly listened.

The subject which I have chosen for our mutual improvement, is, *The object of intellectual education; and the manner in which that object is to be attained.*

I. It hath pleased Almighty God to place us under a constitution of universal law. By this we mean, that nothing, either in the physical, intellectual or moral world, is in any proper sense contingent. Every event is preceded by its regular antecedents, and followed by its regular consequents; and hence is formed that endless chain of cause and effect which binds together the innumerable changes which are taking place everywhere around us.

When we speak of this system as subjected to universal law, we mean all this; but this is not all that we mean. The term law, in a higher sense, is applied to beings endowed with conscience and will, and then there is attached to it the idea of rewards and punishments. It is then used to signify a constitution so arranged, that one course of action shall be inevitably productive of happiness, and another course shall be as inevitably productive of misery. Now, in this higher sense is it strictly and universally true, that we are placed under a constitution of law. Every action which we perform, is as truly amenable as inert matter, to the great principles of the government of the universe, and every action is chained to the consequences which the Creator has affixed to it, as unalterably as any sequence of cause and effect in physics. And thus, with equal eloquence and truth, the venerable Hooker has said, 'Of Law, here can be no less acknowledged, than that her seat is the bosom of God, her voice the harmony of the world; all things in heaven and earth do her homage, the very least as feeling her care, and the very greatest as not exempted from her power; both angels and men and creatures of what condition soever, though each in different sort and manner, yet all with uniform consent, admiring her as the mother of their peace and joy.'

Such a constitution having been established by a perfectly wise Creator, it may be easily supposed that it will remain unchangeable. His laws will not be altered, for our convenience. We may obey them or disobey them, we may see them or not see them, we may be wise or unwise, but they will be rigidly and unalterably enforced. Thus must it ever be, until we have the power to resist the strength of omnipotence.

Again; it is sufficiently evident that the very constitution which God has established, is, with infinite wisdom and benevolence, devised for just such a being, physical, intellectual, and moral, as man. By obedience to the laws of God, man may be as happy as his present state will allow. Misery is always the result of a violation of some of the laws which the Creator has established. Hence, our great business here, is, *to know and obey the laws of our Creator.*

That part of man by which we know, and, in the most important sense, obey the laws of the Creator, is called MIND. I use the word in its general sense, to signify, not merely a substance, not matter, capable of intellection, but one also capable of willing, and to which is attached the responsibility of right and wrong in human action. And, still further, it is one of the laws of mind, that increased power for the acquisition of knowledge, and a more universal disposition to obedience, may be the result of the action of one mind upon another, or, of the well-directed efforts of the individual mind itself.

Without some knowledge of the laws of nature, it is evident that man would immediately perish. But it is possible for him to have only so much knowledge of them as will barely keep generation after generation in existence, without either adding anything to the stock of intellectual acquisition, or subjecting to his use any of the various agents which a bountiful Providence has everywhere scattered around, for the supply of his wants and the relief of his necessities. Such was the case with the Aborigines of our country, and such had it been for centuries. Such, also, with but very few and insignificant exceptions, is the case in Mohammedan and Pagan countries. The sources of their happiness are few and intermitting—those of their misery multiplied and perpetual.

Looking upon such nations as these, we should involuntarily exclaim, What a waste of being, what a loss of happiness, do we behold! Here are intelligent creatures, placed under a constitution devised by Infinite Wisdom to promote their happiness. The very penalties which they suffer, are so many proofs of the divine goodness—mere monitions to direct them in the paths of obedience. And besides this, they are endowed with a mind perfectly formed to investigate and discover these laws, and to derive its highest pleasure from obeying them. Yet that mind, from want of culture, has become useless. It achieves no conquests. It removes no infelicities. Here, then, must the remedy be applied. This immaterial part must be excited to exertion, and must be trained to obedience. Just so soon as this process is commenced, a nation begins to emerge from the savage, and enter upon the civilized state. Just in proportion to the freedom and the energy with which the powers of the mind are developed, and the philosophical humility with which they are exercised, does a people advance in civilization. Just in proportion as a people is placed under contrary influences, is its movement retrograde.

The science which teaches us how to foster these energies of mind is the science of Education. In few words, I would say, *the object of the science of Education, is, to render mind the fittest possible instrument for* DISCOVERING, APPLYING, *or* OBEYING, *the laws under which God has placed the universe.*

That all this is necessary, in order to carry forward the

human species to the degree of happiness which it is destined, at some time or other, to attain, may be easily shown.

The laws of the universe must be *discovered*. Until they are discovered, we shall be continually violating them and suffering the penalty, without either possibility of rescue or hope of alleviation. Hence the multitude of bitter woes which ignorance inflicts upon a people. Hence the interest which every man should take in the progress of knowledge. Who can tell how countless are the infelicities which have been banished from the world, by the discovery of the simple law that a magnetized needle, when freely suspended, will point to the north and south!

Nor is it sufficient that a law be discovered. Its relations to other laws must be ascertained, and the means devised by which it may be made to answer the purposes of human want. This is called *application*, or *invention*. The law of the expansive power of steam was discovered by the Marquis of Worcester, in 1663. It remained, however, for the inventive power of Watt and Fulton, more than a century afterwards, to render it subservient to the happiness of man. From want of skill in a single branch of this department of mental labor, the human race has frequently been kept back for ages. The ancients, for instance, came very near the invention of the printing press. Thus has it been with several other of the most important inventions. It makes a thoughtful man sad, at the present day, to observe how many of the most important agents of nature we are obliged to expose to the gaze of lecture-rooms, without being able to reveal a single practical purpose for which they were created.

But this is not all. A man may know a law of his Creator, and understand its application; but if he do not *obey* it, he will neither reap the reward nor escape the penalty which the Creator has annexed to it. Here we enter, at once, into the mysterious region of human will, of motive and of conscience. To examine it at present is not my design. I will only remark, that some great improvement is necessary in this part of our nature, before we can ever reap the benefits of the present constitution of the universe. I do not think that any philosopher can escape the conviction, that when important truth is the subject of inquiry, we neither possess the candor of judgment, nor the humility of obedience, which befits the relations existing between a creature and his Creator. In proof of this, it is sufficient to refer to well known facts. Galileo suffered the vengeance of the Inquisition, for declaring the sun to be the centre of the planetary system! How slow were the learned in adopting the discoveries of Hervey or of Newton! Still more visible is this obstinacy, when the application of a moral law is clearly discovered. Though supported by incontrovertible argument, how slowly have the principles of religious toleration gained foothold even in the civilized world! After the slave trade had been proved contrary to every principle of reason and conscience, and at variance with every law of the Creator, for nearly twenty years did Clarkson and his associates labor, before they could obtain the act for its abolition. And to take an illustration nearer home,—how coolly do we look on and behold lands held by unquestionable charter from Almighty God, in defiance of an hundred treaties by which the faith of this country has been pledged—in violation of every acknowledged law, human and divine, wrested from a people, by whose forbearance, a century ago, our fathers were permitted to exist! I speak not the language of party. I eschew and abhor it; but 'I speak with the freedom of history, and I hope without offence.' These examples are at least sufficient to show us, that the mind of man is not, at present, the fittest instrument possible for obeying the laws of his Creator, and that there is need, therefore, of that science which shall teach him to become such an instrument.

The question which will next arise, is this:—Can these things be taught? Is it practicable, by any processes which man can devise, to render mind a fitter instrument for discovering, applying and obeying the laws of his Creator? We shall proceed, in the next place, to show that all this is practicable.

1. It is practicable to train the mind to greater skill in *discovery*. A few facts will render this sufficiently evident.

It will not be denied that some modes of thinking are better adapted to the discovery of truth than others. Those trains of thought which follow the order of cause and effect, premises and conclusion, or, in general, what is considered the order of the understanding, are surely more likely to result in discovery than those which follow the order of the casual relations, as of time, place, resemblance and contrast, or, as it is commonly called, the order of the imagination. Discovery is the fruit of patient thought, and not of impetuous combination. Now it must be evident that mind, directed in the train of the understanding, will be a far better instrument of discovery than if under the guidance of the imagination. And it is evident that the one mode of thinking may be as well cultivated as the other, or as any mode whatsoever. And hence has arisen the mighty effect which Bacon produced upon the world. He allured men from the weaving of day-dreams to the employment of their reason. Just in proportion as we acquire skill in the use of our reason, will be the progress of truth.

Again; there can be no doubt that, in consequence of the teaching of Bacon, or, in other words, in consequence of improvement in education, the human mind has, in fact, become a vastly more skilful instrument of discovery than ever it was before. In proof of this, I do not refer merely to the fact, that more power has been gained over the agents of nature, and that they have been made to yield a greater amount of human happiness to the human race, within the last one hundred years, than for ten times that period before. This, of itself, would be sufficient to show an abundant increase of intellectual activity. I would also refer to the fact that several of the most remarkable discoveries have been made by different men at the same time. This would seem to show, that mind in the aggregate was moving forward, and that everything with which we are now acquainted must soon have been discovered, even if it had eluded the sagacity of those who were fortunate enough to observe it. This shows that the power of discovery has already been in some degree increased by education. What has been so auspiciously begun, can surely be carried to far greater perfection.

Again; if we inquire what are those attributes of mind on which discovery mainly depends, I think we shall find them to be patient observation, acute discrimination, and cautious induction. Such were the intellectual traits of Newton, that prince of modern philosophers. Now it is evident that these attributes can be cultivated, as well as those of taste or imagination. Hence, it seems as evident that the mind may be trained to discovery, that is, that mind may be so disciplined as to be able to ascertain the particular laws of any individual substance, as that any other thing may be done.

2. By *application* or *invention*, I mean the contriving of those combinations by which the already discovered laws of the universe, may be rendered available to the happiness of man. It is possible to render the mind a fitter instrument for the accomplishment of this purpose.

In proof of this remark, I may refer you to the two first considerations to which I have just adverted; namely, that some trains of thought are more productive of invention than others, and that, by following those trains, greater progress has, within a few years, been made in invention, than within ten times that period before.

It is proper, however, to remark, that the qualities of mind on which invention depends, are somewhat dissimilar from those necessary to discovery. Invention depends upon accuracy of knowledge in detail, as well as in general, and a facility for seizing upon distant and frequently recondite relations. Discovery has more to do with the simple quality, invention with the complex connexions. Discovery views truth in the abstract; invention views it either in connexion with other truth, or in its relation to other beings. Hence has it so frequently taken place, that philosophers have been unable to avail themselves of their own discoveries; or, in other words, that the powers of discovery and of invention are so seldom combined in the same individual. In one thing, however, they agree. Both depend upon powers of mind capable of cultivation; and, therefore, both are susceptible of receiving benefit beyond any assignable degree, by the progress of education.

3. The mind may be rendered a fitter instrument for obeying the laws of the universe. This will be accomplished, when men, first, are better acquainted with the laws of the universe, and second, when they are better disposed to obey them. That both of these may be accomplished, scarcely needs confirmation.

For, first, I surely need not consume your time to prove, that a much greater amount of knowledge of the laws of the universe might be communicated in a specified time, than is communicated at present. Improvement in this respect depends upon two principles;—first, greater skill may be acquired in teaching; and second, the natural progress of the sciences is towards simplification. As they are improved, the more proximate relations of things are discovered, the media are rendered clearer, and the steps in the illustration of truth less numerous. As a man knows more of the laws of his Creator, he can surely obey them better.

And, secondly, those dispositions which oppose our meek and humble obedience, may be corrected. Candor may be made to take the place of prejudice, and envy may be exchanged for a generous ardor after truth. This a good teacher frequently accomplishes now. And that the Gospel of Jesus Christ does present a most surprising cure for those dispositions, which oppose the progress of truth and interfere with our obedience to the moral laws of our being, no one, who, at the present day, looks upon the human race with the eye of a philosopher, can with any semblance of candor venture to deny.

It would not be difficult, did time permit, by an examination of the various laws, physical, intellectual, and moral, under which we are placed, to show that the principles which I have been endeavouring to illustrate, are universal, and apply to every possible action of the most eventful life. It could thus be made to appear that all the happiness of man is derived from discovering, applying, or obeying the laws of his Creator, and that all his misery is the result of ignorance or disobedience; and hence, that the good of the species can be permanently promoted, and permanently promoted only by the accomplishment of that which I have stated to be the object of education.

I have thus far endeavoured to show, from our situation as just such creatures, namely, under laws of which we come into the world ignorant, and laws which can only be known by a mind possessed of acquired power, that there is, in our present state, the need of such a science as that of education. I have endeavoured to show what is its object, and also to show that that object may be accomplished. I will now take leave of this part of the subject, with a few remarks upon the relation which this science sustains to other sciences.

1. If the remarks already made have the least foundation in truth, we do not err in claiming for education the rank of a distinct science. It has its distinct subject, its distinct object, and is governed by its own laws. And, moreover, it has, like other sciences, its corresponding art,—the art of teaching. Now if this be so, we would ask how any man should understand this science, any more than that of mathematics or astronomy, without ever having studied it, or having even thought about it? If there be any such art as the art of teaching, we ask how it comes to pass that a man shall be considered fully qualified to exercise it, without a day's practice, when a similar attempt in any other art would expose him to ridicule? Henceforth, I pray you, let the ridicule be somewhat more justly distributed.

2. The connexions of this science are more extensive than those of any other. Almost any one of the other sciences may flourish independently of the rest. Rhetoric may be car-

ried to high perfection, whilst the mathematics are in their infancy. Physical science may advance, whilst the science of interpretation is stationary. No science, however, can be independent of the science of education. By education their triumphs are made known; by education alone can they be multiplied.

Hence, thirdly, it is upon education that the progress of all other sciences depends. A science is a compilation of the laws of the universe on one particular subject. Its progress is marked by the number of these laws which it reveals, and the multiplicity of their relations which it unfolds. Now we have before shown that the number of laws which are discovered, will be, in proportion to the skill of mind, the instrument which is to discover them. Hence, just in proportion to the progress of the science of education, will be the power which man obtains over nature, the extent of his knowledge of the laws of the universe, and the abundance of means of happiness which he enjoys.

If this be so, it would not seem arrogant to claim for education the rank of the most important of the sciences, excepting only the science of morals. And, hence, we infer, that it presents subjects vast enough, and interests grave enough, to task the highest effort of the most gifted intellect, in the full vigor of its powers. Is it not so? If it be so, on what principle of common sense is it, that a man is considered good enough for a teacher, because he has most satisfactorily proved himself good for no one thing else? Why is it, that the utter want of sufficient health to exercise any other profession, is frequently the only reason why a man should be thrust into this, which requires more active mental labor in the discharge of its duties, than any other profession whatsoever? Alas! it is not by teachers such as these that the intellectual power of a people is to be created. To hear a scholar say a lesson, is not to educate him. He who is not able to leave his mark upon a pupil, never ought to have one. Let it never be forgotten, that, in the thrice resplendent days of the intellectual glory of

Greece, teachers were in her high places. Isocrates, Plato, Zeno, and Aristotle were, without question, stars of by very far the first magnitude, in that matchless constellation, which still surrounds with undiminished effulgence the name of the city of Minerva.

And lastly, if the science of education be thus important, is it not worthy of public patronage? Knowledge of every sort is valuable in a community, very far beyond what it costs to produce it. Hence it is for the interest of every man to furnish establishments by which knowledge can be increased. Of the manner in which this should be afforded, it belongs to political economists to treat. Let me suggest only a very few hints on the subject. Books are the repositories of the learning of past ages. Longer time than that of an individual's life, and greater wealth than falls to the lot of teachers, are required to collect them in numbers sufficient for extensive usefulness. The same may be said of instruments for philosophical research. Let these be furnished, and furnished amply. Let your instructers have the use of them, if you please, gratuitously; and if you do not please, not so, and then, on the principles which govern all other labor, let every teacher, like every other man, take care of himself. Give to every man prominent and distinct individuality. Remove all the useless barriers which shelter him from the full and direct effect of public opinion. Let it be supposed, that, by becoming a teacher, he has not lost all pretensions to common sense; and that he may possibly know as much about his own business as those, who, by confession, know nothing at all about it. In a word, make teaching the business of men, and you will have men to do the business of teaching. I know not that the cause of education, so far as teachers are concerned, requires any other patronage.

I come now to the second part of the subject, which, I am aware, it becomes me to treat with all possible brevity.

II. In what manner shall mind be thus rendered a fitter instrument to answer the purposes of its creation?

To answer this question, let us go back a little. We have shown that the present constitution of things is constructed for man, and that man is constructed for the present constitution. As mind, then, is the instrument by which he avails himself of the laws of that constitution, it may be supposed that it was endowed with all the powers necessary to render it subservient to his best interests. Were it possible, therefore, it would be useless to attempt to give it any additional faculties. All that is possible, is, to cultivate to higher perfection those faculties which exist, or to vary their relations to each other. In other words, to cultivate to the utmost the original faculties of the mind, is to render it the fittest possible instrument for discovering, applying, and obeying the laws of its creation.

This is, however, an answer to the question in the abstract, and without any regard to time. But the question to us, is not an abstract question; it has regard to time. That is to say, we do not ask simply what is the best mode of cultivating mind, but what is the best mode of doing it now, when so many ages have elapsed, and so many of the laws of the universe have been discovered. Much knowledge has already been acquired by the human race, and this knowledge is to be communicated to the pupil.

All this every one sees at first glance to be true. Nearly all the time spent in pupilage, under the most favorable circumstances, is in fact employed in the acquisition of those laws which have been already discovered. Without a knowledge of them, education would be almost useless. Without it, there could evidently be no progressive improvement of the species. Education, considered in this light alone, has very many and very important ends to accomplish. It is desirable that the pupil should be taught *thoroughly;* that is, that he should have as exact and definite a knowledge as possible of the law and of its relations. It is desirable that he be taught *permanently;* that is, that the truth communicated be so associated with his other knowledge, that the lapse of time will not easily erase it from his memory. It is important, also, that *no more time be consumed in the process than is absolutely necessary.* He who occupies two years in teaching what might as well be taught with a little more industry in one year, does his pupil a far greater injury than would be done by simply abridging his life by a year. He not only abstracts from his pupil's acquisition that year's improvement, but all the knowledge which would have been the fruit of it for the remainder of his being.

If, then, all that portion of our time which is devoted to education must be occupied in acquiring the laws of the universe, how shall opportunity be afforded for cultivating the original powers of the mind?

I answer, an all-wise Creator has provided for this necessity of our intellectual nature. His laws, in this, as in every other case, are in full and perfect harmony.

For, first, the original powers of the mind are cultivated by use. This law, I believe, obtains in respect to all our powers, physical, intellectual, and moral. But it must be by the use of each several faculty. The improvement of the memory does not, of necessity, strengthen the power of discrimination; nor does the improvement of natural logical acuteness of necessity add sensibility to the taste. The law on this subject seems to be, that every several faculty is strengthened and rendered more perfect exactly in proportion as it is subjected to habitual and active exercise.

And, secondly, it will be found that the secret of teaching most thoroughly, permanently, and in the shortest time; that is, of giving to the pupil in a given time the greatest amount of knowledge, consists in so teaching as to give the most active exercise to the original faculties of the mind. So that it is perfectly true, that if you wished so to teach as to make the mind the fittest possible instrument for discovering, applying and obeying the laws of the Creator, you would so teach as to give to the mind the greatest amount of knowledge; and, on the contrary, if you wished so to teach as to give to a pupil, in a given time, the greatest amount of knowledge, you would so teach as to render his mind the fittest instrument for discovering applying and obeying the laws of its Creator.

I do not forget that the discussion of the practical business of teaching is, on this occasion, committed to other hands. You will, however, I trust, allow me to suggest here, one or two principles which seem to me common to all teaching, and which are in their nature calculated to produce the results to which I have referred.

1. Let a pupil understand everything that it is designed to teach him. If he cannot understand a thing this year, it was not designed by his Creator that he should learn it this year. But let it not be forgotten, that precisely here is seen the power of a skilful teacher. It is his business to make a pupil, if possible, understand. Very few things are incapable of being understood, if they be reduced to their ultimate elements. Hence the reason why the power of accurate and natural analysis is so invaluable to a teacher. By simplification and patience, it is astonishing to observe how easily abstruse subjects may be brought within the grasp of even the faculties of children. Let a teacher, then, first understand a subject himself. Let him know that he understands it. Let him reduce it to its natural divisions and its simplest elements. And then, let him see that his pupils understand it. This is the first step.

2. I would recommend the frequent repetition of whatever has been acquired. For want of this, an almost incalculable amount of invaluable time is annually wasted. Who of us has not forgotten far more than he at present knows? What is understood to-day, may with pleasure be reviewed to-morrow. If it be frequently reviewed, it will be associated with all our other knowledge, and be thoroughly engraven on the memory. If it be laid aside for a month or two, it will be almost as difficult to recover it as to acquire a new truth; and it is, moreover, destitute of the interest derived only from novelty. If this be the case with us generally, I

need not say how peculiarly the remark applies to the young.

But lastly, and above all, let me insist upon the importance of universal practice of everything that is learned. No matter whether it be a rule in arithmetic, or a rule in grammar, a principle in rhetoric, or a theorem in the mathematics; as soon as it is learned and understood, let it be practised. Let exercises be so devised as to make the pupil familiar with its application. Let him construct exercises himself. Let him not leave them until he feels that he understands both the law and its application, and is able to make use of it freely and without assistance. The mind never will derive power in any other way. Nor will it, in any other way, attain to the dignity of certain, and practical, and available science.

So far as we have gone, then, we have endeavoured to show that the business of a teacher is so to communicate knowledge as most constantly and vigorously to exercise the original faculties of the mind. In this manner he will both convey the greatest amount of instruction, and create the largest amount of mental power.

I intended to confirm these remarks by a reference to the modes of teaching some of the most important branches of science. But I fear that I should exhaust your patience, and also that I might anticipate what will be much better illustrated by those who will come after me. I shall, therefore, conclude by applying these considerations to the elucidation of some subjects of general importance.

1. If these remarks be true, they show us in what manner text books ought to be constructed. They should contain a clear exhibition of the subject, its limits and relations. They should be arranged after the most perfect method, so that the pupil may easily survey the subject in all its ramifications; and should be furnished with examples and questions to illustrate every principle which they contain. It should be the design of the author to make such a book as could neither be

studied unless the pupil understood it, nor taught unless the instructer understood it. Such books, in every department, are, if I mistake not, very greatly needed.

If this be true, what are we to think of many of those school books which are beginning to be very much in vogue amongst us? There first appears, perhaps, an abridgement of a scientific text book. Then, lest neither instructer nor pupil should be able to understand it, without assistance, a copious analysis of each page or chapter or section, is added in a second and improved edition. Then, lest, after all, the instructer should not know what questions should be asked, a copious list of these is added to a third and still more improved edition. The design of this sort of work seems to be to reduce all mental exercise to a mere act of the memory, and then to render the necessity even for the use of this faculty as small as may be possible. Carry the principle but a little farther, and an automaton would answer every purpose exactly as well as an instructer. Let us put away all these miserable helps, as fast as possible, I pray you. Let us never forget that the business of an instructer begins where the office of a book ends. It is the action of mind upon mind, exciting, awakening, showing by example the power of reasoning and the scope of generalization, and rendering it impossible that the pupil should not think; this is the noble and the ennobling duty of an instructer.

2. These remarks will enable us to correct an error which of late has done very much evil to the science of education. Some years since, I know not when, it was supposed, or we have said it was supposed, that the whole business of education was to store the mind with facts. Dugald Stewart, I believe, somewhere remarks that the business of education, on the contrary, is to cultivate the original faculties. Hence the conclusion was drawn that it mattered not what you taught, the great business was to strengthen the faculties. Now this conclusion has afforded to the teacher a most convenient refuge against the pressure of almost every manner of attack. If you

taught a boy rhetoric, and he could not write English, it was sufficient to say that the grand object was not to teach the structure of sentences, but to strengthen the faculties. If you taught him the mathematics, and he did not understand the Rule of Three, and could not tell you how to measure the height of his village steeple, it was all no matter,—the object was to strengthen his faculties. If after six or seven years of study of the languages, he had no more taste for the classics than for Sanscrit, and sold his books to the highest bidder, resolved never again to look into them, it was all no matter,—he had been studying, to strengthen his faculties, while by this very process his faculties have been enfeebled almost to annihilation.

Now, if I mistake not, all this reasoning is false, even to absurdity. Granting that the improvement of the faculties is the most important business of instruction, it does not follow that it is the only business. What! will a man tell me that it is of no consequence whether or not I know the laws of the universe under which I am constituted? Will he insult me, by pretending to teach them to me in such a manner that I shall, in the end, know nothing about them? Are such the results to which the science of education leads? Will a man pretend to illuminate me by thrusting himself, year after year, exactly in my sunshine? No; if a man profess to teach me the laws of my Creator, let him make the thing plain, let him teach me to remember it, and accustom me to apply it. Otherwise, let him stand out of the way, and allow me to do it for myself.

But this doctrine is yet more false; for even if it be true, that it matters not what is taught, it by no means follows that it is no matter how it is taught. The doctrine in question, however, supposes that the faculties are to be somehow strengthened by 'going over,' as it is called, a book or a science, without any regard to the manner in which it is done. The faculties are strengthened by the use of the faculties; but this doctrine has been quoted to shield a mode of teaching, in which they were not used at all; and hence has arisen a great amount of teaching, which has had very little effect, either in communicating knowledge, or giving efficiency to mind.

Let us, then, come to the truth of the question. It is important what I study; for it is important whether or not I know the laws of my being, and it is important that I so study them, that they shall be of use to me. It is also important that my intellectual faculties be improved and therefore important that an instructer do not so employ my time as to render them less efficient.

3. Closely connected with these remarks is the question, which has of late been so much agitated, respecting the study of the ancient languages and the mathematics. On the one part, it is urged that the study of the languages is intended to cultivate the taste and imagination, and that of the mathematics to cultivate the understanding. On the other part, it is denied that these effects are produced; and it is asserted that the time spent in the study of them is wasted. Examples, as may be supposed, are adduced in abundance on both sides; but I do not know that the question is at all decided. Let us see whether anything that we have said will throw any light upon it.

I think it can be conclusively proved, that the classics could be so taught as to give additional acuteness to the discrimination, more delicate sensibility to the taste, and more overflowing richness to the imagination. So much as this, must, we think, be admitted. If, then, it be the fact that these effects are not produced—and I think we must admit that they are not, in any such degree as might reasonably be expected—should we not conclude that the fault is not in the classics, but in our teaching? Would not teaching them better be the sure way of silencing the clamor against them?

I will frankly confess that I am sad, when I reflect upon the condition of the study of the languages among us. We spend frequently six or seven years in Latin and Greek, and yet who of us writes,—still more, who of us speaks them with facility? I am sure there must be something wrong in the mode of our teaching, or we should accomplish more. That cannot be skilfully done, which, at so great an expense of time, produces so very slender a result. Milton affirms, that what in his time was acquired in six or seven years, might have been easily acquired in one. I fear that we have not greatly improved since.

Again, we very properly defend the study of the languages on the ground that they cultivate the taste, the imagination, and the judgment. But is there any magic in the name of a classic? Can this be done by merely teaching a boy to render, with all clumsiness, a sentence from another language into his own? Can the faculties of which we have spoken, be improved, when not one of them is ever called into action? No. When the classics are so taught as to cultivate the taste and give vigor to the imagination,—when all that is splendid and beautiful in the works of the ancient masters, is breathed into the conceptions of our youth,—when the delicate wit of Flaccus tinges their conversation, and the splendid oratory of Tully or the irresistible eloquence of Demosthenes is felt in the senate and at the bar—I do not say that even then we may not find something more worthy of being studied,—but we shall then be prepared, with a better knowledge of the facts, to decide upon the merits of the classics. The same remarks may apply, though perhaps with diminished force, to the study of the mathematics. If, on one hand, it be objected that this kind of study does not give that energy to the powers of reasoning which has frequently been expected, it may, on the other hand, be fairly questioned whether it be correctly taught. The mathematics address the understanding. But they may be so taught as mainly to exercise the memory. If they be so taught, we shall look in vain for the anticipated result. I suppose that a student, after having been taught one class of geometrical principles, should as much be required to combine them in the forms of original demonstration, as that he who has been taught a rule of arithmetic should be required to put it into various and diversified practice. It is thus alone, that we shall acquire that δυναμις αναλυτικη, the mathematical power which the Greeks considered of more value than the possession of any number of problems. When the mathematics shall be thus taught, I think there will cease to be any question, whether they add acuteness, vigor and originality to mind.

I have thus endeavoured, very briefly, to exhibit the object of education, and to illustrate the nature of the means by which that object is to be accomplished. I fear that I have already exhausted your patience. I will, therefore, barely detain you with two additional remarks.

1. To the members of this Convention allow me to say, Gentlemen, you have chosen a noble profession. What though it do not confer upon us wealth?—it confers upon us a higher boon, the privilege of being useful. What though it lead not to the falsely named *heights* of political eminence?—it leads us to what is far better, the sources of real power; for it renders intellectual ability necessary to our success. I do verily believe that nothing so cultivates the powers of a man's own mind as thorough, generous, liberal and indefatigable teaching. But our profession has rewards, rich rewards, peculiar to itself. What can be more delightful to a philanthropic mind, than to behold intellectual power increased a hundred fold by our exertions, talent developed by our assiduity, passions eradicated by our counsel, and a multitude of men pouring abroad over society the lustre of a virtuous example, and becoming meet to be inheritors with the saints in light—and all in consequence of the direction which we have given to them in youth? I ask again, what profession has any higher rewards?

Again, we at this day are in a manner the pioneers in this work in this country. Education, as a science, has scarcely yet been naturalized among us. Radical improvement in the means of education is an idea that seems but just to have entered into men's minds. It becomes us to act worthily of our station. Let us by all the means in our power second the efforts and the wishes of the public. Let us see that the first steps in this course are taken wisely. This country ought to be the best educated on the face of the earth. By the blessing of Heaven, we can do much towards the making of it so. God helping us, then, let us make our mark on the rising generation.

DR WARREN'S LECTURE.

LECTURE I.

ON THE

IMPORTANCE OF PHYSICAL EDUCATION.

BY J. C. WARREN, M. D.

When I had the honor of being invited to make some remarks at this meeting on the subject of Physical Education, I felt much hesitation in undertaking the task. This hesitation arose from the apprehension that professional occupations would render it impracticable for me to present the subject in such a form as to excite the interest it demands. Aware, however, that the course of my pursuits had put me in possession of facts having an important bearing on the present modes of education, and feeling anxious that these facts should be made known to instructers and parents, and others concerned in the management of the rising generation,—I felt myself called on to wave the consideration of the objections to this labor, and to trust the results of my experience, in such a dress as I could afford to give them, to the candor of those to whom they were to be submitted.

Nature has destined that the physical and intellectual education of man should be conducted in very different modes. The culture of the mind requires the early, constant and well-directed efforts of an artificial system. That of the physical faculties is fully effected by the powers of unassisted nature,

All that she asks, is, that we would leave her free and unconstrained. Unhappily, our state of civilization, while it has copiously supplied the means of intellectual improvement, has, nearly in the same ratio, raised obstacles to the developement of the physical powers; and if we wished to restore to those their original spring, we should either revert to our primitive condition, or find substitutes in art for the modes employed by nature.

Considerations of this description have presented themselves occasionally, as I have been called to observe the evils arising from the prevalent systems of education, and also from too steady an application to literary pursuits in those whose education was completed. At one period, my attention was excited to the unfavorable influence of studious and sedentary habits on health, by the occurrence of alarming indisposition among the members of the sacred profession, a number of whom became its premature and much lamented victims. At another, I witnessed the effects of a mistaken system, on the constitution of multitudes of the fairest work of creative power. I have had the misfortune to behold, when it was too late to apply a remedy, numerous instances of decay in the most vigorous constitutions, and of distortion in the best proportioned forms.

The importance of health to the regular exercise of the faculties of mind, as well as those of body, is very well understood in theory, and very generally neglected in practice. We are daily seen to accumulate the treasures of science on intellects, where the physical machinery is disordered and made useless by the burden. What is the value of a brilliant genius, or a highly cultivated mind, to a weak and laboring frame? Let us suppose the existence of such a case in either of the learned professions. If it occur in the minister of religion, the organs of utterance are enfeebled, and the power of instructing his hearers is diminished or destroyed. The thoughts that should speak, remain unembodied in language, and the words that should burn, are extinguished on his lips. His usefulness is impaired in the moment of his full career; and even if his days are not cut off at an early period, he finds his mental abilities prematurely chained down by bodily weakness.

If it happen in the interpreter of the law,—the powerful workings of the mind in the investigation of obscure points, and the elaboration of profound arguments, break down a sickly and yielding organization, and bring on a train of nervous affections and perverted imaginations, as permanent perhaps as life, and less supportable than death.

Again, a bad constitution in a professor of the healing art, keeps him at variance with all his duties. How can he heal others, in whom the springs of health act feebly and imperfectly? A laborious and active course of duty demands a bodily vigor that can endure all kinds of unseasonable labor; a steadiness of fibre, that can bear without agitation the sufferings of others, while attempting to relieve them; and a firmness of health, able to resist the attacks of those malignant epidemics, that prostrate a whole community.

When we regard the influence of a debilitated body on the more delicate sex, we find it not less distressing. A young female, at the age of twelve or fourteen, presents a beautiful figure, rosy cheeks, an airy step, and the fulness of life and happiness in every movement. As she advances, her vivacity naturally lessens; but, as if it would not be soon enough extinguished, it must be repressed by art. The lively motions of the body and limbs must be checked, the spirits must be restrained, and a sort of unnatural hypocrisy made to conceal every ingenuous movement. The activity of disposition is destroyed; by confinement she loses the inclination for exercise, and passes from her school to a state of listlessness at home, or to frivolous and useless amusements, or perhaps to fresh tasks. By this regular repression of the physical powers, their energy is at last broken. Various organs lose their tone and their healthy action. Even the most solid parts are gradually impaired, and, being unable to support their ordinary burden, they sink under its weight, and bring on unchangeable deformity. Perhaps the exterior of health may remain a little longer, although the destroying principle is working in the heart. Should she be called on to be a mother, then comes the trial of her strength. The fruit, so fair without, is then found decayed within, when scarcely matured. Next, the roses of the countenance wither; the limbs are feeble and tottering; the vivacity is extinguished; the whole system undermined, and ready to fall on the first impulse. Of what use now are all the finery of accomplishment, and the rich stores of literature and of science, the fruits of so many years' labor? They are all wasted, and perish unemployed.

What I have now stated as the result of the mode of female education in use at present, is not a picture of the imagination; it is a fair representation of what we are compelled to encounter, in almost daily experience.

My wish now is, to point out some of the principal ways in which literary pursuits may be destructive to health; and also to show what measures might be adopted to prevent these pernicious consequences.

Action is the object for which organization was created. If the organs are allowed to remain inactive, the channels of life become clogged; and the functions and even the structure get impaired. Young animals are filled with the desire of motion, in order that the fluids of the body may be forced rapidly through their tubes, the solids thus elongated and enlarged, and every part gradually and fully developed.

The immediate consequences of action on the bodily frame are familiar and visible to daily experience. Observe the sinewy arm of the mechanic. The muscles are large and distinct; and when put in motion, they become as hard as wood, and as strong as iron. Notice those who are accustomed to carry considerable weights on the head. The joints of the lower limbs are close-set and unyielding; the frame perfectly erect, and the attitude commanding. In the cultivator of the soil, though the form may be vitiated by neglect, you may observe that the appearance of every part is healthful, vigorous, and well fitted for labor.

While all of us are desirous of possessing the excellent qualities of strength, hardiness and beauty, how defective are our systems of education in the means of acquiring them? In the present state of civilization, a child, soon after it can walk, is sent to school; not so much for the purpose of learning, as to relieve its parents of the trouble of superintending its early movements. As he grows older, the same plan is incessantly pursued and improved on, till a large part of his time is passed in sedentary pursuits and in crowded rooms. In the short intervals of mental occupation, the boy is allowed to follow the bent of his inclinations, and seek in play that exercise which nature imperiously demands. The developement of his system, though not what it was destined to be, is attained in a certain way; and he is exempted from some of the evils, which fall heavily on the other sex.

The female, at an early age, is discouraged from activity, as unbecoming her sex, and is taught to pass her leisure hours in a state of quietude at home. The effects of this habit have been already spoken of in general terms; and I would now point out some of its results in a specific manner.

In the course of my observations, I have been able to satisfy myself that about half the young females brought up as they are at present, undergo some visible and obvious change of structure; that a considerable number are the subjects of great and permanent deviations; and that not a few entirely lose their health from the manner in which they are reared. The proportion of those who fall under the first description, I have already stated. The amount of the two last, it is impossible to ascertain with preciseness. I can venture to say, that it is sufficient to constitute a powerful claim on the attention of those engaged in the management of young persons.

The nature of all the particular affections and diseases thus induced, it would be impossible to describe in this place. I shall venture to direct your views to the details of only one of them.

The weight of the principal part of the body or trunk, the

weight of the neck, the head and the two upper extremities, are supported by a single bony column, called the spine. This column is about three inches in diameter. It consists of twentyfour pieces of bone placed one on the other; and between each two is interposed a substance, somewhat resembling caoutchouk or India-rubber, for the purpose of giving it elasticity. This column is hollow, and contains the spinal marrow. Now the spinal marrow is the origin and source of the nerves, that convey the influence necessary to voluntary motion; and they are sent off in pairs to the various muscles. The bony pieces of the spine are confined together by many small ligaments, by the elastic substance just spoken of, and by numerous muscles, affixed, not only to connect and support, but also to move them.

The bones of the spine, at an early period of life, are themselves in part composed of an elastic, cartilaginous or gristly substance; and are always of a porous and sponge-like texture. In consequence of this kind of organization, the spinal column possesses much elasticity and flexibility, which enable it to yield and to move in different directions, and expose it to receive permanent flexures, when there is a deficiency of natural strength in its composing parts.

Causes which affect the health and produce general weakness, operate powerfully on this part, in consequence of the complexity of its structure, and the great burden it supports. When weakened, it gradually yields under its weight, becomes bent and distorted, losing its natural curves, and acquiring others, in such directions as the operation of external causes tend to give to it; and these curves will be proportioned, in their degree and in their permanence, to the producing causes. If the supporting part is removed from its true position, the parts supported necessarily follow, and thus a distortion of the spine effects a distortion of the trunk of the body.

The change commonly begins at the part which supports the right arm. The column bends towards the right shoulder, forms a convexity on the side where the shoulder rests, and thus elevates the right higher than the other. This elevation, or, as it is commonly called, growing out of the shoulder, is the first phenomenon that strikes the friends of the patient. Often when observed, it has already undergone a considerable change of position; and the change is not confined to the shoulder, nor to the portion of spine immediately connected with it. On examination, it will be discovered that the curvature to the right in the upper part of the column, is accompanied, as a natural consequence, by a bend of the lower part to the left, and a correspondent projection of the left hip. It is perfectly obvious, that the inclination of the upper part of a flexible stick to one side, will leave the lower part on the other; and when, by this inclination, the vertical support is lost, a disposition to yield at the curving points will continually increase, until it be counteracted by some other power. Thus it happens, then, that any considerable projection of the right shoulder will be attended by a correspondent projection of the left hip.

The rising of the shoulder involves other changes in the osseous fabric. For, as the spinal bones support the ribs, when these bones project, they necessarily push forwards the ribs dependent on them. These ribs form the frame of the chest, and of course the right side of the chest is projected forwards, and causes a deformity in the fore-part of the body. Nor do the changes stop here. The posterior ends of the ribs being pushed forwards, and the anterior ends being confined to the sternum or breast-bone, the right edge of the sternum will be drawn forwards, and the left edge consequently turned backwards. The fore-parts of the left ribs will be gradually forced inwards or backwards, and thus the left side of the chest distorted and contracted.

I am aware how difficult it is to have a distinct notion of these intricate changes in the human machinery, without an exhibition of the parts concerned in them; but it is my duty to represent the train of phenomena as they exist in nature; and I think they are sufficiently intelligible to excite consideration and inquiry.

Perhaps it may be imagined, that the cases I have described are of rare occurrence, and that we have no occasion to alarm ourselves about a few strange distortions, the consequence of peculiar and accidental causes. If such were in fact the truth, I would not have occupied your time with the minute details of these unpleasant subjects. Unhappily they are very common. I feel warranted in the assertion already intimated, that of the well-educated females within my sphere of experience, about *one half are affected with some degree of distortion of the spine.* This statement will not be thought exaggerated, when compared with that of one of the latest and most judicious foreign writers. Speaking of the right, lateral curvature of the spine, just described, he tells us, 'It is so common, that out of twenty young girls, who have attained the age of fifteen years, there are not two who do not present very manifest traces of it.'*

As the bones serve to contain most of the great organs, any change in their forms will be likely to produce changes in the condition and healthy action of these organs. The spine gives lodgement, as has been said, to the spinal marrow; and this sends out nearly all the nerves that carry the influence of voluntary motion, and many of those that convey energy to the great organs of respiration, circulation and digestion. When the containing part is distorted, the part contained is likely to be disturbed, and this disturbance must produce important effects on the nerves issuing from it, and of course on the organs to which these nerves are distributed. If the compression be slight, the operations of the organs will be partially disturbed. Hence proceed shortness of breath; palpitation of the heart; the phenomena of indigestion, flatulence, acidity, &c. These again give rise to the uncomfortable feelings

---

* Lachaise, Sur les Courbures de la Colonne Vertebrale. p. 23.

called nervous; though I believe they are sometimes the direct consequence of partial compression of the spinal marrow. When this pressure is considerable, the bad consequences are more obvious and formidable. In such instances, the muscles supplied with nerves from the part below that compressed, lose their activity. The circulation in the lower limbs is retarded, and they grow cold and livid, and swell. Sometimes even a complete paralysis, or loss of the power of motion, occurs in one or in both of these extremities.

The ribs and the breast-bone enclose and guard, as we have said, the organs of the chest. Their position being altered by the deviation of the spine, the cavity they form becomes deranged. Its left part, where the heart is placed, being diminished in extent, this organ is embarrassed in its movements, and, striving to relieve itself, produces painful and dangerous palpitations, and a general disturbance in the circulatory system. The lungs, for the same reasons, cannot fully expand. This function is partially performed, and the blood imperfectly oxygenated—an irregularity of itself sufficient to bring on a low state of health, and a disposition to disease.

The want of conformity between these organs and the bones they are in contact with, causing interference between the parts, an irritable condition of the lungs may be engendered, disposing to acute inflammation, or to the slow developement of chronic disease.

Having given some notion of the nature of the affections brought on by mistakes during the time of education, I shall advert now to their causes.

The general causes of these derangements are those things that weaken the constitution. They may be physical or mental. Among the most important physical causes, are want of the exercise proper to develope the powers of the body, and the taking of food, improper in quantity or quality. The mental causes may be a too constant occupation of the mind in study; the influence of feelings or passions of a depressing nature, &c.

The facts, that show the want of exercise to be one of the greatest causes of these affections and of the weakness that induces them, are very numerous. On the one side, we observe that young people, brought up to hardy and laborious occupations, whether they are males or females, do not suffer in this way. The sons and daughters of farmers and laborers, for example, never exhibit the deformities spoken of, except in cases where there is a great scrophulous defect, by inheritance.

A still more remarkable fact of a general nature may be seen on a comparison in this respect between the two sexes. The lateral distortion of the spine is almost wholly confined to females, and is scarcely ever found existing in the other sex. The proportion of the former to the latter is at least nine to one. In truth, I may say that I have scarcely ever witnessed a remarkable distortion, of the kind now spoken of, in a boy. What is the cause of the disparity? They are equally well formed by nature; or, if there be any difference, the symmetry of all parts is more perfect in the female than in the male. The difference in physical organization results from a difference of habits during the school education. It is not seen till after this process is advanced. The girl, when she goes from school, is, as we have before said, expected to go home and remain, at least a large part of the time, confined to the house. As soon as the boy is released, he begins to run and jump and frolic in the open air, and continues his sports till hunger draws him to his food. The result is, that in him all the organs get invigorated, and the bones of course become solid; while a defect exists in the other, proportionate to the want of physical motion.

A question may fairly be asked why these evils are greater now than formerly, when females were equally confined? The answer, in reference to the young females of our country, is, that they then took a considerable share in the laborious part of the domestic duties; now, they are devoted to literary occupations, of a nature to confine the body and require considerable efforts of the mind.

I shall not, in this place, say anything of the second of the physical causes of weakness, spoken of, as it will be adverted to hereafter. The next of these causes, which presents itself to our view, is of a moral nature;—the influence of too great occupation of the mind in study, and that of feelings and passions of a depressing nature.

The operation of mental causes on the bodily frame is not unknown to any of us; though they may not perhaps have been thought, in regard to education, to be of very great importance. As it is not in my power to enter fully into the subject, I would barely present it for your consideration.

The effect of anxiety, grief, and other feelings, in diminishing strength and wearing away health, are quite familiar. The loss of property and of friends, has been known to bring on diseases; and it has sometimes happened, that an agreeable reverse or a favorable incident has speedily removed them. Confidence in a physician is a great help towards receiving benefit from his prescriptions; and many of the cures wrought by empirical or quack medicines, are to be attributed rather to the operation of the mind, than to the action of the medicines on the disease.

The production of physical changes in a sudden and sensible way, by the action of moral causes, is comparatively rare, and difficult to comprehend. Yet medical men do sometimes have an opportunity of observing changes effected by this power, which might appear incredible, and almost miraculous, to those not aware of the force of mental operations on the human organs. I could adduce many such cases. Perhaps it will be proper to state one or two in detail.

When, some years ago, the metallic tractors were in the height of their reputation for the cure of diseases by external application to the part affected, the following experiment was performed by Dr Haygarth, of Bath. Two tractors were prepared, not of metal, but of a substance different from the genuine tractors, and made to resemble them. These were applied, in a number of instances, with all the good effects of the real tractors. Among other remarkable cures was that of a person with a contraction of the knee joint, from a disease of six months' duration. After a few minutes' application, this man was directed to use his limb, and, to the surprise of all present, he was able to walk about the room. Such instances are not very unusual. Many empirics succeed by calling into action the same principle. The patient, after a number of contortions of the part affected, is directed to make use of his limb; and though this call on his imagination does not infallibly succeed, it is not wonderful that it occasionally does so.

I will relate another case of this kind. Some time since, a female presented herself to me, with a tumor, or swelling of the submaxillary gland of the neck, which had become what is commonly called a wen. It was about the size of an egg, had lasted two years, and was so very hard, that I considered any attempt to dissipate it by medicine to be vain, and advised its removal by an operation. To this the patient could not bring her mind; therefore, to satisfy her wish, I directed some applications of considerable activity to be made to the part, and these she pursued a number of weeks, without any change. After this, she called on me, and, with some hesitation, begged to know, whether an application recommended to her would in my opinion be safe. This consisted in applying the hand of a dead man three times to the diseased part. One of her neighbours now lay dead, and she had an opportunity of trying the experiment, if thought not dangerous. At first, I was disposed to divert her from it; but, recollecting the power of the imagination, I gravely assured her she might make the trial without apprehension of serious consequences. A while after, she presented herself once more, and, with a smiling countenance, informed me she had used this remedy and no other since I saw her; and, on examining for the tumor, I found it had disappeared.

The possibility of operating powerfully on the corporeal organization by moral causes being admitted, it is clear that the long exertion of intellectual efforts, and still more the frequent action of depressing passions, may, and even must, have a great influence on the condition of the body, at the flexible period when education and growth are going on together.—A close and constant occupation of mind, too long continued, lessens the action of the heart; and a languid circulation, thus being induced, prevents the full growth of the body. Depressing passions act more conspicuously. You may possibly have noticed, though the case is rare in this country, the condition of children subjected to a persevering system of harshness at home. They are pale and shrivelled, and their growth is checked.

In the present modes of education, great pains are taken to excite the imagination by competition. These efforts are attended with but too much success in susceptible minds. An anxiety to excel becomes the predominant passion. The health, the sports, and too often the friendships of youth are sacrificed to the desire of surpassing those around. When this becomes an all-absorbing passion, the result is most unfriendly to physical organization; and a multitude of fine constitutions are ruined by it, in both sexes.

Whether any proper substitute can be found, in our sex, for competition and rivalry, I must leave to others to decide. So far as my experience extends, I should give an affirmative answer; and while I do not pretend to be a very competent judge in the case, it is fair to say, that the habit of giving public instructions for more than twenty years, has afforded me some conclusions of a satisfactory nature.

The application of the system of rivalry to the softer sex, I speak with submission to greater experience, appears to me fraught with mischief. It inflames the imagination, festers the passions, and poisons the happiness of the brightest days of life; and since the very highest grade of literary acquirement is not essential to the duties of the sex, it seems as unnecessary as it is pernicious.

I have just made a question whether there is a substitute, which is sufficiently practical to be of general use. I do not know that there is; and if none exists, I think the ingenuity and intelligence of instructers could not be employed on a more important subject, than in devising such substitute. The spirit of improvement has, I imagine, already discovered that the reasoning process may be generally employed with great success in the instruction of young persons. I know individuals, who use it to a considerable extent, and with the most happy results. They endeavour to enforce on their pupils the doctrine that the path of duty is the most easy and most for the interest of the individual to pursue. They do this by conversation and by argument; and the process succeeds with those who are capable of being influenced in any way,—and why should it not? Children of the earliest age are perfectly capable of feeling the force of reason; and I believe it will generally be found that they are under the power of their parents, rather in proportion to the employment of this agent, than to that of the rod or any other compulsory means. If they understand reason, at so early a period, surely they cannot lose their susceptibility to it, at one more advanced. There are, I know, minds, on which the powers of language make no impression, and all the weapons of argument fall as if pointless. But these are to be considered as exceptions to general laws—cases in which all the means of severity and kindness equally fail. They should not cause discouragement. Patience is the everlasting motto of the instructer. With it he performs wonders—without it he can do nothing.

The remarks made above, will give some notion of the most important of what I conceive to be general causes of ill health and imperfect growth, during the educating process.

It may not be useless to say a few words on some of the immediate causes of spinal distortion, which may be called local, in opposition to the former.

The most obvious of the local causes are bad postures of the body and limbs. The habit of bending the neck, while writing or drawing, gradually compresses the vertebræ, and the intervertebral substance on their anterior part, and causes a permanent change in the form of this part of the spinal column. This distortion is so very common among us, that we are apt to consider it a natural formation. In fact, however, it is entirely artificial in a great number of instances. Sometimes it is the consequence of negligence, and not unfrequently of timidity. Whether it tends to impair the health, always, I will not say—that it sometimes does so, I am certain; and its effect in deforming the shape is even greater than a moderate degree of lateral curve.

The immediate cause of the lateral curve of the spine to the right, opposite to the right shoulder, is the elevation and action of the right arm in drawing and writing. This posture pulls the part of the spinal column to which the muscles of the right arm are fixed, to the right side. The convexity of the spine thus produced keeps the right shoulder elevated, and the left consequently depressed. The lower part of the column is thrown to the left side; and this displacement being favored by the disposition to rest on the left foot, while standing to speak or read, there comes to be a permanent projection of the left hip. The postures employed in practising on musical instruments, sometimes bring on these distortions; as for example, a great use of the harp favors the disposition to lateral curvature, from the constant extension of the right arm.

Having adverted to the nature and the causes of some of the defects that arise from want of attention to physical education, I shall now throw out some hints, as to the modes in which it may be improved.

Nature, as we have before said, if left to herself, is all-sufficient to the developement of physical organization. But we live in an artificial state—a state that continually thwarts the course of the native dispositions of the animal economy; and as we must abandon the advantages of these, we must seek for substitutes in an artificial process.

The principles which should form the basis of such a process, will readily be seen, on attending to the nature and the causes of these defects. We shall observe that the remedy, or rather the preventive means, lies in a certain regulation of the sentiments and passions and intellectual operations; in promoting bodily activity; in a salutary regimen, and in some other inferior considerations. In regard to the first of these, that is, to what relates to the mind, I have already said all I intend at this time; and I shall now advert to the others.

Towards a perfect system of education, it is necessary there should be a balance preserved between physical and intellectual cultivation. When the mind is closely occupied, the body should be carefully guarded. If the pursuits of the former are severe and absorbing, those of the latter should be cheerful and relaxing. Instead, then, of abandoning the physical to the intellectual culture, it should be increased in the same ratio, and followed with the same earnestness.

Exercise is so material to physical education, that it has sometimes been used synonymously, though it really constitutes only a part of it. In order that exercise may have its due operation, it must begin at the earliest period of life, and of course, the parent must, in this, act the part of instructer. He must take pains to have the infant carried into the air, every day, and in every season; for, whatever may be the dangers of such a course, they are in the end less than those incident to the accidental exposures of a delicate constitution. In the earlier years, the dress should be arranged so as to allow that use of the body and limbs, to which nature prompts, with freedom, and without impropriety. When children are sent to school, care should be taken that they are not confined too long. Children under fourteen should not be kept in school more than six or seven hours a day; and this period should be shortened for females. It is expedient that it should be broken into many parts; so as to avoid a long confinement at one time. Young persons, however well disposed, cannot support a restriction to one place and one posture. Nature resists such restrictions; and if enforced, they are apt to create disgust with the means and the object. Thus children learn to hate studies that might be rendered agreeable, and they take an aversion to instructers, who would otherwise be interesting to them.

The postures they assume while seated at their studies, are not indifferent. They should be frequently warned against the practice of maintaining the head and neck long in a stooping position; and the disposition to it should be lessened by giving a proper elevation and slope to the desk; and the seat should have a support or back of a few inches, at its edge. The arms must be kept on the same level; and there should be room to support them equally, or the right will be apt to rise above the left, from its constant use and elevation. A standing posture in writing and studying, is not commendable for young persons. The secret of posture consists in avoiding all bad positions, and avoiding all positions long continued.

The ordinary carriage of the body in walking should be an object of attention to every instructer. How different are the impressions made on us by a man, whose attitude is erect and commanding, and by one who walks with his face directed to the earth, as if fearful of encountering the glances of those he meets! Such attentions are even of great importance to the fairer sex, where we naturally look for attraction in some form or shape. If nature has not given beauty of face to all, she has given the power of acquiring a graceful movement and upright form—qualities more valuable and more durable than the other. These qualities are lost or gained at school; and of course they lie, to some extent, within the control of the instructer. It seems to me it would afford a great addition of satisfaction to the superintendent and guardian of the rising population, to be able to send out to the world his annual recruits, not only well imbued with knowledge and virtue, but also endowed with a handsome form and graceful manners.

The influence of an upright form and open breast on the health, has been, I think, sufficiently explained; and what may be done to acquire these qualities, is shown by many remarkable facts, one of which I will mention. For a great number of years, it has been the custom in France, to give to young females of the earliest age, the habit of holding back the shoulders, and thus expanding the chest. From the observations of anatomists lately made, it appears that the clavicle or collar bone is actually longer in females of the French nation than in those of the English. As the two nations are of the same race, as there is no other remarkable difference in their bones, and this is peculiar to the sex, it must be attributed, as I believe, to the habit abovementioned, which, by the extension of the arms, has gradually produced a national elongation of this bone. Thus we see that habit may be employed to alter and improve the solid bones. The French have succeeded in the developement of a part, in a way that adds to health and beauty, and increases a characteristic that distinguishes the human being from the brute.

As young persons advance in age, and as the disposition to motion naturally diminishes, it becomes important to encourage and provide for it, especially in females, and in young men of studious character. Instead of restraining their movements, and blaming the disposition to frolic, they should be allowed and advised to it, at proper times, and in becoming modes.

Next to walking in the open air, the best exercise for a young female is dancing. This brings into action a large part of the muscles of the body and lower limbs, and gives them grace and power. The mode in which I wish to recommend its use, is not in balls and parties and crowded assemblies, but at home, alone, or with two or three friends, or in the domestic circle. As this practice does not give motion to the upper limbs, and as the exercising them is too apt to be neglected, it is important to provide the means of bringing them into action, as well to develope their own powers, as to enlarge and invigorate the chest, with which they are connected, and which they powerfully influence. The best I know of is the use of the triangle.* This admirably exerts the upper limbs and

---

* The triangle is made of a stick of walnut wood, four feet long, an inch and a half in diameter. To each end is connected a rope, the opposite extremities of which being confined together, are secured to the ceiling of a room, at such height as to allow the motion of swinging by the hands.

the muscles of the chest, and, indeed, when adroitly employed, those of the whole body. The plays at ball with both hands, and that of dumb bells, are useful. The parallel bars afford a very fine exercise for the muscles of the body and upper limbs. Battledoor I should recommend to be played with the left hand as well as the right, a habit, like all others, acquired by due practice. While I particularly mention these, I should advise as great a diversity as possible, in exercise and amusement; so that, when the mind or the muscles get fatigued with one, they may take up another with fresh ardor. Every seminary of young persons should be provided with the instruments for these exercises. They are not expensive, occupy but little room, and are of unspeakable importance.

While active exercises should occupy time sufficient to excite the circulation, and to put in motion the organs, there must also be an occasional relaxation. At proper intervals, the whole muscular apparatus should be allowed to repose. I do not mean that the young lady should sleep during the day; but I wish to advise a graceful attitude on a couch or sofa, as a necessary alternation to muscular or mental effort.

The remarks last made have reference principally to the exercises of young ladies, who are more likely to suffer in this respect, in our plans of education, than the other sex.

The necessity of cultivating the physical powers in young men, is sufficiently understood. The establishment of gymnasia through the country, promised, at one period, the opening of a new era in physical education. The exercises were pursued with ardor, so long as their novelty lasted; but, owing to not understanding their importance, or some defect in the institutions which adopted them, they have gradually been neglected and forgotten, at least in our vicinity. The benefits which resulted from these institutions, within my personal knowledge and experience, far transcended the most sanguine expectations. I have known many instances of protracted and distressing affections wholly removed; of weakly organized forms unfolded and invigorated, and of the attainment of extraordinary degrees of muscular energy and elasticity in persons in health.

The diversions of the gymnasium should constitute a regular part of the duties of all our colleges and seminaries of learning; and, to give them the requisite power of excitement, the system of rewards, so dangerous when mismanaged in literary education, might be introduced without any ill effect. Our young men may surely find time to cultivate those exercises, which Cicero and Cæsar, and some of the most studious among the ancient and modern philosophers, considered necessary, and contrived to prosecute in the midst of their studies and affairs.*

If the gymnasium is deserted because it calls for too much effort, let me intreat them at least to adopt a regular plan of walking. Two hours a day must be devoted to this business without relaxation, unless they are willing to carry the mark of disorder in the face while young, and a dyspeptic, nervous, disabled frame through that part of life, which requires health and activity.

I have often been asked, how it is the German literati preserve their health without exercise. Some of them are known to pass most of their time in study, and think not of wasting their precious moments in taking care of their bodies. To this I reply; first, that they are careful to acquire a good constitution by habits of activity while they are young. The

---

* Cicero is described by Plutarch, as being, at one period of his life, extremely lean and slender, and having such a weakness in his stomach, that he could eat but little, and that not till late in the evening. He travelled to Athens, however, for the recovery of his health, where his body was so strengthened by gymnastic exercises, as to become firm and robust; and his voice, which had been harsh, was thoroughly formed, and rendered sweet, full, and sonorous.

In regard to Julius Cæsar, the same author informs us, that he was originally of a slender habit of body, had a soft and white skin, was troubled with pains in his head, and subject to epilepsy; but, by continual marches, coarse diet, and frequent lodging in the fields, he struggled against these diseases; and used war, and the exercises and hardships therewith connected, as the best medicine against these indispositions.—*Sir John Sinclair.*

organs are properly developed, and confirmed in healthy action. Secondly, they do not break down their strength by luxurious ways of living, and the free use of stimulant drinks, in early age. Thirdly, which is the great secret, they live most abstemiously. The digestive organs are not overburdened with food, and stand not in need of extraordinary efforts to relieve them.

Let those who are compelled to sedentary pursuits, seasonably lay aside one half of their ordinary food; and they will experience no loss of time in combating the horrors of dyspepsia.

The inhabitants of the Philadelphia Penitentiary, confined to a uniform regimen, which of course limits itself, enjoy uninterrupted health. Those who were diseased from bad habits before they became its tenants, are effectually cured after a short residence.

Regulation of the food is of primary consequence towards the formation of a good constitution. The most common error in relation to it, consists in the use of too much food. Nature has given us organs of a certain capacity, on the presumption that, being called on to manual labor, we should then require a large quantity of food. Muscular effort exhausts the strength, and requires renovation by nutritious substances; but when the muscular efforts are small, the quantity of nourishment required is comparatively trifling; and if, in consequence of the capacity of the gastric organ, a large quantity is taken, the result will be pernicious, directly or indirectly. Parents are uneasy when their children eat but little, and would encourage them to eat against their inclination. No mistake can be more pernicious to health; and if persevered in, disease will infallibly result from it. When the child wants appetite, instead of being compelled to take food, it must be compelled to take exercise, unless positively ill, and then it must be compelled to take medicine.

The quantity of liquid given to young persons is decidedly injurious. The principal agent in the digesting process, is a solvent juice. The more this is diluted with fluids, the weaker it is, and the less perfect the digestive action. Animal food should be sparingly taken by young persons who use little exercise; and children generally do not need it. Bread and milk, and fruit are the best articles for those who do not labor. Wine is highly pernicious to young persons. It is a slow but certain poison. Before the body has attained its full growth, there is an overplus of excitability; and if to this is added the powerful agency of wine, or any other stimulating drink, the constitution cannot fail to be hurt. Females are more injured by stimulating drinks than males, because their system is more susceptible of physical excitement. The nervous power is more energetic; the pulse and respiration are quicker; and the developement of animal heat greater. Hence, I suppose, it is, that they require less covering in cold weather; and suffer more inconvenience from the heat, than the other sex.

Females are unfortunately compelled by fashion to adopt partial and unequal coverings of the body. A part of the chest is very much covered, while another part is wholly exposed. The dangers which spring from fashion are more easily pointed out, than avoided. They serve at least to place in a clearer light the necessity of inuring young females to exposure, and invigorating them by exercise.

There is one part of female dress, the dangers of which have been made known, but which still, I fear, continues to be practised; I mean the girting the chest.

In what notions of beauty this practice took its origin, I am unable to discover. The angular projections formed by a tightly drawn cord, are in direct opposition to the models of Grecian or Roman beauty. In the flowing robes of the Juno, the Vesta and Diana, every part is light and graceful. Nor have I been able to discover, in the representation of the Muses or the Graces, any habiliment which would lead us to believe they wore stays or corsets. The taste of the other sex is uniformly opposed to the wasp-like waist and the boarded chest. Yet, strange as it seems, there is scarcely a young lady of fifteen, who has not imbibed a disposition for this species of application, and scarcely a well dressed lady of any age, whose chest is not confined in such a manner as to impede the motions of respiration and the free use of the muscles of the upper extremities. It is true we are constantly told that they are uncomfortable without these appendages; but this only shows, what great inconveniences, we can, by habit, become accustomed to. The Indian nations, who consider the flattened forehead to be a beauty, confine the heads of their infants between two pieces of board corded together, and the child exists under this pressure and may grow up. Yet there can be no doubt that diseases are generated by it; that some lose their lives and others their intellects. Still the fashion continues from age to age; for I have now in my possession flattened heads, which must have lived some hundreds of years since, and others which have belonged to individuals of the existing generation.

Nature has so contrived the human chest that there is no superfluous play of the parts composing it. Its movements are just sufficient to give such an expansion to the lungs and such an extent of oxygenation of the blood, as are adequate to the wants of the individual, under different occurrences. In females, the chest is shorter than in males; and to compensate for this, the motion of the ribs is naturally more extensive and more frequent. Whatever limits this motion is therefore peculiarly injurious to the sex; especially as they are more disposed to consumption and other chronic affections of the lungs. Now the ligatures in the fashionable dress are placed precisely on that part, where the motion should be greatest; that is, the lower part. It is precisely here, that, in case of fracture of the ribs, when we desire to stop the movements of the chest, we apply a tight bandage;—though rarely do we venture to make it so tight as the ordinary corsets. The effect of such pressure, begun at an early period of life, will be understood from what has been stated in regard to the spine. The bones must yield to it; their shape becomes permanently altered; the lower part of the breast contracted; the space destined by nature for the heart and lungs diminished; and what the fatal results of all this on these tender and vital organs are, every day's experience shows us. The influence on the health, though slow, is certain. It may not at once produce consumption; but it lays the foundation for ills it would pain you to hear, and me to describe. I will only say by way of specification, that, among other diseases of which this is the fruitful germ, I have known three instances of perpetual headache, at last bringing on insanity and terminating in death. The immediate cause of the disease was the compression of the heart and great blood vessels, and the consequent accumulation of blood in the head.

As young ladies are disposed to this practice, probably by fancies communicated by their companions, those who have charge of them, should not only prohibit these applications—they should, for themselves, observe whether anything is wrong; and after the young ladies have reached the age when dress is considered a primary object, they should resolutely oppose every encroachment on the rights of the vital organs, beyond what is required by a decent attention to the prejudices of the day.

If I might call your attention to other topics of interest connected with this subject, I should advert to the constant use of cold bathing, especially the shower-bath, as very conducive to invigoration of the body and to lessening the susceptibility to the injurious effects of cold on the surface of the skin. I would speak of the advantages of regular frictions over the whole surface, and especially the chest and the neck, those parts, which are constantly to be exposed to the air. The judicious use of the voice by reading aloud, I should highly commend. It invigorates the lungs, and gives action to the whole digestive apparatus; but I should not speak so favorably of singing—a delightful accomplishment, indeed, but only to be pursued by those whose chests are ample, and pulmonary organs vigorous. These subjects I can barely allude to, without entering into the details of their particular application, having extended these remarks much beyond my original design.

Let me conclude by intreating your attention to a revision of the existing plans of education, in what relates to the preservation of health. Too much of the time of the better educated part of young persons, is, in my humble opinion, devoted to literary pursuits and sedentary occupations; and too little to the acquisition of the corporeal powers indispensable to make the former practically useful. If the present system does not undergo some change, I much apprehend we shall see a degenerate and sinking race, such as came to exist among the higher classes in France, before the revolution, and such as now deforms a large part of the noblest families in Spain;* but if, as I trust it will, the spirit of improvement, so happily awakened, continue to animate those concerned in the formation of the young members of society, we shall soon be able, I doubt not, to exhibit an active, beautiful, and wise generation, of which the age may be proud.

* I am informed, by a lady who passed a long time at the Spanish court, in a distinguished situation, that the Grandees have deteriorated by their habits of living, and the restriction of intermarriages to their own rank, to a race of dwarfs, and, though fine persons are sometimes seen among them, they, when assembled at court, appear to be a group of mannikins.

MR CARTER'S LECTURE.

ADVERTISEMENT.

The subject assigned to the author of the following Lecture, by the Committee of Arrangements for the late Convention of Teachers in Boston, was simply, Teaching Geography. In enforcing the claims of geography to attention as a branch of elementary instruction; and particularly, in stating the peculiar advantages of the method of teaching it, adopted and recommended by the author, he was necessarily led to make a brief analysis of the infant mind, in order to show what intellectual powers would be successfully developed by the study. Under the impression that the Cultivation of the Intellectual Powers was to be the subject of a distinct lecture, the author, in the original preparation of his performance, felt constrained to forbear making his analysis of the mind so full and complete as his inclination would have prompted, lest he should encroach on the province of another.' After the Convention had assembled, however, it was ascertained that the anticipated lecture on the Cultivation of the Intellectual Powers, would not be delivered, and the author was, then, invited to occupy as much of that ground as this late notice and his indispensable engagements during the sittings of the Convention, would permit. These circumstances are stated, in the hope that they will afford a sufficient apology for the great length of the lecture, and the apparent diversity of its subjects, as well as for the introduction of one or two paragraphs published by the author a few years since, in a literary periodical then under his care, and particularly devoted to the cause of popular education.

LECTURE II.

ON THE
DEVELOPEMENT OF THE INTELLECTUAL FACULTIES,
AND ON
TEACHING GEOGRAPHY.

BY JAMES G. CARTER.

Before entering particularly upon the subject of Teaching Geography, I propose to offer a few remarks upon the Developement of the Intellectual Faculties, as the proper purpose of early instruction or elementary studies, generally. When I enter upon the second topic of my lecture, I shall briefly trace the progress of the science of geography, if science it may be called in this humble form, to its present condition in our schools. Then I shall state one or two of the great defects, which widely prevail in the common systems upon the subject. Afterwards, I shall sketch what I conceive to be the best arrangement of elementary geographical works, and describe with some minuteness the best method of teaching them. And, lastly, I shall endeavour to illustrate the peculiar adaptation of this method of instruction to the exercise and consequent developement of the various faculties of the youthful mind. Though this arrangement may divert me for a few moments from the original purpose of my lecture, yet there seems to be more than a mere propriety in it; because the mode of teaching any subject would naturally be somewhat varied according to the objects for which it was to be taught, and according to the scope and comprehension given to it.

What, then, I am led first to inquire, is the proper purpose of early instruction or early education? At what end are parents aiming, when they lavish their cares and anxieties, and expend abundant treasures upon their children? And when may they consider their reasonable hopes as in the progress of fulfilment? What are the great body of teachers throughout our land—a profession more numerous than any other liberal profession, and requiring untold sums levied upon every class of the community for their support—endeavouring to accomplish? Why, certainly, to educate the rising generation. And what is it, the question recurs, to educate the rising generation? The answer to this momentous question is essentially involved in a preliminary and apparently more simple one;—what is it to educate successfully one individual human being? It is by counteracting adverse influences, and by the application of judicious means, to produce where it does not already exist, or to preserve where it does, a sound and healthy state of the whole body; particularly of all those parts of it, which constitute, or on which depend, the external organs of the mind,—the organs of sensation. The avenues of the mind, by which it holds intercourse with the material world, being thus cleared, it is the next business of education to present nature in its simplest forms to the incipient and undisciplined senses; to watch and regulate, by directing and strengthening the attention, the formation of the corresponding impressions, and the modifications of them by reflection; and to vary and enlarge this experience of the youthful mind, so as to call forth in their natural order its various faculties, and render them healthful and vigorous by exercise. A sound mind being thus in the progress of developement, in a sound body, *mens sana in corpore sano*, the principal remaining point of attention is simultaneously to regulate the affections of the heart,—to direct them to their proper objects; first, to those who are immediately around them,—to those earthly benefactors, whose kind offices are most obvious; and thence gradually and solemnly upward to our heavenly Benefactor: for, in the right exercise of this latter class of affections consists not only the essence of all moral excellence, but the only sure foundation of all intellectual greatness.

It will be perceived, that, in this view of the objects of early instruction, I have said nothing of imparting knowledge,— even of useful knowledge. And who that has reflected much upon the subject, will say, that it is the sole, or even a main subject of early and elementary education to fill the mind with facts, be they as useful in themselves or practical as they may? Who has not seen, even in this practical age, too many living examples that knowledge of facts is not wisdom,—that it is very possible to store the mind of a child or youth with a vast amount of learning, and yet leave him but poorly educated? But limited and superficial as his views of the science of education must be, who could for a moment think of estimating his success in instruction by the amount of knowledge imparted? At what other objects do teachers generally, and the prevailing systems of instruction, seem to aim? Or by what other standard do parents and the public estimate the abilities and success of a teacher?

So far is the acquisition of knowledge from being the main object of early or elementary instruction, that it is not, in my view, even the best criterion by which to judge of an individual's progress in education. Although it would not be possible to regulate the external impressions upon the infant mind, or the modifications of those impressions formed in the mind itself, in the course of its developement, so as not to give it much knowledge both of the natural and the intellectual world; yet, I apprehend, this knowledge, useful and important as it may be, is only to be considered as incidental to education, or at most but accessary to it. The main object, so far as it can be influenced by any direct efforts of parents and teachers, is, the successful developement and discipline of the several moral and intellectual faculties of man, in their natural order, and each to its due degree of strength and maturity. All other objects, about which the busy writers and talkers upon education are so much engaged, are but subsidiary to this. They are, therefore, to be regarded only as means, and are important or pernicious in a course of instruction, just in proportion as they tend to facilitate or retard the attainment of an ulterior and higher purpose. That youth is not necessarily the best educated, who knows the most, or knows that which will be most useful in his intended situation, or even who knows it most thoroughly; but he whose faculties,—physical, intellectual, and moral,—are most perfectly developed. These constitute the man, and give him his own individual and peculiar character. It is by means of these, and these only, that he will be able to learn a profession, to acquire knowledge, and make himself estimable by his virtues. And every arrangement of studies and every plan for the education of children and youth, which makes not the developement of the faculties and the enlargement of the natural capabilities of our nature, its main aim, seems to me to be essentially defective. And every parent and instructer of youth, who keeps not this aim constantly in view, and makes not his arrangements, and directs not his discipline accordingly, is in imminent peril of wasting, or probably worse than wasting, his efforts.

In vain will you put into the head of a child the elements of all the sciences; in vain will you flatter yourselves that you have made him understand them. If there has been no endeavour to develope his faculties by continual yet moderate exercise, suited to the yet weak state of his organs, if no care has been taken to preserve their just balance, so that no one may be greatly improved at the expense of the rest, your child will have neither genius nor capacity; he will not think for himself; he will judge only after others; he will have neither taste, nor intelligence, nor nice apprehension; he will be fit for nothing great or profound; always superficial; learned, perhaps, in appearance, but never original, and perpetually embarrassed, whenever he is put out of the beaten track; he will live only by his memory, which has been diligently cultivated, and all his other faculties will remain as it were extinct or torpid.*

The powers and faculties of our nature, physical, intellectual, and moral, are developed only by slow degrees and by repeated and varied opportunities for exercise. These opportunities for the exercise of our powers in the very earliest stages of education, are afforded in the ordinary course of nature without any direct efforts of parents or teachers. And a kind arrangement of Providence it is, to check our presumption, and prevent the rude interference of men with the delicate and subtile operations of this noblest work of God. But soon, man has a part to take in the most momentous and responsible business of giving form and direction to the opening faculties of a fellow being. And it becomes him to approach his duty in this regard with great deliberation, and with that awe, which he cannot but feel, when he reflects that he is about to blend his imperfect means with his Maker's, and cooperate with Him in giving form and character to an immortal mind.

The organs of sensation, only, are born with us; their use, which alone gives them their value, is acquired by intercourse with the material world. And this intercourse is carried on, partly in the ordinary course of nature, above and beyond the reach of human interference; and partly by means, which lie distinctly within the sphere of our control. The child hears, sees, and feels things as they are, only by practice, by repeated efforts, trials, and alternate failures and successes. It walks not with a firm and elastic step, till the several muscular organs employed in the operation have been disciplined, tried and strengthened, one by one, and in more limited combinations; nor even then, till large experience and many failures have taught it where greater strength and agility are wanting. It walks and moves not gracefully, till a still later peri-

* See 'Journal de Genève,' 1790. also 'Bibliothèque Universelle' of Professor Pictet, Feb. 1817.

od,—till it feels the luxury of a perfect control of all the muscles and limbs of the body.

So it is in the developement of the several intellectual faculties. No one of them is born with us, nor have we even an idea, upon which they may employ themselves, till the material world is presented to the physical senses. They are brought out but gradually, by slow degrees and by gentle use; and they are prepared for high and masculine efforts, only by a long series of healthful and vigorous exercises. We have not the power of steadfast attention, till we have been baffled many times by its waywardness. We are not quick in comprehending, exact in reasoning, sound in judgment, sagacious and original in invention, till we have much exercised, one by one, and in their more limited combinations, all the elementary powers of mind, on which its highest efforts, of course, essentially depend.

The affections, and all our moral faculties, too, on the character and exercise of which depend not only the well-being of society, but all the absorbing interests of the individual, are not less the creatures of habit; which is only the results of education, in its widest sense, combined. Where exists, but in the benevolence of God, filial affection, till it is called into exercise by the mother's smiles? How can we conceive of gratitude, and how does that affection receive a character and become a habit within us, till our hearts have been touched by the varied and repeated tokens of kindness in those about us? How does it receive its highest and holiest direction, till we have largely experienced and deeply realized that protection and those mercies, which men cannot give? Or how do our hearts rise spontaneously upward in prayer, till we have been placed in circumstances beyond the control of human means, and perhaps beyond the reach of human sympathy, and there felt the utter impotency of man to relieve our keenest wants, or satisfy our highest aspirations?

I have, perhaps, said more than enough to bring before my fellow laborers in the cause of education, some of the main grounds of my belief, that the prevailing systems of instruction have been formed upon a somewhat mistaken principle; that the selection of subjects on which to employ the young and tender minds of children, and the arrangement of those subjects in our text-books, have been too often made with reference to what I cannot but consider a mistaken purpose of elementary studies. They seem to have been made upon the supposition, that the acquisition of knowledge is everything, and the discipline of the mind nothing; or, at best, that the acquisition of knowledge is the main thing, and the discipline of the mind a secondary or subsidiary consideration, which may be regarded or neglected without essentially affecting a system of instruction. Now, if the principles I have stated be correct, these two purposes of early education have been misplaced in regard to each other. The discipline of the faculties is the main and legitimate object of elementary instruction; and the acquisition of knowledge is a secondary and inferior consideration, which may be, and should be, neglected, whenever it would interfere with the main aim. When professional education begins, the main object of instruction is changed. The faculties being fully and harmoniously developed, the individual now properly seeks to acquire that knowledge, which will be most useful to him in his intended course.

I have thought it worth while to be thus explicit in stating the proper purposes of elementary studies; because, in forming plans and devising means for the attainment of any remote object, it is the part of wisdom first to place the object itself as distinctly in view as its nature will admit. With a clear and well defined idea of what we would attain, constantly in the mind, we shall be much less liable to mistakes, either in our choice of means to be used, or in our manner of applying them. The necessity of this cautious mode of settling a plan of operations becomes more obvious, just in proportion to the remoteness of the object, and the variety of the means to be used for its attainment. It must, therefore, be peculiarly important in devising and adopting a system of practical education. For here, no reasonable parent or teacher looks for a conclusive result of his labors, till the object of his solicitude has taken his place among the busy actors in the scene of life. Indeed, though we may see enough in the progress of education to inspire us with high hopes, or fill us with painful apprehensions for the result of our efforts, we cannot know the full measure of our success or failure till a decision is made upon the characters of the immortal beings, we have contributed to form, beyond the grave.

The means to be used, too, in the education of the young, requiring a cool and watchful discretion in their selection, as well as in the time and manner of their application, are as various as the forms of visible creation,—infinite, even, as the states of the ever changing spirits within us.

If this view of the proper object of elementary instruction be correct, the foundations of the science of intellectual and moral education, are to be found in the phenomena and principles of the infant mind. And a deep and thorough knowledge of these is as essential to the accomplished and scientific instructer, as the maxims of a system of morals are to the moralist, or the definitions and axioms of mathematics are to the mathematician. The foundation of a teacher's professional skill being laid in an intimate acquaintance with the condition, states, and wants of the youthful mind, and his object being the developement of all its powers and faculties, in their natural order, and each to its due degree of strength and maturity—the superstructure of his science must embrace a thorough knowledge of the various means, direct and indirect, suitable to be used in the attainment of the desired end.

It will at once be perceived that I do not pretend to have found out, either for pupil or for teacher, any royal road to learning. No such thing. On the contrary, though I have laid down principles, which would somewhat smooth the way for pupils, I have greatly magnified the duties and the responsibilities of the teacher. And I hope something may be found in the remarks I have made and may hereafter make, to discourage the temerity of inexperienced teachers in assuming the labors of a profession, upon which they have never bestowed a thought, and for which, of course, they are totally, totally unfit. What! will you require a seven years' apprenticeship, before you will allow a man to drive a nail in the shoe of a horse's foot, or set a stitch in the shoe of your own foot, and yet commit the training of an immortal mind to one who has served no apprenticeship? Will you always be so inconsistent as to lay your hands upon the heads of little children, and invoke the blessing of Heaven upon them, and then send them to a knave to learn morality—a debauchee to learn chastity—or a dunce to learn philosophy? I hardly know which most astonishes me, the presumption which ventures heedlessly upon such high responsibilities, or the folly and inconsistency of parents in committing their children to be educated, to those who can know nothing of their business and duties. I do believe the time is coming, when a more due estimate will be formed both of the difficulties of conducting education, and the consequence to be attached to those who do it successfully. I do believe the time is coming, when he, who has devised means for enlarging the capacities of happiness both here, and hereafter, will be considered as great a benefactor, as he who has invented gunpowder or engines for destroying them.

The study of the youthful mind, the first branch of the science of education, or of a teacher's preparation for his profession, is one of uncommon difficulty. It is not an easy matter to analyze the infant mind, even so far as to enumerate its elementary powers, and state the natural order of their developement, and their mutual connexion and dependence, with intelligible precision. However interesting and alluring it may be, I am not about to make a deliberate essay upon this virgin field of philosophy; nor shall I even enter it, farther than by and by to describe a few of those powers, which I think the correct method of studying geography peculiarly adapted to develope.

It may be new to some of my hearers, even now, to hear

the subject of education spoken of as a science.* I am sure it was new to me but a few years ago. And it must be confessed that the term is applied to it, rather in consideration of

---

* For the leading reflections contained in this and some of the subsequent paragraphs, the reader is referred to an article, published by the author, in the United States Literary Gazette for Dec. 1, 1825. The author takes the liberty to add in this form, and as pertinent to the subject brought under discussion in this part of the lecture, the following remarks published by him, in the same article, to which he has already referred.

'We hold and have held for many years, undoubting belief that the science of education is capable of being reduced, like other sciences, to general principles. By a particular induction, or a long series of discriminating observations, the infant mind may be so far analyzed or its phenomena classed, as to enable us not only to define accurately its several powers with their mutual connexions and dependences, but to fix with precision the natural order of their developement, and to adapt to them such exercises as will develope them most successfully. It might perhaps seem presumption to call in question the axioms of the science; and it certainly would not be easy to point out in a few words the false principles which lie at the foundation of our systems of instruction. Moreover, we should not lightly undertake to calculate the perplexity, and time, and perversion of talents they cost the young—the waste of money they cost parents and the public,—and the waste of patient and laborious effort they cost instructers. We shall name only two false principles, which seem to us to lie at the root of the matter, believing that if they could be reformed the whole subject would assume a new aspect.

'1st. Education is understood to consist in the acquisition of knowledge. This we infer from the pompous catalogues of books and subjects, which are arrayed and set forth as constituting the course of every petty school in the land. They are subjects oftentimes for which the youthful mind is not at all prepared, and by which of course it must be baffled and discouraged. When a subject is presented to a pupil, which requires the exercise of an intellectual faculty not yet developed, he must be as much confused as a blind man would be, if called upon to criticise colors. Education, we believe, at least elementary education, does not consist in the acquisition of knowledge, but in the developement of mind. And subjects should be selected and arranged with reference to this object, the acquisition of knowledge being only incidental.

'2. When the subjects are selected, perhaps judiciously, they are presented in a form which neither affords a salutary discipline to the mind, nor facilitates the acquisition of knowledge. They are all too abstract, or are generalizations of facts, which are themselves unknown to the pupil. Particularly the whole course of the physical and exact sciences, to use a common but expressive phrase, come precisely the wrong end foremost,—first

what it should be, than of what it really is, or is understood to be, even by some who have been long engaged in its practical details. But is it incredible or even improbable, that a new science may yet be disclosed? The searching spirit which is abroad, has developed within a few years several new sciences, which before were almost unknown, or were made up of a few scattered facts, and those not systematically arranged, or reduced to any general principles. Within the short period of my recollection, political economy was despatched in a few paragraphs under some subdivision of the science of politics. Geology and mineralogy have recently sprung up and assumed the dignity of separate sciences. And chemistry has declared independence of natural philosophy. These are now, all of them, sciences, which are found to have important bearings upon the interests of society; and all of them are sciences, which now engross a liberal share of the public attention. And even these may be again subdivided, and others spring out of them which do not now exist even in the imaginations of men.

the general principle, then the particular instances illustrating it. Lord Bacon has taught us that this is not the method by which the human mind takes in knowledge, and it is time we had attended to his instructions. Upon all new subjects of which we have no knowledge or experience, we must first have the particular cases, instances, or facts, abstracting the qualities or points of resemblance, common to them all; then a description of those qualities or points of resemblance, which constitute a general principle.

'We have no room to enlarge upon these topics, but believe they will be found to reach the evils and defects, which have been so long and so severely felt. For, if the purpose of early education be the developement and discipline of the mind, then all subjects must be selected and arranged with reference to this purpose. And if Lord Bacon's philosophy is sound; then the subjects so selected and arranged must be put in that form, in which alone the mind can successfully encounter them.

'If these views are correct, and these principles philosophical,—and we do not see how any one can doubt that they are so,—the question occurs, how they can soonest be developed in all their details, and be made thoroughly effective in all our public as well as private instruction. It seems to us, as we have before intimated, that it can only be done by making the subject the ground of a distinct profession.'

So I believe it will be with education as a branch of moral and intellectual philosophy. There is a whole science wrapped up in that mysterious thing, the infant mind, which has never been developed, nay, hardly yet been discovered to exist;—a science, too, which will have a stronger influence upon the condition and prospects of men than any other. I say a stronger influence, because it relates to that part of ourselves which is susceptible of the highest, perhaps of indefinite improvement, at a period of our lives when every bias is soonest felt, and every impression made, most permanently remains; and because it has for its object to call forth those moral and intellectual powers, that constitute the very instruments with which we must proceed to accomplish whatever is within the reach of man.

Moral philosophy has been studied, reduced to principle, and inculcated in all systems of public instruction; but it only teaches *men* their duty and the reason of it. We have a moral nature and moral feelings, which are susceptible of influence, developement, and direction, by a series of means, before we can reason upon them ourselves. This is the field for the moral philosophy of education. It opens almost with our existence, and extends through all the stages of childhood and youth, till our intellectual faculties are so far developed as to enable us to excite, suppress and control our feelings, and regulate our actions with a reference to distant motives. Then we may begin the *study* of moral philosophy. Before that time we must act from motives, placed before us by those who control our education, without being able to comprehend the ultimate tendency or the reason of our actions; and his moral education is most perfect, whose feelings and habits are so formed, that he needs not to change them when his reason comes to decide upon their fitness with reference to his being's end and aim. The skill of the instructer, therefore, in this department of education, consists in comprehending the temperament and disposition of his pupil, and in addressing those motives only to him, which will induce such actions as he approves, and lead to the formation of such habits as he wishes to establish. If this view of the subject be correct, it must occur to every one, that there are several stages in the developement of our moral nature, and the formation of our moral character, which have never been subjected to a sufficiently minute and rigid examination.

General principles in the moral education of youth, must be established, like all other general principles, by a regular process of induction. And in order to this, a great variety of particular cases must occur, and a great many discriminating observations be made; or, in other words, we must have at hand large experience either of our own, or of those upon whose observations we may safely rely. With sufficient materials for philosophy, or the necessary facts of the case, I know not why we may not establish general principles upon this subject as well as upon any other of a similar nature. And when they are so established, they must be of incalculable utility to those of slight experience in the management and government of youth; and such there must always be, while men attain only to threescore years and ten.

Metaphysicians have analyzed the human mind often enough, and perhaps minutely enough; but it has always been the mind in a state of maturity. This class of philosophers always open their subject, and vindicate its claims to extraordinary dignity, by saying that the materials to be analyzed and the instruments to be employed upon them are all within themselves. So indeed they are within themselves. And for that very reason they describe only those faculties and those operations, of which no one can be conscious, whose mind is not yet in the same advanced stage of developement. But there is a series of years, and important years, in our education, of the intellectual operations peculiar to which we can in manhood have no recollection, and of which we can form no adequate conceptions by reference to the operations of a mature mind under similar circumstances. The analogy between the feeble and fluttering motions of an infant mind, with its faculties partially and unequally developed, and the steady operations of a mature one in full and vigorous action, is by no means so close as to enable us to infer, that what is true of the latter will necessarily be so of the former. The kind of evidence, on which our general principles are to be formed, in the two cases, is almost entirely different. When we attempt to describe the operations of a mature mind, we do it by a *consciousness* of the movements of our own minds under given circumstances; and we strengthen our conclusions by appealing to the *consciousness* of other mature minds under the same circumstances. But whatever we learn of the intellectual habits of children we must learn by very different means. Our own consciousness will do no more than suggest the direction of our inquiries; and we cannot appeal to the consciousness of the child, because it has not yet learned to call off its attention from the external objects of sensation and fix them upon the operations of its own mind; much less has it learned the language suitable to convey to another, ideas, which it has not yet itself received.

Here, then, although the instruments of observation, to use the language of metaphysicians, are within the philosopher, the subject upon which they are to be employed, is not. And this important circumstance constitutes the difference between the science of metaphysics, as it has usually been understood and defined, and the new branch of it, which is about to be developed as the *basis* of the science of education. Nature proceeds by uniform laws in the developement of the infant mind as well as in everything else. What then are these laws, and how shall we trace them? This is a field where there is scope for the exercise of the highest degrees of discrimination and sagacity. Before we can approach with any degree of rational confidence to conclusions in regard to the operations of a child's mind, we must direct the most patient and scrutinizing observations to all the external indications of thought; such as broken sentences, to be made intelligible only by our own ingenuity; the words; the actions; the unconsciously changing countenance, and the beaming eye.

We are upon a level far above the object of our severe scrutiny, and must look down upon its shadowy, complicated, and varying operations, as we look down upon a landscape, whose shades and lines are almost too minute to be traced by our blunted sight. We must observe and arrange, by our own ingenuity, the circumstances which excite it, and trace its operations, or rather the results of its operations, when it is excited, somewhat as we observe phenomena and trace laws in chemistry, by noticing the results of given combinations of elements, when we cannot see the operations going on, or comprehend the mode of them.

What may be the effects of a full developement of the science of education, upon our present systems and modes of instruction, cannot be foreseen. For, that sagacity, which could foretell and minutely describe the changes and improvements that are to be made, would almost necessarily make them. The developement of a new science in all its ramifications and details, must be a slow process, and the work of many minds. But the work is already begun; ay, and it is going forward with a motion as steady and irresistible as that of the spheres. The advances are, indeed, as yet almost unseen; for our systems of instruction, it must be confessed, remain, in almost all essential particulars, as they were left by the revival of letters two centuries ago. But they are now undergoing a severe ordeal; a test, which they cannot stand. The focus of public opinion is upon them; and we have only to hold steady our broad lens, and they must give way. If one effect of the discussions, which are now going on, should be a thorough conviction, that the legitimate purpose of elementary studies is the discipline and developement of the faculties, rather than the acquisition of knowledge, this change of the main object of early education, would necessarily bring in its train, great changes of some kind, both in the subjects to be taught, and in the manner of teaching them. I do not by any means despair of seeing this principle prevail. Indeed, I as firmly believe, as I ardently hope, that the time is soon coming, when we shall see it carried out into all its practical details, not only in our higher schools, but in every common school throughout this wide-spread empire. And then, instead of seeing classes called up, one after another, to exhibit their proficiency in the acquisition of a knowledge of grammar, or rhetoric, or logic, or astronomy, we shall see them classed according to the developement of their minds. And their exhibitions will be so conducted as to show the progress made in the developement and discipline of this or that intellectual faculty. The instructresses of our infant and common schools, will then present their younger classes for examination, and at the same time state to their employers or examiners, that the children are very young, and have been in school but a short time; that they have attended mainly to the developement and discipline of the five *senses*, more particularly, perhaps, to the senses of hearing, seeing, and feeling; that to discipline these senses, they have used such and such means, or exercised them upon such and such subjects. Then she will proceed to exhibit the result of her skill, by showing the strength and accuracy of the several senses in question, by practical examples. No matter, not the least, whether the children have learned to name the senses. They had better learn to use them than to name them. They had better, for the present, learn the names of external objects, and let impalpable abstractions alone.

That the senses are susceptible of cultivation and improvement, even in manhood, admits of no doubt; much more are they so in childhood. But they can be brought to perfection only by repeated exercises adapted to each one of them. Here nature does, indeed, somewhat relieve our ignorance; for the variety of objects and occasions for the use of the senses presented to a child, in almost any situation, are sufficient for the training of the senses, in some degree, to their proper use. But we may, and do frequently, detect one or more of the senses in delinquency. It is then, that skill in the science of education can be most efficaciously applied. The delinquent must be sought out with the keenest scrutiny, and appealed to frequently and earnestly, till it habitually and perfectly performs its proper function.

Having exhibited the proficiency of her youngest class, our instructress will then introduce one a little older, and state to her employers, that this class, having all their senses accurate, developed in harmonious proportion, and each to a considerable degree of strength, has been attending to the cultivation of *perception*, or of the perceptive powers. Their exercises have of course involved those of the preceding and younger class. She will then proceed to exhibit their proficiency, by showing, by examples, with how slight opportunities for sensations they will get distinct perceptions of things.

Upon the vividness of the sensations, to which I have already alluded, depends, in a considerable degree, the accuracy of the consequent perceptions and ideas. These constitute the first furniture of the mind, and the materials for all mental effort. And if they be loose and unformed, not only will all the subsequent modifications of them, and conclusions derived from them by the higher mental operations, be unsatisfactory and unsafe, as modes of belief and rules of action; but the powers of the mind themselves, will receive the greatest detriment from being employed upon poor materials. If the very elements of knowledge are so compounded of truth and error, no wonder so much of the latter ingredient remains to be eradicated in later life by bitter experience; and that the mind itself, from long familiarity with the compound, loses the power of nice discrimination between the component parts.

The cultivation of the perceptive powers, therefore, should begin with the very dawn of intellect, and extend through all subsequent stages of education. Both the power and the habit of getting clear perceptions of all objects and upon all subjects presented to the youthful mind, are absolutely essential to the perfect developement of the later and higher intellectual faculties, as well as to the rapid and easy acquisition of knowledge. To this part of mental culture should be attached the very highest importance, and to it should be directed our earliest and steadiest efforts. Our ultimate success in aiding and directing the developement of a youthful mind, is essentially involved in the degree of perfection, to which we can bring it, in habitually forming clear and distinct perceptions of things.

Though sensation, to a certain degree, at least so far as external objects affect the mind, is essential to every perception, yet, I apprehend, clearness of perception, as a habit, generally depends much more upon attention than sensation. And this brings the formation of the habit more completely within the control of judicious means of education; for no power or habit is susceptible of more cultivation than that of attention. All children, at least so far as my observation and experience have extended, have sensations vivid enough for the ground of distinct perceptions, if they are properly attended to. The pupil, for example, immured in a close and uncomfortable school-room, never mistakes the number of strokes of the clock which is to set him free; though the same sounds, and even much louder, will often pass unheeded, when he is more agreeably employed. The reason is obvious. In one case the sensation is attended to; in the other, not. So we often see children, and youth, and even men, of the most lively habits, and apparently of the quickest sensations, have the most confused perceptions imaginable. The reason is equally obvious. The sensations succeed each other with such rapidity, that they are blended one with another. The volatile and lively mind glances a hasty and wavering attention over the whole, but does not dwell long enough upon any particular part, to get a distinct impression of it; while he of slower mould and duller sensations, having learned the necessity of making the most of them, will carry away from the observation of the same object, under the same circumstances, a very distinct perception.

This distinction in the intellectual habits of children, is among the first that appears, and seems to spring originally and chiefly from physical causes. In its turn, it becomes itself a cause, and gives rise, more than any other single one, to that infinite diversity of talent and disposition, discoverable among men. This view of the origin of habits of confused perception, suggests the different courses of discipline, to be adopted with each class of individuals, as the confusion arises from too dull sensations, or too fickle attention. The child whose sensations are constitutionally dull, requires to be aroused and stimulated by gentle excitements, not only that his sensations may be more vivid, but that, by increased efforts of attention, he may make the most of them, defective as they are, in obtaining clear perceptions; while the child of lively habits and quick sensations, requires to have all excitements taken away, even those he may create for himself. For the very difficulty lies in the flickering attention arising from excessive excitement and sensitiveness. The latter is by far the most common fault of youthful minds, and requires the utmost skill for its modification and correction. And what will you do to correct it? Will you treat it harshly? Will you lay a weight of unyielding restraint upon this tender little being, and thus, as it were, grind to powder a germ of intellect? Oh no! God forbid! It is an immortal mind! We must deal gently and carefully with it; for our impressions upon it are indelible as eternity is enduring.

These obstacles to clear perceptions vary so infinitely, both in kind and degree, in different individuals, that we cannot rationally hope wholly to remove them by any general principle applied without discrimination to large classes. We may do much to strengthen and confirm habits already formed in the youthful mind, by the courses of discipline pupils are subjected to in classes or large numbers; but the habits must be commenced by particular attention to the condition of every individual mind. We must rely chiefly, therefore, on our personal intercourse with individuals, for discovering their wants and weaknesses, and applying the proper remedies, suggested by the peculiar circumstances of each case. If, for example, you have in hand a pupil, or a class of pupils, of sluggish mould, and apparently of dull sensations, and would form in them the habit of clear perception, seize an opportunity in your daily intercourse with them to take them up with considerable promptness and energy in your manner, to some striking but complex object of sense. They will irresistibly imbibe somewhat of your own spirit and energy from example, contact, and sympathy. Direct this attention to the object, and if you would produce a little more excitement, limit the time allowed for getting a precise idea of all its parts, or suspend some consequence upon success, and then require a description of the whole. You will gain something by every instance of such discipline; and the pleasure of success will soon aid you so far as to set your pupils upon trying the same exercise by themselves.

On the other hand, if you would form the same habit of clear perceptions, in a pupil whose confused perceptions arise from volatility,—and this is the common fault,—you should, with a very cool and deliberate manner, request him to observe some complex object, and with plenty of time before you, to enumerate with great minuteness and describe with great precision, in the presence of the object, all its parts. He would soon learn that a gleam of general attention to the whole would not answer his purpose. He must fix his mind, with unfaltering energy, successively upon every minute part of a complex object, before he can obtain perceptions of them all, with their relations to each other, so distinct as to enable him to describe them intelligibly, even while the object itself is before him to attract his fluttering attention and refresh his confused sensations. At a later period, and when the difficulty has been partially conquered, you may gradually withdraw the external object from the senses, and require of your pupil a description scrupulously exact, from his conceptions alone.

I have spoken of sensation and perception, and shown their susceptibility of cultivation, especially in the early stages of education. I have noticed the importance of those powers, as the foundation of intellectual and moral culture, and alluded briefly to some of the means, by which we may hope to develope them. But though the degree of perfection, in which these powers are possessed by any individual, will indicate, with considerable precision, the strength and energy of his mind, they are not more important to him than *attention*, which we may suppose would be the next in order to receive cultivation. If there be any power of the youthful mind more completely within the control of judicious means of education, or more essential to the healthful developement of the higher faculties, and to the easy and rapid acquisition of knowledge, than others, it is the power of voluntary attention. However perfectly all other powers and faculties may be possessed, the mind can do but little, without the direction of this severe and wary controller of its movements. The effectiveness of an army, depends not more upon having its able-bodied men subjected to the command of a skilful general, than the energy of a mind does upon having its faculties under the control of voluntary attention. We should hardly exaggerate the importance of this power of the mind, if we should say, that the main business of early education consisted in watching the natural developement of the other faculties, and subjecting them, as they rise, to the control of attention.

No time of the pupil and no pains of the teacher, therefore, are wasted, if judiciously appropriated to the cultivation of the power and the formation of the habit of attention. And while engaged in exercises upon any subject for this purpose, all considerations of the value in itself of that subject, or the acquisition made in it, should give place to the precise object in view. Considering its importance, we deserve, and considering the difficulty of its attainment, we need, all the aids we can derive from every quarter. Not among the least of these is it to take subjects for the mental exercises, designed to cultivate attention, in themselves interesting. For no principle in education is more obvious, upon the slightest consideration, than that the mind is most easily fixed upon what is most agreeable to it. It should be a prominent motive, therefore, in the selection of topics on which to employ the minds of young pupils, to take such as interest them. No matter what the subject is, if it be but attractive. It is chiefly through inattention to this plainest principle of education, that so many youths pass the period of all direct instruction, with such a feeble control of their own minds. We certainly discover great diversities in the interest, which children and youth manifest in different objects of nature, as well as in different subjects of speculation; and though their taste may not seem to mature minds the best, and though they may not be able to give any satisfactory reason for their choice, it is the part of wisdom to indulge, for a season, even their caprice. We want the control of their attention, and we must have it, at almost any sacrifice of time. If a horse, unaccustomed to the bit, will not, at first, move with us in the precise direction we wish, we allow him to prance and curvet and to take his own course, till he has learned to submit to the bit and to bear us; then we can easily turn him where we wish. And it will be a matter of but small concern, if he have, in the course of his discipline, carried us a few miles out of our way, provided we secure by the sacrifice a perfect control of him during the remainder of his life.

But though the interest of the pupil in what he may be employed upon, be essential to the successful cultivation of the power of attention, fewer sacrifices in the choice of subjects will be necessary to secure it, than might at first be imagined. For the interest of the youthful mind depends much more upon the obvious aspect of an object than upon its nature. Hence the skill of the teacher lies in always placing the learner on the sunny side of what he would secure his attention to. So in a later period of education, when the thoughts begin to grow discursive, and to range through wider fields of observation and experience, the chief interest felt by the pupil in the various subjects presented to him for reflection and speculation, depends upon the view he takes of them, and the associations he forms with them. Hence the efforts of the teacher should be directed to making the associations with a subject in which he would create an interest, agreeable. And in order to effect this, he should, if possible, and it generally is possible, display some more or less immediate practical bearing of it upon the pupil's own happiness. Subjects not naturally interesting may frequently, by the exercise of a little discretion of the teacher, in forming associations with them, become so, or at least not intolerably revolting.

The power of attention is most successfully cultivated in the early stages of education, by employing the mind upon objects of sense. Every part of the sensible creation has the charm of novelty to the infant mind; and the eagerness, with which it flies from one thing to another, shows how strongly it is attracted by new objects, and how much it is predisposed by curiosity to rest upon them. But the very freshness of nature, and particularly of animated nature, which proves so attractive to the untrained senses and the opening faculties of the mind, is also a warning to us not to attempt to keep the attention long upon the same object. A child is incapable, however interesting the object may be at first, of long continued and undivided attention to it. It is the part of wisdom, therefore, to yield to the teachings of nature, and not attempt to counteract her laws by requiring long efforts of the youthful mind upon the same thing. Children have a natural aversion, too, to rigid system in their mental as well as in their physical exercises, because the very novelty of objects and of the motions of the muscular organs, is constantly attracting them in every direction; and as the combinations of these are infinite in variety, they war effectually against all rules, till novelty is by degrees abated by experience. The power of attention is often weakened by requiring its exercise too long upon the same thing. Every attempt to fix the mind upon an object, beyond the point when interest declines and fatigue begins, will not only fail, but the very restraint forms a disagreeable association, which will render the next effort more unpleasant and consequently less likely to succeed.

Children rush with animated gambols and shouting from the mental exercises of the school-room into the open air, not because there is naturally more pleasure in the motions of the body than in those of the mind,—this would be a reflection upon the wisdom and the goodness of God, and is absurd on the very face of it,—but because they are generally free from rigid system in their physical exercises, and may take what course best pleases them; while the school-room is rendered intolerable to them by its restraints upon their restless spirits, by the rigidness of its rules, the sternness and tyranny with which they are executed, or perhaps the cruelty with which their slightest violation is avenged. These all form disagreeable associations with mental exercises, which no skill in the teacher can wholly counteract. Hence the buoyant and elastic spirits, which rebound from the leaden atmosphere of the school-room with such irregular explosions, are instantly quelled and compressed by the summons to their disagreeable duty. At the first stroke of the bell, which subjects them to rules, their joyful countenances assume the air of one without hope. And they return to duty in a procession as solemn as one of friars, and with much the same feelings as we may suppose to animate the affected solemnity of the professional mourners of Italy.

Though the commencement of the formation of the habit of attention must be made by means of sensible objects, a second stage in the process soon succeeds, when we must take subjects which are of a mixed nature, requiring the exercise of attention partly upon ideas of reflection and partly upon those of sensation. The pupil is now supposed to have acquired a considerable stock of ideas from external objects, and to have performed many operations upon them in his own mind. He can now hold his mind for very short periods upon trains of thought, when all objects of sense are withdrawn; nevertheless, he requires the aid of sensation, if an effort of attention be demanded for any considerable time. And by such means the mind may be kept steadily upon trains of thought much longer than could otherwise be done.

Habits of attention for short periods of time, are early and naturally formed in children, by exercising their minds upon those objects of sense which interest them. But these feeble habits are usually destroyed or very much impaired by teachers, as soon as they begin the work of systematic education. For they make a sudden transition from exercises of the mind wholly upon objects or ideas of sense, to those upon ideas of memory or reflection; and seem to expect the same degree of continued attention to the latter, which has hitherto been paid only to the former. I once knew a little child taken from his toys and playthings in the nursery, and sent to school for the first time without a knowledge of his letters. His teacher, a gentleman of liberal education and of distinguished attainments as a scholar, marked off the seven first letters of the alphabet, and sent our little pupil to his seat to learn his lesson. Do you think it strange that the child found it difficult to confine his attention to his book?

This is unreasonable. The principal means of exciting an interest, and thereby keeping up the attention, has been suddenly withdrawn, viz. the sensations produced by the presence of interesting external objects. The transition should be more gradual. While the subjects, upon which the minds of children are employed, before what is called direct instruction begins, are almost exclusively those arising immediately from the objects of sense presented to them, those employed by teachers in their instruction are as exclusively abstract. The moment the child passes from the hand of his parent to that of a professed teacher, the requisitions upon his attention are greatly increased, while his facilities for yielding it are diminished. A disagreeable association is thus formed by the pupil with everything and everybody, which has been thus accessary to making him unhappy; and all the ordinary means of overcoming the association increase rather than weaken it, till that common consummation arrives—the proverbial irksomeness of study.

I have described the powers of *sensation, perception,* and *attention,* and discussed, in general terms, some of the means to develope and improve them. I have been more copious, perhaps, than courtesy to your patience would have suggested; but certainly more brief than the interest and importance of the subjects demand. I could have wished time and strength to discuss in this connexion, also, the powers of *memory, conception*, and *judgment*, as among those early faculties of the mind, which I think the study of geography upon the correct principle is peculiarly adapted to develope. But the extent of the subject seems more suited to the purpose of a treatise than the compass of a lecture. And the length to which my more general remarks, and my imperfect analysis of these few powers of the mind, have carried me, warns me to presume no longer upon your patience, but to proceed to the consideration of the subject of geography, and the best method of teaching it.

In this part of my lecture, particularly, I shall endeavour to be plain and practical, even at the expense of every other consideration. I must here also necessarily adopt the ideas, and, perhaps, I shall in some instances use the same language, which I have before used and published, more than six years ago. If I should, and what I say have not the charm of novelty with all who hear me, I trust it will be a sufficient apology for me to state, that I have nothing better to say upon this subject now than I said then, and that it seems necessary something should be said upon the point, in this place.

Children are very early capable of describing the places, mountains, and rivers, which pass under their inspection. And they commonly do it with an enthusiasm, which shows how lively an interest they take in the subject, and how deep an impression the peculiarities of new places make upon them. 'Oh! father, we saw a great river three times as wide as our river.' This is the common language of little children, and when they have thus learned, by actual *perception*, a few of the features of the face of the earth, at a period a little later they are capable of feeling a similar interest in forming a *conception* of places, mountains, and rivers, from representation and description. Then may with propriety commence the study of geography; because then they can understand it, if it is presented to their minds in its simplest forms.

This is an elementary study, which has been more neglected, till within a few years, than its importance deserves, whether we consider the value of the knowledge obtained, or whether we consider the adaptation of the study to the early developement of the mind. As commerce and letters multiply the mutual interests, relations, and dependences of distant places, and especially as the facilities of intercourse among them are increased, some knowledge of those places becomes almost indispensable to all professions and classes of society.

Till within a few years, however, there has been but little order in the arrangement of the books, which could be used as text-books. Facts and descriptions were selected with no very great care or attention to their importance, and with less, if possible, to their authenticity. These materials were thrown together upon some plan adopted from the caprice of the author, but with not the least reference to the learner. Consequently, the whole subject was almost totally neglected;—so much depends upon the manner, in which knowledge is presented to the learner. But within a few years great improvements have been made in the elementary books upon this subject, which have brought it into notice. It is now very generally, though I am far from believing very successfully, taught in our schools. The manner of teaching it by question and answer, which is the manner adopted by the books most approved at present, is objectionable, although it enables the young learner *to seem* to have acquired great knowledge of the subject. The questions direct the learner to the most important facts, no doubt; but that is of little consequence to him, so long as he is unprepared to comprehend them. He connects the question and its answer by some artificial association, and will repeat a passage containing important information, with verbal accuracy. To the hearers, who have already acquired a knowledge of the subject, and who attach to the words a definite and correct meaning, the child seems to have an astonishing fund of knowledge. But

I apprehend, that many a child, who thus delights and astonishes his parents, and gains his books and instructer great renown, would make as sorry a figure, on more careful examination, as the child mentioned by Miss Hamilton. After answering to all his questions, and giving an accurate account of the statistics of Turkey, on being asked, 'Where is Turkey?'—a question not in the book—he replied, '*In the yard with the poults.*'

But, notwithstanding the strong objections to printed questions in our elementary books, when the alternative comes to be between questions well shaped by the author, and the marking-off and committing-to-memory system, which was formerly and is yet sometimes practised, there can be no doubt that the former is the lesser of the evils. If the instructer understand both the subject and his pupil's mind well enough to ask *judicious* questions, I should much prefer that printed questions were wholly omitted. They are an evil, and were better avoided, unless, by adopting them, we avoid a still greater evil.

The improvements in our school-books upon this subject, have consisted in greater attention and accuracy in the collection of authentic and important facts, and in a more consistent arrangement of them. But by far the most important improvement, made in the last twenty years in teaching geography,—and it has hardly been taught at all longer than that in our common schools,—is the introduction of maps. The principle of using maps deserves unqualified approbation. For when the object and meaning of a map are thoroughly understood by the pupil, it aids him to confine his attention, and form a conception of the relative magnitude of towns, countries, states, and continents, and also of the relative length and breadth of rivers, and the situation of places with regard to each other, much better than the most elaborate and minute descriptions, without such aid. But the plan, and especially the principle of arrangement, upon which almost all the most popular books upon this subject have been made, I must beg leave to object to strongly, and decidedly. And while I hold my own opinions upon this subject, and claim the right to state, to explain and to vindicate them; if others hold different opinions, they have the same rights. Our difference of opinion in this age of free inquiry is not surprising, and implies no mutual disrespect.

The pupil, by some of the most approved systems, is presented in the onset with a map of the whole world, reduced to the size of a hat-crown. In connexion with this, he is directed to read a description of the largest rivers, mountains and seas; and also to learn some accounts of the character and manners of the principal nations.. Perhaps he will now be required to learn the amount of exports and imports of the most commercial nations, to the accuracy of a farthing.

Some, not content with presenting the whole earth to the first and single glance of the young learner, and as if determined to push the absurdity of the plan to the utmost, have given the whole solar system to the child, for his first lesson in geography. This is called setting up landmarks, and getting a general knowledge of the subject; but so far from that, in my view, it is getting no knowledge at all. It is only a confusion of words, without any definite meaning attached to them whatever.

The subject is begun precisely at the wrong end. If it is addressed to the understanding of the young learner, this arrangement seems to presume that he will take a deeper interest in, and better comprehend the general features of the world, embracing the largest mountains and rivers, and the characters of nations, of whose existence he has perhaps never before heard, than the roads, hills, and rivers of his own neighbourhood, and the boundaries of his own town, county, or State. Besides, upon the strictest philosophical principles, it is perfectly demonstrable that he can get no adequate idea of the magnitude of the largest mountains and rivers of the world, except by comparing them with the mountains and rivers which he has seen, and of which he has formed some definite idea. 'A river three times as wide as our river!'—this is the natural language of children, and it is philosophical language. In forming a conception of a distant mountain or river, which we have never seen, we proceed precisely as we do in forming a conception of any other magnitude. We fix upon something of the same kind, which is known as a unit of measure; and then compare, and discover the relation of what is known with what is unknown. So the child could form some idea of a mountain twice as high as the hill before his eyes; or he could form a tolerable conception of a river three times as broad as the brook, which runs before his father's door, or the river he may, perhaps, have seen in a neighbouring town; but talk to him at once of a mountain many thousand feet high, and a river a hundred miles wide, and I am much mistaken if he forms the least conception of what he is told.

When God created Adam, we are told that he placed him in the Garden of Eden. What do you suppose Adam wished to know first after he opened his eyes on the fair face of the earth, over whose inhabitants he was newly appointed lord? And what course do you suppose he took to become acquainted with his dominions and his duties? Did he stand in conscious dignity, and carefully survey the objects around him on that part of the earth's surface on which he found himself; or, did he sit down and sigh for a book treating of America or the moon? If he had a particle of unperverted reason, he first surveyed the Garden of Eden, and that from the point on which he stood. He soon became acquainted with every part of it. He knew every tree. He examined every hillock and every precipice. He found every spring, and followed the course of every rivulet within his little territory. Then and not till then would he naturally begin to look abroad beyond his immediate enclosures, and see whether the streams, which fertilized the Garden of Eden, were common to other places. Then and not till then would he naturally begin to inquire whence they came, and whither they went.

The correct plan for an elementary work on geography,

would, therefore, enable the learner to begin at home, with a description, and if practicable with a map, of the town in which he lives. Or if that should be thought too particular, the instructer must supply the description, and the map begin with the pupil's own county or State, in which he will of course be most interested. From this he may proceed to the whole country or kingdom, and thence to the more general divisions of the earth. The maps will of course be reduced in their scale, and the descriptions grow less and less minute, as the places are further removed, or from any cause become less interesting. This presents the geography of the earth in perspective. And it should be so. We need to know most, other things being equal, concerning those places, which are nearest to us.

Having traced the progress of geography to its present condition in our schools, and having stated my views of the best arrangement of elementary geographical works as perspicuously as I am able in the brief space I can assign to this part of my lecture, I proceed to explain how I should recommend that the subject be taught. Each pupil* should be provided with a small, light, black board, say eighteen inches long by fifteen broad. If this cannot easily be procured, a common slate and pencil will very well answer the purpose. Each pupil should also have a map of the country lying immediately around him, on a distinct and large scale; for here he is to begin his study. After explaining the points of compass, let his attention be directed to the map; explain to him by some famil-

* Children of common capacity, of five or six years of age, may with advantage begin the study of geography upon the plan here recommended, provided they can be supplied by their teacher or otherwise with a description of the country immediately around them, in such simple language as they can understand, and with a full map of the same region on a large and distinct scale. The acquisition of useful knowledge, even by children of this tender age, will be very considerable, and the habits of mind formed will be found to be of incalculable utility in pursuit of all other subjects of education, to which their attention may be simultaneously or subsequently directed.

iar illustration the meaning of a map, and inform him that the top is north, the bottom south, the right hand east, and the left hand west. Let him find on the map the town or the village, where he resides, and observe carefully its shape, its ponds, its rivers, and its hills or mountains. All these he is to draw from the map upon his slate or small black board, and to draw them over and over again upon a variety of scales, till he can do it accurately from his memory and conceptions, without the aid of his map. Next, direct the pupil to observe on the map the boundaries of his town; and to observe them so carefully as to be able to name the places which lie around his own drawing, when his map is withdrawn from him. He may now lay down his map and small black board, and see what he can find in his elementary book, or in any book, concerning the place he has been drawing. To show the pupil that this is a matter for investigation, and that it is one for which he is fully competent, his teacher should encourage him to consider whether he knows anything about this town, whose shape and features he has been drawing. Whether there are any small streams, mills, factories, or public institutions in it, which he cannot find in any description. He will probably be able to draw the road, which passes by his own schoolhouse, and to place a mark at least for the position of the schoolhouse. If he can do this, he will be greatly gratified with his acquirements and success. And well he may be; for he understands much more of the use of a map and the meaning of the term geography, than if he had merely learned to say that 'geography is a description of the earth.' If the teacher can add anything to the pupil's knowledge of the place, relate any event or anecdote of history, which happened there; or if he can refer the pupil to any correct sources of information upon the subject, he will not only add variety to the exercise, and thus fix the attention, but will inculcate the very important habit of investigation. And this habit may be formed while children are yet very young.

This is learning the lesson. And when one or two lessons

have been learned in this way, the teacher will have very little more trouble with this part of the business, whatever may be the number of his pupils. The lesson being thus learned, all books and small black boards may now be laid aside, and the pupil is ready to recite.

For recitations a large black board should be used, at least three feet wide and three and a half feet long. This, if possible, should be so placed in the school-room, that the pupil standing before it, may have his face to the north; when of course his right hand will be to the east, his back to the south, and his left hand to the west. If the class consist of several, and be now assembled for recitation, let them stand round, fronting the black board, in such a manner that each, as well as the teacher, may see every line that may be drawn. Direct one pupil to draw the north line of the town or portion of the earth's surface, which he has been learning, on as large a scale as the board will admit. As soon as he has done it, let him step back to his place, and let it be distinctly understood that it is the privilege and the duty of every pupil in the class to criticise the work. They have all a direct interest in seeing that it is done correctly; because, if it be incorrect, it will affect every line they attempt to join to it, and thus prevent them from being accurate themselves. Besides, they have another motive to steady attention to the business, perhaps as strong as that of interest. Such is the perversity of human nature, we are very willing to see each other's faults. If no one has any amendment to offer, and the teacher is satisfied with the work, he may call upon another to draw the east line, and subject the work to the same critical examination. There is a new difficulty comes into the work in drawing this line, because it must be drawn in exact proportion to the first boundary. The pupil must not only have an accurate conception of each line, and each part of a line, in his mind, but he must judge of their proportions to each other; and so must the whole class when they come to criticise. Observe now the various and distinct powers of the mind, that have been called into exercise thus far only in the process of reciting. There is sensation, perception, conception, discrimination, and judgment; and all of them under their strict marshal, attention.

Having completed the outline of the lesson in this manner, let a pupil be called upon to name the towns on its borders, marking the place of each as he names them, mentioning its direction from the town drawn, and pointing to its actual position with reference to the place in which he stands. Then let the hills, mountains, streams and ponds be laid down upon the drawing, and require the pupil to point with his hand to their true position from him. Having thus recited what has been learned from the map without its aid, and from the mind alone, you may be sure your lesson is understood. There can be no mistake. And if the lesson cannot be so recited, you cannot be sure that your pupil understands what he has been about. For we have not distinctly conceived the situations of places, till we can form our conceptions alone, and represent those places in a drawing.

With the black board and their drawing still before the class, questions should now be asked to elicit all the historical, botanical, geological or any topographical information, which may have been obtained in the course of the investigations to which I have before alluded.

It will be perceived that in reciting a lesson in geography, I call for historical information, and I improve the opportunity to remark, that I think children should always learn the particulars or facts of history in connexion with geography. And this is as far as children can go in history. The particulars, the facts or events are naturally and strongly associated with the places where they happened. You cannot separate them, if the child perfectly understands them both. You must let them go into his mind together. For example; if a child have a distinct conception of the shape and situation of Bunker-hill, and have also in his memory an account of the interesting and important event, which happened there, they will always suggest each other. The association is the natural one, and therefore it is the best one, which can be found for a child. The infant mind cannot associate the events of history by cause and effect, which is always the principle of association in philosophical history. Therefore, general and philosophical history is not adapted to the youthful mind. Children can understand detached events, and they will always be most interested in them, and consequently be most likely to understand them perfectly, in connexion with the places where those events happened. At a subsequent and a late period in their mental developement, they can associate these particulars together by the principle of cause and effect. Then, and not till then, can they study to advantage a philosophical and general history. All history before that is to them chronology.

Having thus completed the pupil's own town, the next exercise may be one or more of the adjoining towns, according to their difficulty. At reciting this second lesson, the shape of the town or towns may be drawn upon a variety of scales. This exercise will be found to be exceedingly useful, as a severe discipline of the mind is involved in producing accurate proportions. And the whole class should be kept constantly on the alert, in judging of the truth of the proportions between the several lines drawn by each one of them. When greater ease has been acquired in drawing, and several towns can be despatched at a lesson, there will be a wider field for this exercise in adjusting the relative size and shape of different towns. Let the class thus pass through their own county, taking for each lesson a group of contiguous towns; and there should be a review of their work as often as once for every four or five lessons.*

I will not detain you longer upon the details of teaching geography, than barely to observe, that besides my more gen-

---

* If this process should be thought too minute, the pupil has only to begin drawing by counties, and proceed to the completion of his own State, in the same manner as he would by the above process complete his own county.

eral remarks just made, I have gone through above, very minutely, the process of learning and reciting one lesson. *Ex uno discite omnes.* You will, perhaps, inquire, if it takes so long to describe the process, and a still longer time for the pupil to perform it, where we shall find time for the study of geography, upon this plan. A whole life would be consumed in the process. So, indeed, it would, if we were to go over the whole earth's surface with the same minuteness, with which we learn our own town. But this is neither necessary nor desirable. The whole empire of China would, perhaps, be despatched by pupils here in less time than would be necessary to draw a county. So that on the whole we shall not lose much time. On the contrary, in one respect at least we shall gain time; for we shall find appropriate employment for children, who now waste, worse than waste, their years upon studies not suited to their capacities.

While I do not concede that a minute and accurate knowledge of geography yields to that of any other science in practical utility as an acquisition; and while I do not concede that this particular mode of teaching it, is less likely to leave permanent valuable knowledge in the mind of the pupil than any other, but, on the contrary, contend that it will enable him to retain his acquisitions much better than the common methods, or any method with which I am acquainted; still it is not upon either or both of these considerations, that I mainly found the claims of geography to attention, as an elementary study for young children. It affords, when studied in the manner I have described, the best of discipline for several of the powers earliest developed in the infant mind. And, *therefore*, they should be employed upon it. I do not know that I should go too far, if I should say, that,—if the vast amount of geographical knowledge they will acquire, were entirely useless in itself, and if every fact, description and interesting event learned, were utterly obliterated from the mind, the moment they close their book,—I would nevertheless put them upon the study for the discipline it affords the mind alone. I know of no one elementary study within the range of subjects adapted to the capacities of children, which calls into exercise so many of their faculties, and trains them in such an agreeable manner, as geography, when it is properly studied. The sense of seeing and the perceptive powers in examining the shapes of geographical delineations,—the power of conception, in forming in the mind the image of objects, when the objects themselves are withdrawn, —the powers of discrimination, comparison and judgment in adjusting the relative proportions of lines,—memory in relating the facts and events of local history,—are among those early faculties which are most exercised and disciplined by this elementary study. And last and greatest of all is the advantage of it in forming the invaluable habits of investigation, accurate observation, and attention. Being partly employed upon ideas derived immediately from the senses, and partly upon those of memory and reflection, it forms, in a course of early discipline, a convenient link between the playthings of the nursery and the abstractions of the school-room.

I have now said all that I intended to say upon geography, and the best mode of teaching it. A word to my brethren of the profession, and I have done. We are about to leave here upon record our names and 'a pledge of our zealous efforts to promote the cause of popular education.' May that pledge be redeemed in spirit and in truth. It is a great cause; none can be greater. Our progress must, indeed, be slow, with all our efforts; but then, with them, it may be sure. Bacon, our great benefactor, has thrown forward an anchor for us, with which the world has not yet come up. And if you will consent to seize hold and pull, you will produce a much more sensible motion, than to be hoisting your sails and flourishing your pennants in a dead calm. Science now sits solemnly in her temple afar off. The ways of approach are dark and devious. A few votaries, only, by chance or untired perseverance, gain access, till, at the expense of half their lives, they are warned by experience, like an inspiration from Above, to become as little children, that they may enter. But when the influence of education is more duly estimated; and when the cultivation of the head and heart shall be united, and, indeed, form one distinct and dignified profession, drawing to its practice the greatest and the best of men; then we may hope that a proper direction will be given to the opening minds and expanding hearts of the young, and that all the deep and permanent prepossessions of childhood and youth, will be upon the side of truth and virtue. Science, philosophy and religion will then be blended with their very natures, to grow with their growth, and strengthen with their strength.

In this great work we can all participate. But what *we* do must be done quickly. We are passing rapidly on upon the great high road of life. Other generations are coming forward in crowds to take our places; and soon, very soon, instead of the fathers shall be the children. We ought to meet them, to meet them in their cradles, and extend to them, to every one of them, the blessings of a good education.

I call upon you, whose dominion is in the domestic circle, you, who send your influences unseen into the rugged recesses of sterner hearts, to lend us your aid. You, who hold in your arms and lead by the hand the hope of the present and the strength of the coming generation, lend us your aid. You, who minister at the altars of religion, warn us of our sins, and reassure our feebler virtues, lend us your aid. You, who are appointed to rule in the land, and to whom is committed the ark of our free institutions, lend us your aid.

MR RUSSELL'S LECTURE.

LECTURE III.

THE

INFANT SCHOOL SYSTEM OF EDUCATION,

AND THE EXTENT

TO WHICH IT MAY BE ADVANTAGEOUSLY APPLIED

TO ALL

PRIMARY SCHOOLS.

BY WILLIAM RUSSELL.

The establishment of schools adapted to the condition and capacities of infancy, is an important event, whether regarded as the commencement of a new era in the exertions of philanthrophy and charity, or the source of extensive improvement in elementary education. These schools are the field of a most interesting experiment in morals. The question is here to be answered, whether much of human evil may be avoided or averted, rather than remedied; whether, in the treatment of the mind, as well as of the body, a preventive may be substituted for a curative regimen. The momentous results connected with this new order of things, are developing in gradual but sure and encouraging succession. The physical frame of man is beginning to receive a portion of that care which is due to it, as a production of creative wisdom; the human heart begins to be regarded as the native soil of virtue, which early culture is to keep free from encroaching weeds; and the intellect begins to be treated as a self-impelling power, which education is to aid, rather than to check.

The general effect of methods founded on such views of education can, as yet, be imagined only. But even the slight progress already made, affords a wide scope to just expectation. The rational education of infancy seems destined to effect vast, though silent and unostentatious, changes on the condition of man. His physical strength and activity, his intellectual and moral tendencies, may, by this means, be brought under the influence of such modes and habits of action as shall renovate his whole character; substituting intelligent, spontaneous, and habitual virtue, with its attendant happiness, for the struggle of self-conquest, or the pain of conscious failure,—the two extremes between which the human heart has hitherto vibrated, under the influence of arbitrary education. No doubt, at least, remains, that the most successful as well as the most natural method of removing many of the evils of social life, is, to impart active habits, and an elevated character, to the minds of the poor, and to do this effectually and extensively, by means of universal early education.

As little doubt seems to remain, that the modes of elementary instruction, prevailing previous to the introduction of infant schools, were, in general, defective and inadequate; that, under their influence, the health of the body, and the natural action of the mind, were neglected; the affections left uncultivated or ill-regulated; the intellect forced into arbitrary channels, and accustomed to mechanical influences and morbid habits.

It is unnecessary to enter at present into a particular statement of the common defects of elementary education, previous to the introduction of the methods adopted in infant schools. They may be briefly summed up in the great neglect of physical accommodation, of comfort, and of health; in the small size, defective ventilation, inconvenient arrangement, and gloomy aspect of most school-rooms; their uncomfortable seats; the long continued and painful sedentary attitude of the little pupils; the entire absence of appropriate visible objects, addressed to the active feelings and restless imagination of childhood; the want of cheering and invigorating exercise;

a mechanical routine of application, producing little effect but on the memory, and leaving the understanding and the imagination nearly inactive; lessons presented, in general, in the form of compulsory tasks; modes of discipline retrospective rather than anticipative, repulsive, therefore, and arbitrary, not founded on reason and affection, and influencing the imagination only through the medium of fear or restraint; no social intercourse between the pupils permitted; and consequently the natural opportunities for influencing feeling and character precluded.

A well-regulated infant school furnishes a happy contrast to these defects: it exhibits a spacious, airy, cheerful, and comfortable apartment, prepared expressly for every good influence on the infant being; a frequent change of attitude and of employment; the presence of pictures and other objects calculated to inspire the mind with activity and delight, or to diffuse tranquillity and tenderness of feeling; mental employments interspersed with appropriate juvenile exercise, or judicious intervals of entire rest; lessons adapted to the capacities and desires of infancy; mental exertion rendered agreeable and voluntary; discipline consisting chiefly of rational and affectionate measures addressed to sympathy and moral feeling, and, as far as practicable, to reason, and turning upon the incidents arising from the pupils' intercourse with each other. Such are the prominent features of the system adopted in infant schools, and which, as might reasonably have been anticipated, at a time of unusual thought and inquiry on the subject of education, have commended themselves to the minds of all who have had opportunity to observe them,—which have already, to some extent, been introduced in primary and other elementary schools, and which have become a subject of peculiar interest to all who are, in any way, concerned in early education.

Before attempting to speak more particularly of the extent to which these improvements in instruction may be introduced in primary schools in this country, it will be necessary to advert to the circumstances in which the infant schools originated, and under which they still exist, in England. There, they were introduced as a charity, designed for the benefit of the poor. Experience soon suggested, in some instances, the advantage of allowing them, in part, at least, to depend on a slight contribution from the parents of the children who are taught in them. But they continue, in general, like some of those established in cities in this country, to present themselves as institutions of benevolence, patronized by the bounty of the richer classes of society, rather than supported by the voluntary exertions of the poor themselves, or by the choice of parents in better circumstances, who prefer them to other schools, or to the common course of domestic education.

Another circumstance deserving consideration towards a proper estimation of infant schools, and the methods of instruction adopted in them, is the fact, that these schools were originally established for the benefit of a class of society among whom the advantages of any form of education had scarcely been felt,—for parents whose circumstances were, in general, such, that they felt it necessary to have their children put, as early as possible, into the way of earning something towards the support of their families. People in such a condition naturally regard even the slightest acquisition in education, as a new and unexpected benefit, and are not generally solicitous about the attainments made by their children at an elementary school, as introductory to education at schools of a higher order. But even in those cases in which infant schools are expressly intended as a preparatory step to the national schools of England, (corresponding in some respects to the primary and common schools of New England,) the initiation required at the infant schools is limited by the narrowness of education at these higher schools themselves; in few or none of which the branches of instruction, or the extent to which they are carried, are equal to those of the New England common schools, when conducted by a teacher of enterprise and intelligence.

The attempt, therefore, to transfer the infant school system, as it is called, to the first stages of instruction in this country, would seem to require a consideration of the difference of the state of education here, and in England. The children of every parent in New England, may, by the auspicious arrangement of the system of public schools, receive the benefit of instruction, as soon as they are old enough to walk to the schoolhouse. What is here needed, then, in the way of improvement, is not the introduction of a new system, but the better adaptation of that which already exists, to the education of the youngest classes of scholars. All the advantages of the methods of instruction in infant schools, would be attained by adopting the *spirit* of these methods, in *primary education*. Every village school in New England, may, during the summer, if not the winter months, become an infant school, as far as such a change is desirable.

That the result, in this case, would be highly advantageous, is a point which needs no proof to those who have ever visited an infant school, and observed the intelligence, the cheerfulness, and the infantine innocence and goodness which they cherish, even when taught in a very imperfect and mechanical way.

The extent to which the infant school system may be applied to all primary schools, should be measured, not by the extent to which its routine may be borrowed or copied. The mechanism of the infant school system is, indeed, excellent in many respects. Its whole aspect is happy and inspiring, and favors the expansion of the intellect and the heart, while it promotes a healthful vigor of body. But a literal copy of its minutest details, is neither practicable nor expedient. It is of the utmost consequence, in this case, to look beyond the external routine to the internal principle. If we secure the latter, we shall not lose the benefit of the former, although we may modify it by new circumstances. Excellent as is the spirit which pervades the general system of the infant schools, there are some points in which their details of instruction admit of much improvement,—some in which they are radically defective, or, at all events, unsuitable for the purposes of early education in New England, and, perhaps, in other parts of this country.

The objectionable points now alluded to, are chiefly comprehended in the injurious habit of learning by rote. This defect in the prevailing modes of instruction at infant schools, pervades most of the lessons, from the sublime topics of religion, or the sciences of geometry and astronomy, to the tables of arithmetic. Proof of this point may be found in the unintelligible matters of religious theory, and the obvious peculiarities of faith, which form a large portion of the catechetical instruction of infant schools,—in the fact that the lessons in geometry and astronomy are but a course of recitations in nomenclature, aided by ocular or tangible illustrations, while the tables in arithmetic are made a mere mechanical succession of sounds, dependent on an arbitrary effort of memory. By such methods of instruction children may be made to appear intelligent in subjects naturally far beyond their grasp; but the result is mere outward show. The intellect is still dormant; it must be waked, if at all, by very different expedients.

Leaving these points, which concern the understanding and the heart, we shall find, if we proceed to the departments of imagination and taste, a want, not only of felicity, but of truth and correctness, in the expedients adopted for the cultivation of this part of the intellectual constitution. Poetry, music, and pictures, might exert a fine influence on the unfolding mind of infancy, were they appropriately employed. But used as, in general, they now are, their effect is rather to degrade and pervert, than to elevate the associations of the infant mind.

The hymns prescribed as infant school exercises, are, with a few exceptions, a succession of verses which possess none of the attributes of poetry, and often fall into absolute doggerel. It is exceedingly difficult, no doubt, to find good poetry for children and infancy; but this is no reason for using that which is bad;—better that imagination should remain uncultivated, than become degraded or perverted.

The music at infant schools is seldom what it should be,—perfectly simple and perfectly correct. The ear of infancy should be attuned to the purest and best forms of music, or should be left uninfluenced. The high polish of consummate skill in this branch of art, is not necessary, it is true, in leading the voices of infants. But an early fault of taste and habit, caught from bad example, is a misfortune for life; since it entails corruption on all the mental associations connected with music.*

Of the drawings or engravings in common use at infant schools it is impossible to speak with truth, unless in terms of strong reprehension. The subjects are very often badly chosen, presenting to the eye of infancy the exhibition, sometimes, of the most degrading and horrid crimes, instead of such objects as should shed a serene and happy influence on the heart. Pictures delineating scenes in which infants cannot naturally take any interest, or which they cannot comprehend, are also in very common use. But an objection more general exists in the gross inaccuracy of the forms, and the inappropriate colors, in most pictures prepared for children. Here is an injury not barely to taste, but actually to the power of perception,—to truth and accuracy in the habits of the mind. Much improvement, it is true, has taken place, within a few years, in this branch of art. But children's picture books still abound in the most striking errors of delineation, and tend generally to hold back or mislead the mental powers, rather than to incite or assist them.

The distinguishing points of excellence in the infant school system, are found in the general plan of education on which

---

* Specimens of what music adapted to children should be, were given by a class of children, during the lecture of Mr Woodbridge. No person who had the happiness of hearing those simple and touching strains, can doubt in regard to the great influence of music on the juvenile mind, and the possibility of its being early and scientifically taught, or forbear to wish that such exercises may be speedily and extensively introduced in all schools for young children.

it is based, rather than its execution in detail: they consist, chiefly, in the blending of physical and moral culture with the exercise of intellect, and the embodying of all in simple and attractive forms, addressed to the imagination. The infant school system is, in these respects, an immense improvement in modes of education, which every friend to the best interests of man must wish to see transferred to all elementary schools.

To appreciate rightly the improvement effected by the introduction of this system, we must contrast its operations with those of the common modes of elementary instruction. Looking into an infant school, we observe the children employed in healthful and pleasant recreation, or enjoying a temporary repose; listening to a story inculcating the virtues of childhood; admiring a picture, or joining in a song; yielding a cheerful obedience to affectionate management; asking the artless questions which are prompted by the natural curiosity of infancy, or listening, with deep interest and attention, to their instructer's answers.

Let us turn to inspect, for a moment, a primary school, taught in the common way,—and we see usually a number of little sufferers, confined to one uncomfortable posture, for hours in succession; enduring an irksome restraint, as the condition of an escape from penalties; conning mechanically a memory lesson which they do not understand, or reciting it as mechanically; controlled in every look and action by the aspect of authority;—the whole nature of the little beings put under a discipline of repression and restraint.

To supersede this repulsive system by the other, would certainly be a most desirable step in the progress of human improvement. This result, however, is not to be attained by merely exchanging one routine for another, but by entering into the spirit of rational, affectionate, and congenial methods of early culture.

To secure the benefits of the improved system, teachers and others who can exert an influence on primary education, should not look merely to a change of books or the introduction of apparatus, but to a general reformation of methods of education. Attention should, in the first place, be given to *the influence of health, activity, and happiness, on the developement of the infant powers.*

The situation, the size, and the arrangement of the school-house, should be the first objects on which to commence improvement. These should be divested of every hinderance to health, and, by every possible means, rendered conducive to happiness. The school-room, without and within, should favor cheerfulness and freedom, and be propitious to intellectual association.

Teachers cannot perhaps succeed in changing the situation of school-houses, so as to have them placed in spots, adapted, by retirement, shade or shelter, to a good influence, moral and intellectual, as well as physical. But they might sometimes succeed in obtaining, for the use of their little charge, permission to cultivate an adjoining piece of ground, as a happy opportunity for inculcating a practical lesson on the fruits of industry, and of leading the young mind to watch the growth and trace the forms of plants, or to observe the frame and habits of insects. Imagination and taste might here be brought under the best of influences.

But circumstances may render it impossible to attain the aid of such advantages in education. The teacher should therefore devote an assiduous attention to *the internal arrangement of the school-room ;* the adaptation of its furniture to convenience and comfort ; the decoration of the walls with objects calculated to exert a useful and happy influence on the mind,—especially, in the proper season, with shrubs and flowers, and other productions of nature, which necessarily excel pictures, and all forms of imitation, as the original does the copy. Pictures, however, if well executed and well chosen, are among the best means of awakening and interesting the mind of infancy; and a few books of engravings, prepared for the use of infant and primary schools, with or even without, the addition of appropriate letter-press, would be a very interesting and useful source of thought and conversation between teachers and children. A book of this description may be made by every teacher for his own use, by procuring a number of good cuts or drawings, and forming them into a volume, by inserting them between the leaves of a blank book of suitable size,—cutting out every other blank leaf, and pasting the picture on the next. This expedient has been found very serviceable for interesting and employing children too young to be able to read.

A *play-ground*, enclosed sufficiently for the safety of very young children, and provided to some extent with playthings of such a kind, and of such size and form, as would conduce to healthful exercise, and furnish agreeable and perhaps instructive employment, would be a valuable aid to early education. Health, cheerfulness, and tranquillity, are not merely important things in themselves, as means of immediate happiness—they are indispensable in infancy and childhood to the natural moral action of the feelings, and the successful developement of intellect. Moral energy and self-control may well supersede such aids with the adult. But the dependent condition of infancy cannot dispense with them. They are, in fact, its birthright; in a natural form of life, it is surrounded with them in abundance; and, in depriving it of these, we thwart the nature of the infant being more seriously, perhaps, than we should by withholding food and rest, or by perverting the forms in which these means of life are administered.

It should never be forgotten, that, in the education of infancy, and especially as conducted in cities, a great violence is generally done to the constitution and character of man. We take the being who is born to inherit the free air and the spacious earth, with all their wide variety of forms and colors, of motion, change, and life,—a theatre of grandeur, and beauty, and delight; we take this being, and shut him up from the healthful and fragrant atmosphere, and the inspiring light; we cut off his communication with the varied face of the earth, with the great worlds of vegetable and animal life, and all the pure and natural pleasures of his own sensations, with the varying but ever happy thoughts to which these give rise; and we confine him to a small and perhaps disagreeable room, place him on an uncomfortable bench, put a book in his hand, and compel him to look on it, and, as far as we can, chain his mind to its mechanical influence.

To the careless eye of him who is content with the present condition and past attainments of man, and whose indolence or timidity of nature would lead him to submit to all the load of imperfection which he has himself inherited, or whose own inactivity of mind leads him to regard with a skeptic eye every attempt to render education the means of a general improvement of the intellectual and moral condition of society,—to such a mind the accumulation of evils under which infancy and childhood have been left to labor, may seem a picture of fancy. But to the eye of the mother and the teacher, whose office it is to watch the progress, and observe the impediments of the young mind, these hinderances appear in their true light. It is to these close observers only, that truth, in this form of it, can appear. And the infant school system is based on the observation and experience of mothers and elementary teachers, when it prescribes, for infant education, the use of a large, airy, cheerful room, and enjoins a frequent change of attitude, with occasional alternations of active play and of rest, or even of sleep.

The modes of city life leave very little in the power of the teacher, in regard to the happy influence of nature on the young mind. But the obligation of teachers is, in such circumstances, only rendered stronger, to use every exertion which may counteract the evils of confinement and discomfort, and to take all possible measures for cherishing in the mind those propitious states of feeling, which education so limited and embarrassed is apt to repress. A school-room in a city or a large town, may be necessarily excluded from a free access of air and light. The attentive teacher will, on this account, double his efforts to have the internal arrangement and appearance of the room made convenient and comfortable; he will endeavour to have the children seated at as great a distance as possible from each other, and their seats contrived with express regard to free and varied postures of body; he will reserve, if possible, a clear space sufficiently large for simultaneous exercise in walking, running, and the other forms of motion natural to early childhood, and conducive to mental activity and enjoyment; he will be strictly watchful of ventilation, both in summer and in winter, so as to preserve a moderate and healthful atmosphere, in an apartment in which so large a part of every day is spent by young children; he will gratify and cheer the mind, through the medium of the eye, by agreeable and instructive pictures and other objects, suspended on the walls, since every aid to cheerfulness is a favorable impulse to the habits of mind and of body.

Primary schools in the country are exempted from the unfavorable influences of restricted space and unwholesome atmosphere. But care should be taken, in such circumstances, to keep pace, in interior arrangements, with the happy influences existing without. There is danger of the child feeling that all his pleasures lie out of the school-room, and that here alone he is to be confined and restrained, or surrounded by dulness and monotony. Teachers in the country should make liberal use of the advantages which they enjoy, for attracting the attention and impressing the imagination of childhood, by the productions of nature. These only can fully impart that silent instruction, and that innocent delight, which, although they cannot be measured by definite and tangible marks, form the most natural and the most effectual developement of mind, whether we regard its intellectual or its moral habits.

Teachers of primary schools ought, in a word, to attend to, and, as far as possible, regulate, everything that may influence early habit;—remembering that their peculiar duties render them, next to mothers, responsible for the welfare of man;

and that if there is any object for which no sacrifice of time and of exertion is too great, it is the early direction of the affections, the intellect, and the health of human beings. Teachers who are disposed to take these matters on trust, and quietly to follow in the track of custom, are unfit for the office they have assumed, and would do well to relinquish it, in favor of an employment less responsible in its nature.

The school-house or room having received its due share of attention, as a tacit but powerful influence on the mind and corporeal frame of infancy, the next step, in the order of importance, is to reform *the moral management* of the school,—to adopt a preventive, instead of a retrospective care of the mind; to act upon the individual by means of general sympathy; to break loose from the plan of observing and repressing single faults, for the moment, and to adopt a liberal and generous management, which appeals to affection and conscience, identifying itself with imagination and with character; moulding the disposition by the genial and voluntary influence of individual intellect; avoiding in every word, and tone, and look, a single expression which may indicate the presupposing of evil intention, in infantine 'faults', as they are called, but, on the contrary, rendering the teacher's measures an appeal to the heart, and a model to the imagination; and throwing, by every means, a cheerful aspect on whatever comes under the name of duty. In all these respects, the infant school system forms a striking contrast to the literal and mechanical modes of discipline, prevailing in elementary schools taught in the ordinary way.

The great moral defect in primary schools, is, that in them the management of childhood is regulated by a few arbitrary rules, and a corresponding scheme of various stages of punishment. By this narrow method, the child whose constitution inclines him to stillness of body, and negative action of mind is invested with a false merit; while the active, the buoyant, and the enterprising, carry with them, into the school-room, a load of native guilt, which soon brings down upon its possessors the punishment which they are told it deserves.

A discipline characterised chiefly by a series of restraints, represses the action of the mind, takes away its freedom, and the whole merit and conscious pleasure of voluntary virtue. A discipline consisting principally of infliction, presents to the young mind the mean animal motive of present pain, and brings forth all the lower attributes of character,—fear, duplicity, and cunning.

The distinguishing excellence of the infant school method, is, that it addresses itself to the heart, and presents to the child the same class of motives that are employed by maternal love: it cheers and leads onward the young mind, presupposing that infant morality will always be correct, if not turned from its natural course. To create a pure and healthful conscience, which may serve as a sure guide and protecting guardian in later years, is one great aim of this happy mode of management. The teacher, therefore, does not rest satisfied with prescribing rules and penalties, but endeavours to enter into the inmost feelings of the infant being, and preserve them in their original freshness and force.

The common system of general rules and prohibitions, is faulty as a means of early culture; since it ever must fail of touching the springs of individual character. By its generality alone, not to speak of other defects, it merges the individual in the mass, and takes away much of personal responsibility and individual character, which are the only sure foundation of virtue. Its utmost limit of success is a negative compliance with a principle of convenience; and its prohibitory character, tending to repress inquiry and activity, renders it, for the most part, utterly ineffectual as a means of improvement to the mind.

The method of the infant schools appeals, on the contrary, to thought and feeling in the individual breast; it implants and cherishes those principles of rational and affectionate obedience; it cultivates those feelings of cheerfulness or of tranquillity, from the absence of which rules and penalties become necessary: it is thus enabled to dispense with these formal and mechanical aids, and, rising to a higher class of mental motives, exerts a more propitious influence. It fastens on the individual mind by methods resembling those of judicious maternal management, which are always addressed to the affections or to reason, and operate not as laws but as principles.

An infant school, when rightly conducted, is made to resemble a family; the teacher taking, for a time, the place of the parent. In a word, the mind and character of the teacher are brought into direct contact with those of the children; and the management of the school depends not on a preestablished system of rules or routine of exercises, but on the immediate action of a presiding mind. No dependence is placed on formalities of any sort. The teacher endeavours rather to avoid these, and trusts to his influence over reason and affection. Instead of repressing the mind by a rule, or restraining it by a penalty, he endeavours to lift it up to intelligent views of order and duty, and to inspire it with the conscious pleasure of rectitude and self-control. To this end, he reasons and persuades; he appeals to sympathy; he calls in the aid of imagination. If the quickness of infantile emotion has, for a moment, overthrown reason, he calmly and gently endeavours to raise it again. If waywardness arises, the little offender is never made to feel the discipline of systematic resentment: he is directed to a new train of thought, by means of new objects; he is placed amidst a cheerful group of his associates, and is allowed to take part in their employments; he is presented with a picture calculated to raise an agreeable or tranquil state of feeling; or is told an appropriate and interesting story, which wins him back from his temporary mood of pain, and restores to him that balance of his infant powers, which circumstances had disturbed.

The teacher of an infant school does not come to his employment with an apparatus of regulations, prohibitions, and penalties, contrived beforehand, and happily calculated to operate as a general prescription and infallible remedy for all moral disorders: he comes to watch the infant mind in its action and tendencies, to aid and befriend it; he occasionally ventures to guide and direct it, but never thwarts it, and seldom checks it. His methods spring up at the moment; they arise out of particular occurrences, and vary with every aspect of the mind. He cherishes infantile virtue by giving it free scope and generous encouragement, rather than by soliciting or exciting it by any particular expedient: vice he anticipates and prevents, by taking away the occasions of it. *

The intellectual instruction attempted in infant schools, is not so successful, perhaps, as the moral management. It is sometimes carried much farther than the infant capacities admit, and so becomes nominal and apparent, in some particulars, more than real or beneficial. I allude, here, to the inculcation of dogmatic theology, to lessons in the nomenclature of geometry and astronomy, and to the exercise of chanting tables in arithmetic. Much, I admit, is apparently done in this way: the memory is called into use, and the children are made to seem very intelligent. But the memory thus cultivated is verbal merely; and the knowledge is that of words rather than things. This is but the exploded system of teaching by rote, revived and applied to science, instead of the columns of the spelling-book. There is no intellectual gain in such instruction; or, rather, there is no instruction given in such cases.

Leave the infant being to nature's tuition; and what a contrast is exhibited to the common, unmeaning, and mechanical process of elementary education! As soon as the infant can walk, he manifests that he has learned to discriminate forms and colors, odors and sounds, without teaching. If left to himself, he walks about in the field, picking the most beauti-

---

* The humorous and eccentric moralist, John Newton, has left a great legacy for teachers in that shrewd saying of his, ' Let me first fill the bushel with wheat, and then I defy any man to fill it with chaff.'

ful and fragrant plants around him. He prefers one shape of a leaf to another: he selects the most brilliant blossoms. He stops to listen to the natural melody of the birds. He watches, with sympathetic delight, the varied forms, and the free and graceful movements of the different animals he sees. In all these employments he is undergoing a discipline of attention, judgment, memory, imagination, and feeling, which the superficial observer may not trace, but which is not the less real, useful, and practical.

Appropriate instruction for infancy would be such as should follow out and regulate these tendencies of nature,—not preclude them, by an arbitrary and formal routine, as is commonly done, in what is called regular education. The infant school system is not, as yet, what it may be expected to become, after a few years more of experiment and observation shall have shed their light on this new department of instruction. It needs a still greater freedom from the shackles of previous custom. But it is deserving of all praise, in its tendency to afford a natural and generous scope to the young mind,—in its compliance with the obvious predilections of juvenile taste, in its liberal supply of those objects on which the affections of infancy and childhood naturally fasten, and by means of which they are invigorated and expanded. Pictures, and such playthings as are calculated to have a salutary effect on mind and body, are freely used in the infant schools. But it is much to be desired that the branches of knowledge, and the practical exercises, which are introduced in these and similar schools, should be such as even the infant mind could appreciate,—that *natural history*, in all those branches of it which are accessible to childhood, should be still more extensively introduced, and *taught by means of specimens or pictures, and other representations*. The capacities and propensities of the infant mind would, in this way, be equally consulted; and a vast deal of useful mental discipline on the forms and colors of objects might thus be imparted. The elements of number and combination might be drawn from the same source. Attention and discrimination would, by such means, be successfully cultivated; memory would be usefully employed; the affections would be interested and refined; imagination would be exercised; and the whole mind would receive an intellectual impulse, favorable to elevation and purity of character.

Instruction in this department of science, however, would need to be divested of system and of nomenclature, and to be modified, in all respects, by the condition of childhood. The teacher's aim should be to elicit thought and reflection, rather than to furnish the appearance of scientific acquirements; early cultivation being regarded by him merely as a preparative for intellectual habits, and not requiring, therefore, the terms and the apparatus which belong to later stages in the pursuit of knowledge.

The rudiments of several useful accomplishments, may, no doubt, be successfully taught in early childhood. Among these would certainly be *reading, writing, and arithmetic;* —but the last two as comparatively unimportant at the early stage of infancy, and the first, rather as a happy means of promoting general habits of intelligence and of pure morality, than as a thing urgent or indispensable. A child may be well informed, comparatively, may be accustomed to excellent moral habits, may have been, in fact, well taught, without being able, as yet, to write or read or spell; and the success of a teacher who is engaged in the instruction of young children, should never be measured by the letter of attainment, even in these practical branches, but by the extent to which he has imparted the power of attention, and by his endeavours to create an inquisitive and discriminating turn of mind, or a delight in mental occupation.

The true idea of an infant or elementary school would be most fully realised by that of an infant 'lyceum,' (so to term it,) in which the main object is not to peruse any one volume, or exhaust any one science, but rather to select the instructive and the entertaining from all, to excite a general interest in the rudiments of knowledge, and to produce a relish for intellectual pursuits.

There are but few *books* which could be mentioned, as suited to the wants of the infant mind, or successfully adapted to the business of elementary instruction. The current volumes of natural history are too extensive in their plan, or are so largely devoted to rare and foreign animals, as to be unsuitable for very young children. A book of domestic animals, with correct and neat engravings, would be very useful in this department. *Worcester's Primer* will be found serviceable to children old enough to use it. But a simpler book still would be better. *Fowle's Child's Arithmetic* is, on the whole, well adapted to its objects; so also is *Emerson's North merican Arithmetic*. A *slate* and *slate pencil*, put into the hands of children who are capable of using them, with permission to draw and print, are an excellent means of employment and of improvement. The *Child's Song Book* will be found useful in any attempt to teach simple tunes to little children, and a volume of suitable drawings or engravings, selected as already mentioned, would afford much useful instruction, as well as entertainment. Such, however, is the scantiness of supply in all these departments of publication, that no book can be mentioned with exclusive or unqualified approbation. The teacher must expect to find all such aids in need of modification and improvement. He must look to the minds of his little charge themselves, to ascertain what he and they need; and he must, after all, draw largely from his own resources for methods and materials.

The great means, indeed, of improving elementary education we must look for in *the character and qualifications of teachers themselves*. One prevalent and fatal error must first be corrected,—the impression that little is required of an elementary teacher, and that any person is competent to such an office. No mistake could be more prejudicial to education than this. To teach an elementary school, with even a moderate degree of success, demands a depth and variety of intellectual and moral qualifications, which no other office in education, in any of its departments or stages, ever requires. Eminent attainments in a single branch of science or of literature, with a facility in imparting knowledge, are all that can be justly held indispensable to instructers in what are called the higher branches of education, or in the higher order of institutions. It is not so with the elementary teacher: he must possess, in the first place, a degree of moral perfection which no other teacher has occasion to exercise; he must understand the nature of the young mind on which it is his business to operate; he must have an extensive knowledge of the physical and moral, as well as the intellectual nature, of the human being; he must possess an active imagination, an affectionate disposition, a mind judicious and ready in expedients;—in a word, a truly intellectual character. Persons who do not possess a good degree of all these qualities, are unfit for this employment; though they may become useful and respectable, and enjoy a solid happiness in pursuits less trying to the texture of the soul.

The female sex are especially adapted to the office of early instruction, by their native tenderness, their ready observation, their apparent adaptation to occupations demanding a minute and varied attention. But where shall we find that range of thought, that disciplined perfection of mind, that untiring corporeal strength, which are all indispensable to the successful teaching of infancy? To improve early education, we must afford more liberal advantages of instruction to the generality of the female sex. They themselves must take more vigorous measures to secure and prosecute the best opportunities of intellectual advancement,—not those merely which can be commanded by resorting to a distinguished school, but those, rather, which alone are worthy of the name;—extensive reading, thorough investigation, vigorous application of the individual mind to all that concerns the happiness of human beings.

To the question, 'How far can the infant school system be advantageously adopted in primary schools?' a general answer only can be given. Methods and exercises which might be both appropriate and useful in one school, and under the management of one teacher, might not be so in other circumstances; as must obviously be the case in the different condition of schools in the city, and those in the country,—of those which can be liberally supplied with books and pictures, and other means of interesting and instructing the infant mind, and in those in which the supply of materials of this description is limited. The main point to be desired, is, that the teacher should possess, in his own head and heart, the *spirit* of infant education, by which he will be enabled, in a great measure, to create the aids of which he stands in need, and to make up, by fertility in mental resource, what may be lacking in external means.

To the teacher who possesses the proper qualifications for early instruction, materials will not be scarce or difficult to command; a flower, a leaf, a grain of sand, even, if rightly presented to the attention of infancy, will afford ample materials for thought and conversation, and embrace more elements of useful knowledge and of mental pleasure, than ever can be derived from the routine of common books and formal tuition. An exact prescribed course of operation is not desirable in the instruction of young children. Their nature craves variety and change; and a judicious mode of education will regard, with as ready attention, the obvious appetites of the mind, as those of the body.

The chief things to be done, for the improvement of primary schools, or with a view to assimilate them to infant schools, may be briefly recapitulated under the following heads.

1. The attendance of very young children should be encouraged.

2. A suitable play-ground or play-room should be provided for every school.

3. Every exertion should be made to render the school-

house or room, and the school furniture, conducive to health and comfort.

4. The school exercises should be often varied, and the attitude of the children frequently changed.

5. Motion, at short intervals, should be a part of regular school exercise.

6. The school should be controlled by management rather than government.

7. A mild, affectionate, and judicious treatment of individuals, should be substituted for general laws and penalties.

8. Conscience, judgment, affection, sympathy, and not fear, should be employed, on all occasions, as means of moral influence.

9. Pictures, conversation, and stories, and, if possible, plants and animals, should be the chief sources of instruction; formal lessons being carefully avoided.

10. Exercises or lessons of any description should be very short as well as perfectly simple.

11. All lessons should be strictly adapted to the existing powers and capacities of infancy or childhood: nothing should be taught which is to be understood by and by. The true way of teaching a child is not to anticipate or to inculcate anything, but to exercise his faculties on objects to which they are at present equal; leaving the result to take place in its own good time.

12. All learning by rote should be most carefully avoided.

13. Whilst uniform succession of employments, and mechanical routine, are strictly shunned, regard should always be had to the different states of mind and body in which school hours can be most advantageously spent. The first part of school time should be devoted to the direct influence of the teacher's mind on his pupils, by conversation or instruction; the second portion, perhaps, to the action of the children's own minds, in telling again to their teacher the story he has read or told to them;—in writing, (if old enough,) what they remember of it, on their slates; in reading, drawing, counting,

or in any other form of mental activity. The third portion may be given up to play or recreation of any proper kind. The fourth to the contemplation of pictures, or to hearing or joining in simple strains of music, or hearing or saying appropriate pieces of poetry. Bodily exercise should be connected with many, if not most, of these exercises; and rest and sleep, if necessary, should be interspersed with action. But much of all such arrangements must be left to circumstances, or rather to the exercise of individual judgment in the teacher.

14. Children old enough to be instructed in the common elements of school education, should be taught, as nearly as may be, in the manner adopted with the youngest class of pupils,—by rational, interesting, and practical methods.—Few or no books being exactly adapted to the instruction of children in reading, an expedient such as the following may be advantageously adopted. Let the teacher be provided with a large black board or slate; and when he can find a large, well drawn and well colored picture of an animal, or of any other object intelligible and interesting to childhood, let it be suspended over the black board: let the children be asked a few simple *questions* about the form, the color, and the habits of the animal,—if such is the object selected. The ideas elicited by these questions, should be embodied, by the teacher, in a few short and easy *sentences* of familiar words, and *printed*, in large and distinct letters, (capitals, perhaps,) on the black board. Every sentence, (and there should be very few,) should then be slowly and distinctly *read aloud* by the teacher, and repeated several times; the children being permitted to join their voices with his. The next stage of the exercise is, that the teacher should select a few of the prominent *words* of the lesson, and place them in a column by themselves clearly and distinctly printed. These the children should compare with those contained in the regular sentences, pronouncing them distinctly along with the teacher. Two or three of the *letters* which happen to occur oftenest in the words printed, should now be selected and placed by themselves, in large and dis-

tinct form, and be compared with those which occur in the words of the lesson, and their names, or rather, their sounds, distinctly repeated by the teacher and the pupils. Those of the children who are of sufficient age and ability, should now attempt to transcribe the whole or part of the lesson, on a large black board or slate, placed conveniently for them. The youngest should be furnished, each with a few sets of letters pasted on small blocks of wood, or with plates of tin with the letters of the alphabet stamped upon them. With these letters they may 'set up,' or compose, the lesson for themselves on the flat part of the surface of their desks, or on a common school slate. Reading and spelling may thus be taught simultaneously, and in the form of active and pleasant employment, while counting the letters and telling their forms may serve, if rightly managed, to impress on the mind some useful elementary ideas in arithmetic and geometry. These exercises should be continued, perhaps, during the whole of the time that children are employed in learning to read; the nature of the exercise being adapted progressively to the capacity of the learners, and embracing the elements of intellectual and moral discipline, by a proper attention to the subject of every lesson.

Books, when suitable ones can be obtained, may be ultimately employed instead of the lesson on the teacher's board; and the pupils may now be accustomed to vary the language of the story by substituting their own forms of expression. A few of the words of every lesson may be selected to be defined and embodied in sentences, on the slate, by the children themselves. Clear and distinct conceptions will thus be acquired, and the meaning and force of language receive their true and full value. Subsequently, the pupils may be permitted to write a letter or story, on their slates, and read it to their teacher. By this means the false tones of voice usually acquired from the formality of school exercises, may be avoided, and a natural and appropriate elocution acquired; the basis of it having been already secured in the distinct and correct enunciation of words and letters, in the elementary lessons before mentioned.

15. The elements of penmanship may be very conveniently taught, so far at least as regards the forms of letters, by the use of the black board and the slate.

16. Simple exercises in arithmetic may be prescribed in the same way.

17. Formal lessons in geometry and astronomy can only prove useless, or worse than useless, to very young children. But a few of the solids, corresponding to the shapes of common objects, may be used, to good advantage, as the basis of correct ideas of form. Thus far apparatus and other illustrations may prove highly useful.

18. Teachers of elementary schools should, if possible, prepare themselves for teaching the rudiments of drawing and singing.*

19 A great means of immediate improvement in the business of teaching, may be found in the opportunities afforded by the instruction imparted at the meetings of Lyceums and teachers' associations; if these are aided, as they always should be, by the use of an extensive and well-selected library, and are regarded as merely the outer gates of knowledge, whose inmost treasures are never to be won but by the efforts of individual diligence and personal investigation.

---

* Much assistance, in relation to vocal music, may be justly expected from a work now in press, compiled by Mr Lowell Mason, from materials collected by Mr William Woodbridge, during his residence in Germany and Switzerland.

MR THAYER'S LECTURE.

LECTURE IV.

ON
THE SPELLING OF WORDS,
AND A RATIONAL METHOD OF
TEACHING THEIR MEANING.

BY G. F. THAYER,
PRINCIPAL OF CHAUNCY-HALL SCHOOL, BOSTON.

The subject on which I have been appointed to address you, is, I am aware, when compared with many others, of inconsiderable moment. Still, it was thought to be worthy the attention of this Association; and, in accepting the invitation of your Committee to treat upon it, my duty to them and to you, requires, that it should receive all the consideration which its intrinsic importance demands.

I shall detain the Institute but for a very short time, in this lecture, because its subject is one very simple in its nature, and not fairly admitting that scope, which those of a more diversified character might seem to invite.

It is a matter of fact topic, which demands simple statements, rejecting all ornament and amplification. I shall, therefore, be brief, plain, and direct; and not aspiring to offer a single new idea on this branch,—lying at the very threshold of the temple of education,—to those who have ministered any long time at its altar, I shall hope rather to aid those who have been recently invested with its robes.

Experience would perhaps suggest to most minds, seeking for improvement, a course of teaching not dissimilar to that which I intend to present to you; but to save the time to the young teacher, and to enable him at once to avail himself of the experience of others, that the progress of his pupils may not be retarded while he is acquiring a personal knowledge of his art, cannot, as it appears to me, but be a desideratum.

Correct spelling I shall assume to be *necessary;* 1. because on that, in a degree, depends our understanding of written language; and it would not be difficult to show, that, in a language like ours, derived from so many sources, the very opposite idea from that intended to be conveyed, may be expressed by the omission or transposition of a single letter.

2. Although correct spelling is more rare than a thorough acquaintance with the sciences, still every man is a critic in it, and inflicts the penalty of ridicule upon those who transgress its rules.

3. It is important in the education of the young, as it leads to habits of accuracy in other things, in which the want of accuracy might be far more fatal to our own interests and happiness. He who is exact and careful in trifling affairs, seldom, if ever, fails to be so in more momentous concerns.

4. The state of literature generally, and especially the estimation in which thorough education is held, may be inferred from the correctness or inaccuracy of the manner of spelling a language.

5. Good spelling is essential to the permanency of a language. By this alone are we able to trace many words to their etymology, without a knowledge of which,—although we may understand their current use,—we may be entirely ignorant of their signification when originally adopted into our language, and consequently fail to enjoy the authors of past times.

6. It is also important as it respects the effect of our works on nations speaking other languages, both as to the conveni-

ence of foreigners in learning the English, and especially as it relates to translations into other languages, in which the author's fame and a nation's improvement may be implicated.

Some men of rare genius have, it is confessed, delighted the world with their sublime conceptions and harmonious numbers, or illuminated it with the results of their philosophical researches, or dazzled it with their metaphysical speculations; though, from neglect in their primary education, they have been very defective in the elements of their native tongue. But this offers no plea for neglecting to acquire a correct orthography. Their mental achievements were not the result of this deficiency; and however the splendor of the works of genius may have obscured or hidden their defects for a time, we are compelled to admit them as defects, and hence to abate some portion of our estimation of the authors.

Having established the utility and necessity of correct spelling, I proceed to point out what I consider the best means of conferring on the young so desirable a benefit.

Being chiefly an exercise of the faculty of memory, it should be one of the first studies undertaken at school; and should be persevered in, with unremitting constancy, till unfailing accuracy crown the labor.

It is a great mistake to permit the higher branches of learning to supersede this, before it be thoroughly acquired; for, if it be not attained in the first few years of school education, the individual will probably remain deficient in it through life.

Numerous as are the innovations in, or, to adopt a more acceptable term, new methods of, teaching the various branches of education, at the present day, I hold those only to be *improvements*, which present the subjects in a more practical form; which will require the least change from the school method to that to be pursued in the business of life.

If, then, we look for a moment at the common mode of teaching spelling; viz. to assign one or more columns of words, in a *spelling book*, to be 'committed to memory,' and uttered by the voice, letter by letter; we see one entirely at variance with practical instruction, tedious to the pupil, expensive in time to the instructer, and *never to be used in after life;* of course, one that needs reformation, and in relation to which almost any change would be an improvement.

A preferable course would be, to assign a portion in the reading book of each class, to be written on slates to dictation, and subsequently examined by the teacher or monitors, who, after checking any errors that might occur, should return the slates to their respective owners for correction—by the book, or otherwise.

By this method, a whole school may be simultaneously engaged in the exercise, and a hundred pupils, in five distinct classes, may write twenty words each, in fifteen minutes or less—every class from its respective reading book—the teacher naming the *number* of the class, with its respective word to be written, and passing on to another class; so that, by the time five words have been given out to as many classes, the first of them will be prepared for another word.

And here let me urge upon the teacher the indispensable necessity of a *perfectly distinct* articulation, especially as to the vowel sounds. Without it, the pupil will often misunderstand the word, though several times repeated; and with it, he is able not only to understand the word at its first announcement, but catches from his master that clear enunciation and correct pronunciation, which constitute the clearness and efficacy, I may say the great charm, of spoken language. If this be neglected, and the word be uttered in that careless and slovenly manner which we too often hear, even from teachers themselves, no censure should attach to the scholar, how numerous soever may be his errors. For example;—let the word be *disposition;* let it be pronounced, as it is in a majority of cases, *disp'sition* or *dispŭsition,* and I defy any man to say, at once, which of the five vowels would best supply the doubtful syllable.*

* A little work, entitled 'Lessons in Enunciation,' by Wm. Russell, has recently been published, which presents the current errors in pronuncia-

If the school under my own care has made proficiency in anything, it is in this department; and I attribute it not more to the general method of teaching pursued by us, than to the great exactness in the mode of pronouncing, and the invariable rigidness with which a clear and distinct articulation is exacted and enforced.

If the pupil be required, after correcting his failures, to transcribe the words missed, into a book kept for the purpose, he will be less liable to repeat the errors when the same words shall again occur, and will, in time, have made a collection of those that require his greatest care in their application, and which might, in themselves, furnish profitable lessons for review.

In this connexion, I would suggest, that the transcribing of good composition, beside aiding to furnish the mind with various other knowledge, is of essential service in fixing, by habit as well as by memory, correct methods of spelling.

In spelling lessons, at first, the pupils should be required to write every word containing as few as *two* letters; but as they advance, the more difficult words only should be selected. In this selection, the attentive teacher will soon be led by his own experience to perceive, that it is not the *longest* words which scholars are most liable to mispell, but rather those that are common in sound to many others in the language, of a different combination of letters: such, for example, as receive, believe; compeer, cohere, grenadier; the verb *hear* and the adverb *here*; the pronoun *their* and the adverb *there*; a regular noun in the nominative or objective case plural, and the possessive case singular; participles of regular verbs, in which a doubt may exist whether the consonant preceding the final syllable, be double or not; as in committed, benefited, &c. Also, in words where *able* is added to *c soft*, as in *peaceable*, and

---

tion and articulation in so distinct a view, as to be highly valuable to teachers and all persons of taste in these branches of elocution. Teachers of reading, especially, would derive important aid from its rules and suggestions.

to *g soft*, as in *changeable*; in words beginning with *in* and *en*, as inquire, enclose, indorse, entrap; in words ending in *er* and *or*, as instructer, preceptor, visiter, sailor.—Many of these have been thrown into distinct exercises in spelling books, and may, with much advantage, be learned by pupils at a very early age; a recurrence to them, however, as they may be met with in the reading book when used for spelling lessons, will always be found useful. Some of Murray's rules, as given in his book of Exercises, especially the fifth, ninth, and tenth, would afford much aid; although the exceptions are so numerous, as to forbid an implicit reliance upon them.

Beside these *classes* of words, there are many of irregular formation, which are more frequently spelled wrong than right; among these are the following—wagon, pony, balance, saddler, wo,ay (meaning yes), basin, buffalo, expense, absence, melancholy, lily, ennoble, possess, disappointment, recommendation, until, off (adverb), oblige, trousers, separate, too (adverb), college, &c.—To these may be added several proper names of persons, such as Catharine, John, Eleazer, Eleanor, Jesse;—and of States, such as Louisiana, Pennsylvania, Mississippi, &c.

I have said the lessons in spelling should be given from the *reading* book, for the following reasons; 1. most spelling books contain many words which are seldom found in English composition, hard to learn, and almost useless when learned—to the exclusion of simple, common, and consequently useful words.

2. Few spelling books, if any, are adapted to the capacity of very young children; but in general, excepting a few of the first pages in the book, are made up of long and difficult words, much above the comprehension of the scholar.

3. They are, for the most part, so encumbered with notations for accent, pronunciation, &c., that although the teacher may be aided by them, the pupil is perplexed and embarrassed.

The department of reading books, on the contrary, is very fully supplied with such as would meet the wants of every class of children; especially in their primary instruction. A difficulty, however, exists here, and one, too, of no trifling consideration. The compilers of these reading books, spell certain words very differently. We find in some, positive errors; here, an author, whose book is perhaps in the hands of your youngest class, adopts the orthography of Perry; there, is a book used by your next class, which follows Johnson; another takes Walker for his standard; and a fourth varies in some points from all three; while a fifth, professing to follow rigidly the most *fashionable* guide, either from ignorance or carelessness, deviates, most widely in many cases, from his own criterion; beside spelling the same word variously, in different parts of the book.

It is true, an attentive teacher may meet the evil by oral explanation and remark; but while the pupil has the printed guides in his hand, he must inevitably be confused, in many instances, by the inconsistency he discovers. Besides, in numerous cases, instruction in the department of spelling, must be entrusted to the elder scholars; in monitorial schools almost wholly so. Hence, very imperfect instruction will be the result.

Among the good reading books, in use with us at the present time, are, the American First Class Book, the National Reader, and the Introduction to the National Reader, all by the same author, who has not only compiled them with very great care and taste, as to the style of the compositions as well as to their moral tendency, but who has given more than ordinary attention to the spelling of the words; so that they form a series for three classes, containing as few variations from the standard assumed—and that the most popular among us at the present day—as can be found in any other three books in the language. In the spelling of some classes of words, which I shall have occasion to advert to hereafter, I should not perhaps adopt the same rule which he has adopted; but as they are few and very distinct in their character, the variations can be easily explained, and remembered by all pupils, sufficiently advanced to use these books.

The same gentleman would render the cause of education a service, by continuing his labors, until all classes of pupils, from the oldest to the youngest, should be supplied with books for reading and spelling, from one source—by which a uniform standard might be observed throughout.

The wishes of those teachers who might be unwilling to forego the use of the *spelling* book, could be attained by a series of books, prepared with reference to each particular lass; beginning with one containing the alphabet and such simple words as the child himself would naturally understand and use, and advancing, by very gradual steps, in several separate books to the most difficult words in the language.

The words to be spelled might first be embodied in interesting stories, and afterwards arranged in columns,—in the manner of Worcester's Primer,—which, presenting them in two different aspects, would make a more permanent impression on the memory.

Several advantages would arise from this plan; 1. the various books would necessarily be quite small, and a child could entirely master the contents of each, before it would be worn out; which is far from being the case with the spelling books now in use. Hence the plan has economy to recommend it.

2. The pupil's advancement would be much more agreeable to himself, and consequently more rapid; as he would *travel in the light*, comprehending all he learned. He would be stimulated to effort, by passing onward from book to book, as he would realize a promotion at every change.

In the use of the spelling books now in our schools, it becomes necessary to *review*—to pass through them several times; and after all, the lessons are not retained, for the pupil becomes tired of the book; he has used it too long; it has been a dull companion to him. He never studies it the second or third time with the same spirit as at the first; whereas, a new book is taken up with an eagerness and freshness that the novelty of it inspires, and produces proportionally increased benefit.

Another advantage will be suggested, when I come to speak of *defining words*, which was a subject connected with that of spelling, assigned to me by your Committee.

Were spelling books, such as have now been recommended, once introduced, I am not sure but that the advantage would lie on their side, even when compared with books exclusively for reading. One superiority they might be made to possess, especially with the younger classes; I mean that which would arise from methodical classification of words. By arranging the lessons analogically, the manner of spelling would be more easily learned, and on the mnemonical principle longer retained, than if taken up promiscuously. Still, I would not have the lessons entirely unaccompanied by exercises from the reading book. And from what book soever or by whatever mode they might be *studied*, the *evidence* of the study should, in all cases, be rendered *in writing*.

On this point I would venture one general remark; which is, that in all branches susceptible of it, the exercises—the results of study—should be presented to the *eye*, as the best organ of communication with the mind. Whatever is acquired through this medium, is better retained than when entering through any other. It may be said, *the eye remembers*. It is more *attentive* than the ear. Its objects are not confused. It takes in a single and perfect image of what is placed before it, and transfers the picture to the mind. Hence all illustrations in our teaching, which can possibly be addressed to this accomplished organ, should be so applied.

The mode of performing orthographical exercises now recommended, is not, it will be observed, a mere substitution of a more expeditious and effective method of accomplishing a spelling lesson. It implies the adoption of a different principle of operation from that which generally prevails. It proceeds upon the great principle of calling the mind into action in a practical and useful way, instead of one which is arbitrary and mechanical. It demands of the pupil, not a mere listless attention, or a transient effort of recollection, but an active exercise of his powers, such as corresponds to the occasions of business in after life. The senses, even, are employed, and the perceptive power in young minds is so slight and evanescent, that such aid is to them indispensable. Attention and memory are made to keep pace, in such forms of exercise, and it is the dissolution of their natural connexion, which, in any case, gives rise to errors in orthography. What is needed in this department of instruction, is, that the pupil have prescribed to him such forms of exercise as shall prevent that mechanical and abstracted attention, which belongs appropriately to a higher stage of his advancement—that in which memory, having become perfectly true and faithful in its office, the power of attention may be safely permitted to glide into a comparatively dormant or unconscious state.

One of the great intellectual benefits of instruction in this department, is to keep the mind in wakeful, voluntary, and efficient attention—a result which can be attained only by practical expedients. The usual mode of performing spelling lessons, fails entirely in this respect, and indeed much of the pupil's success in it depends on an inactive state of mind, in which all the faculties are merged in an arbitrary flow of memory. Practical methods of instruction, involving the cooperation of our pupils themselves, in all that we require as exercises or lessons, have in all cases the recommendation, which, though not always a primary one, is, nevertheless, important in a high degree—I mean the immediate happiness and cheerful diligence of the young. The prevailing method of managing lessons in spelling, is commonly attended with a comparatively dull and languid state of mind, which contributes, along with other things, to render school exercises listless and wearisome. The effect of such states of feeling, is to be dreaded, not merely because it is less favorable to immediate improvement, but because it tends to entail on the mind, habits which are injurious to its powers, unfavorable to their free and generous developement, and at the same time, silently destructive of that freshness and vigor of corporeal sensation, which is indispensable to happiness in youth, and to habitual activity in manhood. All exercises in every department of education, should, as far as possible, be of an active, and not of a passive nature.

Organization, we have heard, bespeaks a design for action.* This should not be forgotten, even in those employments which are purely mental; and perhaps we should find less injury resulting to health from school education, were school exercises of an active and enlivening nature to an extent which is easily practicable. It is perhaps too true of all the stages of education, from the lowest to the highest, that they are planned with too much reference to a recipient and passive state of the mind; that they presuppose and demand *inaction* as a matter of habit, and thus tend to produce a mental character, which, although it may be of occasional advantage in a given branch of study, is precisely that which is not required in the business of life, nor in those stages of intellectual pursuits, in which the student is required to advance for the purposes of discovery and invention, carrying with him all his energies in full and constant activity.

I may be pardoned, I hope, this brief digression; for it is of inexpressible moment, that, in the whole course of education, and especially in its elementary departments, and in its operation on the susceptible faculties of early life, we should keep a constant eye on the probable *result* of all our methods, and their influence on mind and character. In the humble routine of the daily exercises of school, there are principles at work on the intellectual habits of the young, which may give a color or determination to the whole mental being; which may lead to intelligence, moral purity, and happiness for life; or to results of the opposite character, and as lasting in their effects.

The existing diversity in the modes of spelling English words, each defended by high authority, will present to the

---

*Vide Dr Warren's Lecture on Physical Education.

young teacher—who may be desirous of escaping from the shackles of local custom, and establishing for himself, a standard independent of considerations so narrow—much perplexity. Especially when he perceives that fashion is as fickle in this matter as in any other. In this dilemma, I would recommend to him, to adopt the style that is *coming up*, rather than that which is *going down*. Johnson's authority is perhaps better than that of any other lexicographer,—but in several classes of words, his mode of spelling has had its day and has become obsolete.

Many of the writers of this metropolis and vicinity, have adhered to the *k* in the terminations of polysyllables, as in *musick, ecclesiastick*, and the like; and to the *u* even in words like *errour, terrour*, &c. until, in this respect, they stand alone, or nearly so. Most of the accomplished writers of our own country and in Great Britain, have dropped the *k*, and very many the *u*, in these two classes of words. The best periodicals in both countries have done so; and it is plain to perceive, that this mode will eventually prevail to the exclusion of the other. I consider it the *improved* mode, because any method which tends to simplify, without doing violence to etymology or the genius of our language, is a decided improvement.

The letter *s* is also taking the place of *z*, in words having the *z* sound, and so continually is this change going on, that one can hardly decide which is right *to-day*, from knowing what was so *yesterday*. The best periodicals incline to a very general use of the *s*, although there are still many exceptions, and—as a foreigner must be led to think—much caprice on the subject. For, what good reason can be offered in defence of the practice of spelling surprise with an *s*, and apprize with a *z*?

Some have ventured to drop the *z* altogether, in words of this class, and even in words like organization, to substitute the *s* for that letter.

This fluctuating state of things existing, and there being

good reason to believe that the changes enumerated will become general, both as it respects the pronunciation of words and the new mode of spelling them,—why should not we attempt to effect a uniformity at once? Why should not this Association fix for itself and its members, some mode of spelling—especially as it regards the classes of doubtful words above alluded to—which we would be willing to use, to teach, and defend? If the mode were a good one, we might hope to have it generally adopted in our country. And by publishing a cheap manual on the subject, the variations might be easily placed within the reach of all who feel any interest in it.

It seems to me that we could hardly do the community so acceptable a service, with so little labor, or make one of the subjects of primary education more simple, with so little inconvenience to ourselves. The public are not tenacious of particular modes of spelling. With few exceptions, no prepossessions exist. They wish for *consistency;* they desire to find the English language the same, wherever written or spoken. They need only a responsible leader in the matter. They ask for some standard—some authority,—and if that standard be respectable—that authority worthy, they are willing to be guided by it.

Who then shall constitute that standard? Are any more naturally so than men of education, engaged in the profession of educating others? If teachers are what they ought to be in this distinguished office, they are most competent to decide on the question under consideration. I hope they will decide it for themselves, whether the community at large acquiesce or not in their decision.

I cannot, without injustice, omit to mention, in this place, the name of NOAH WEBSTER;—a man who has devoted more time, labor, and profound research to the English language, than perhaps any other man who ever studied it. Twenty-five years—the most vigorous in mental power, of his whole life—given to an examination into its genius, structure, etymology, and current use among the best educated persons who speak it, having stored his mind with a fund of the most valuable information on the subject, invest his opinions with a claim to consideration beyond that of most other men of this or any other age.

The result of his labors is the voluminous and excellent dictionary recently published by him, which, as far at least as any other now known, deserves to be adopted by his countrymen, as the standard of orthographical accuracy. For, although many innovations have been admitted into it by him,—some of which being peculiarities of his, we could have wished he had suppressed,—yet a large share of them must be deemed positive improvements, and as such we may hope ere long to see them come into general use.*

On the subject of defining the words of our language, my opinion is, that the only effectual method of doing it with young pupils, is, 1st. by oral explanation during a lesson in reading or recitation. And no word should ever be passed over, from the first of a child's reading in sentences, without his comprehending fully and distinctly its meaning. For which reason, I am the more in favor of the kind of books—before alluded to—resembling Worcester's Primer, by which the pupil's interest in the story comes to aid him, and renders the teacher's assistance more seldom necessary. If these stories are illustrated by drawings, the advantage is increased, especially in the first two or three books of the series.

2. When the reading lesson, accompanied by all the necessary explanations, shall have been completed, the pupil should be

---

*Since the delivery of this lecture, Mr J. E. Worcester of Cambridge, has given to the public a Dictionary which is better adapted to the wants of the American community in general, than any we had before seen. It contains 43,000 words; is very neatly printed, and brought within the compass of 400 pages. It has an appendix containing copious vocabularies of scripture and classical proper names, with their proper accent and pronunciation; and a collection of most of the words of doubtful orthography in our own language. It is admirably calculated for the most advanced pupils in our schools, and is highly worthy of general attention.

required to define to the teacher, such words from the lesson as may be given to him, and subsequently to write them on a slate for a spelling lesson; if he be directed to write the *meaning* also, so much the better will it be for his progress in the language.

3. The next exercise I should recommend, would be a paraphrase of the story, in the pupil's own language, according to his understanding of it; by which the teacher could ascertain whether he had a correct idea of the whole, as well as of individual words, and also furnish a good opportunity for laying the foundation of the scholar's style.

This exercise would, with the aid above suggested, be found a very agreeable one to the pupil, who would, in no long time, be prepared for the use of the dictionary. This might be first put into his hand, as soon as he should be able to distinguish synonymes. Until then, for the lesson in question, he had better be without one.

4. The teacher now having marked in the reading lesson, such words as he deemed most suitable and useful, the pupil should seek in his dictionary for such as could be substituted for them, without changing the import of the sentence; when he might either write the original words with their synonymes on a slate, or *read* the latter in lieu of the former—incorporating them into the sentence.

This practice continued for a while, prepares the scholar for reading, with unhesitating fluency, the supplied synonyme for the original word,—in the same manner that a good linguist translates a language at sight, and looking on a page of French,—for example—reads it in correct English.

A sure and satisfactory method of ascertaining that the pupil has acquired the *meaning* of every word along with its *definition*, and to invest him with the highest and most important benefit arising from this exercise, is to require of him to embody every word he is asked to define, in a sentence of his own composing. Such exercise, it is hardly necessary to observe, calls into action all the resources of the mind, and produces a readiness of thought which is an invaluable acquirement.

It is not to be expected that the pupil will accomplish all this without many failures, and much occasional aid from the instructer, but every step of his progress will tend to make the next more easy, and will, beside giving him a correct understanding of the subject of the lesson before him, lead him to observe those nice shades of difference in words and expressions, without which, he can never write his native tongue with purity and precision.

These methods of teaching spelling and defining, are not merely theoretical. They are the results of positive experiment, practised under my own superintendence, for eight or ten years. And as far as my opportunities have enabled me to compare results with those of other methods of teaching, in these departments, I am satisfied that such as have been recommended,—if not the *only true* ones—are of that practical character, without which all methods must be useless, if not worse than useless.

I have said nothing of the practice, once so common, of assigning lessons in spelling and defining from the columns of a dictionary, sweeping through the whole, from the letter A, to the last word under Z,—if the pupil continued long enough at school to accomplish it,—for I cannot suppose it to have come down to this day. If it had, however, I should feel impelled to pronounce it one of the most stupid and useless exercises, ever introduced into a school—compared with which, the 'committing to memory' indiscriminately, of all the pages of an almanac, would be agreeable, beneficial, and instructive.

To say that it would be impossible to remember the definitions thus abstractly learned, would be to assert what must be perfectly obvious to every one. And even if they could be remembered, they would be of little utility; for as the right application of a definition must depend entirely on the situation of the word to be explained and the office it performs in a sentence, the repeating of half a score of meanings as obscure perhaps as the word itself—conveys no definite thought, and serves rather to darken, than illuminate the mind.

As a book of reference, a dictionary is useful ; although, it must be confessed, that even with the best, one often finds himself obliged to make his own explanation, in preference to any furnished by the lexicographer : and the teacher or the pupil who relies exclusively on his dictionary—without the exercise of much discretion—for the definition of whatever words he may find in the course of his studies, will not unfrequently fall into very awkward and absurd mistakes.

Experience and common sense must lend their aid ; the former to teach us what is practicable ; and the latter, what is appropriate and useful. And the teacher who has the improvement of his pupils and the great interests of education generally, at heart, will not content himself with what he has already attained, but be perpetually striving to add to his stock—by however small degrees, and in however insignificant departments—whatever may make him more accomplished in his profession, and consequently, more worthy of the charge entrusted to him.

MR CLEAVELAND'S LECTURE.

LECTURE V.

ON
LYCEUMS AND SOCIETIES
FOR THE
DIFFUSION OF USEFUL KNOWLEDGE.

BY NEHEMIAH CLEAVELAND,
PRECEPTOR OF DUMMER ACADEMY, NEWBURY, MASS.

AMONG the schemes of an age fertile in expedients, one of the most recent and striking, is the establishment of societies to promote the general diffusion of useful learning. In the old world, the experiment was not only novel, but bold—evincing in its projectors no small share of moral courage, as well as active benevolence. With us the case is widely different. Rarely, in this country, and in a degree comparatively small, are the advocates of popular education called to contend with that aristocratic pride, or those long-established prejudices, which impede the efforts of its friends abroad. Neither is the task to be accomplished by us, of equal magnitude with theirs. Much has already been done to prepare the way. We have not that Augæan mass of superstition and folly to remove, before an entrance can be effected, or a proper foundation laid. No project, perhaps, could meet and gratify public sentiment among us, more fully than this—of promoting by social effort the mental improvement of the community, down to the humblest of its classes. It is, in fact, but the expansion—the final developement of that broad system of education, which was founded by the settlers of New England. It is the illustration, the practical enforcement of that which we acknowledge as the only conservative principle of our free institutions.

While, however, we find in a comparative estimate much to encourage exertion, we find also much that calls for it. We cannot go far, from even the most favored spot in this favored land, without finding enough of ignorance, of prejudice, and of false opinion, to justify all that has yet been said or done in favor of popular improvement. And though it is true, that we have not here a privileged class,—families, from whose claims to patrician origin, opposition naturally flows to everything that tends to lessen the interval between the high and the low,—yet even with us may be found those who regard with coldness or dislike, all attempts to enlighten the mass of the community. I stay not to inquire, whether these feelings proceed from unworthy motives, or from honest though mistaken views, or from a conviction of the total inadequacy of all efforts to effect the object. I propose, at present, to consider the question as, in effect, settled. The experiment has been begun. The institution is in actual operation. On both sides of the water, a host, powerful in intelligence as well as in numbers, have engaged in the cause, with a zeal that promises much for its success. Do I hazard anything in presuming, that the great majority of my auditors, have already given it their sanction, and lent it effectual aid?

In considering the subject of Lyceums and Societies for the Diffusion of Knowledge, I will inquire,—what are their proper objects,—and what methods of conducting them, are most likely to obviate objections, and ensure their usefulness?

Their design is evidently different from that of philosophic and academic associations, founded to promote and make known new discoveries in science. Neither is it to be identified with the aims of propagandists in politics or religion. The efforts of these institutions are intended to benefit that large portion of every community, who, from various causes, have hitherto done but little towards their own mental cultivation. It aims to awaken among them a spirit of inquiry; to excite a desire for knowledge, not only on account of its position and practical advantages, but for its own sake —the pleasure it gives, and the true dignity, which it confers. By lectures, discussions, and illustrations, it proposes to furnish an effective stimulus, and, having awakened desire, to supply the means of gratifying it, by the multiplication and distribution of books.

It is with diffidence that I enter on an inquiry into the best methods of effecting these highly important objects. The subject is as yet, in a great measure, unexplored. The institution has not been long enough in extensive operation, to furnish us, in any considerable degree, with that only safe guide in matters of practice, the light of experience. There has been, indeed, a general similarity in the modes of procedure, adopted by different associations;—but no fixed plan, or uniform system. This is, on the whole, a happy circumstance. From it must result a great diversity of expedients and methods, as varying circumstances and ingenuity shall prompt; and thus, far more effectually than if uniformity had prevailed in the outset, will eventually be furnished the materials of a complete system,—embracing, in its details, all the peculiarities, which may be required by the particular wants and condition of different communities.

The formation of associations, where none yet exist, very naturally claims our first attention. By those, who have not witnessed the process, this is generally supposed to be a difficult task. They cannot believe, that a people, long sunk in apathy, as to every object of education and self-improvement, can, at once, and, by means so simple, be roused to feel an active interest in them. Yet the testimony of a hundred cases, shows that it may be done. Let but one individual in a place know something respecting the object, and set himself heartily about it, and he will be sure to succeed. Let him assemble a few of his neighbours, and make known to them the plan of a Lyceum and its benefits. Let him encourage them to form themselves into a club, with a few simple rules for their regulation. Let general attention be directed to the subject, by a public address from some intelligent gentleman, such as every vicinity will furnish. Let them begin operations with a familiar lecture on some subject of science or art; or, in lack of that, with friendly discussions,—reading,—and efforts to procure and circulate books. Their Lyceum is now organized; and theirs will be a case of singular exception, if they do not soon find that the excitement is spreading, and their society advancing in numbers and usefulness.

The details of constitution, bye-laws, and mere business concerns, must be adjusted by each society, according to its own convenience. In reference to these, however, there are two or three general principles, which appear to me of primary importance.

From the whole scope and design of societies for the diffusion of knowledge, it is certain that their terms of admission should be so fixed, as to render their privileges universally accessible. This will not be the case, where there is a high entrance fee, or heavy annual tax. Yet we are not to lose sight of that common principle of our nature, that men prize their acquisitions by the cost, more frequently than by the value. Let us avail ourselves of that strong and universal motive,—the consciousness and love of property. If you would sustain an effectual interest, after the first excitement has gone by, let every man pay something; and let those, whom no higher impulse urges, be led to seek their share of intellectual, as some do of grosser aliment, by the desire of securing their money's-worth.

Another consideration, founded on observation of human nature and its tendencies, has been thought of great importance by some of the warmest and most judicious friends of this cause. I refer to placing the management of these institutions chiefly in the hands of those, for whose immediate benefit they are designed. In most of the societies, which have been formed in England, it is established as a principle, that a majority of the committee of management, shall be of the class of mechanics, or working men. Such a measure, it is thought, has a tendency to promote their independence. Thus constituted, these institutions cannot easily be made instruments in the hands of the designing, for the advancement of selfish ends. But a more important result is the confidence, which it inspires, and the direct, personal interest, which it creates and sustains. In confirmation of what we should naturally expect, we have in favor of this plan, some testimony from experience. In Glasgow, a society for imparting knowledge to mechanics, has been in operation for thirty years, and may be considered the parent of all similar establishments. Here then is the longest and fullest trial that has yet been made. The institution set out without adopting the principle in question. The interest was kept up for a few years, and then subsided. It was at length revived, by giving the management to the mechanics, and has continued, ever since, unabated, and increasing. Mr Brougham, referring to the regulations of the London Mechanics' Institution, says—'Of these, by far the most important, and one, which, in common, I believe, with all my colleagues, I consider to be altogether essential, provides that the committee of management shall be chosen by the whole students, and consist of at least two thirds working men.'

It will be urged, perhaps, that the circumstances of England and America are widely different; that we have not those diversities of rank, or distinctions in society, which create the necessity for such measures. But the difference is of degree, rather than of kind. Are there not here, as everywhere, the distinctions of rich and poor, educated and uneducated, men of leisure and men of labor? Is it not plain to every observer, that there is in all parts of our land, a vast amount of prejudice and wrong feeling, springing solely from this cause, be it real or fancied? If it be not so, what must we think of the growth and professions of that new political sect, which styles itself 'the party of working men?' One of the most valuable benefits to be hoped from societies for diffusing knowledge, is a removal of the misconceptions, on which such passions and parties are founded. Let them then be so constituted, that they shall not be stumbling-blocks in the way. Let the principles, on which they are started, and by which they are conducted, be such as to ensure the cooperation, and keep alive the interest of those, who most need their influence, and they will furnish the surest antidote to the evil just mentioned. By shedding light on the important subjects of political, social, and personal rights and duties, they will directly counteract the only radicalism, which we need to fear,—the radicalism of ignorance and vice.

There is another provision, of sufficient moment, I conceive, to demand general attention;—I mean the insertion of an article in the constitution of every Lyceum, excluding from its lectures and discussions all topics of controversial divinity, and party politics. The effect of introducing such subjects into societies, whose usefulness, not to say existence, depends upon harmony of feeling and action, must be evident to every one. I know not that evil has yet resulted from this cause. But in a land abounding with zealots of every sect, and prolific of demagogues, is there not reason to fear? Will it not be easier to anticipate, and prevent the evil, than to wait for and to cure it? On these disputed and irritating themes, let us be content with what the newspapers and magazines will furnish; with what we shall be compelled to hear from the pulpit, in the hall, and at every place of public resort. Let there be one spot of neutral ground, where rival combatants may meet in peace, and unite their efforts, in the cause of mutual improvement, and true philanthropy.

Instruction furnished through the medium of such societies as we are now contemplating, may be considered in reference to manner and kinds. Thus far, in this country, the instruction of Lyceums and Mechanics' Institutions, have been confined, chiefly, it is believed, to lectures. It was natural that this mode, in the outset, should be the most prominent. The first object is to awaken interest where it does not exist, to attract and fix attention. Many may be induced to listen to a discourse, and thus passively receive ideas, who would make no other effort to acquire them. Nor is the advantage slight, even should this prove all. A great amount of valuable information may be imparted by oral lessons. They are aided by the tones of the living voice; and who knows not how effective they *may be* to enlighten, impress, and persuade. Often, too, they are accompanied by sensible illustrations, models, and experiments, addressing the eye as well as the ear; rendering intelligible and delightful many subjects, which, without such aid, are either dark or dry. But, whatever we may think of these advantages, it is on influences less direct, and on ultimate results, that we must depend most. If the thousand popular lectures now annually delivered in our country, are destined to produce any truly valuable and lasting effect, it must be by rousing the public mind; by creating a new taste,—the love and industrious pursuit of knowledge, where now all is apathy and indolence; by prompting men, in fine, to mould and educate themselves. We have, already, gratifying evidence of some such results; and may we not confidently anticipate a great deal more?

In the accomplishment of this object, much will depend upon the fidelity, ability, and good judgment of those, who lecture; much, on the judicious choice of subjects, and a plain, perspicuous treatment of them; much, in those on scientific topics, upon experiments, or other sensible helps,—and in all, it will be desirable, that the limited and true uses of this mode of instruction be frequently pointed out. Let those, who attend upon lectures, be often reminded, that they are not meant to be, and never can be, substitutes for patient investigation.

The inquiry here arises,—In what other ways may social effort be directed to the accomplishment of the object in view?

Fully and satisfactorily to answer this question, we need the aid of a longer and more extended experience.

Familiar discussions have been recommended, and, in some instances, adopted. These, if rightly managed, promise much good. But they must differ materially from the exercises of a mere debating club. A Lyceum can hardly subserve its true design, if made the arena where a few champions display their adroitness, in making 'the worse appear the better reason,' or showing that 'even though vanquished, they can argue still.' Its design is to elicit truth, to convey information; not merely to make able debaters, to whet the weapons of forensic warfare, or to add a single incentive to the general rage for speech-making. The aim, in such an exercise, should be, to make it easy and familiar, and to encourage as many as possible to engage in it. It will succeed best where the number assembled is small. It may then resemble the animated conversation of a circle of friends, possessing knowledge, and seeking more, not avoiding collision of opinion, yet never contending for victory alone.

Probably much benefit will be found to result from the division of large societies into classes of moderate size. The principle of classification may be similarity of pursuit, contiguity of residence, parity of age, or any other, as circumstances shall indicate. At the class-meetings, reading, conversation, and instruction may be introduced without difficulty. The classes may select their own branches of study;—or, to them as so many standing committees, the managers of the Lyceum may assign special topics for consideration. The thorough investigation and discussion of these, will be of the highest service to the individual thus engaged, while, at stated times, in the form of reports, or otherwise, the concentrated results may be given to the whole body. As branches of Lyceums, or in connexion with them, associations of school-teachers have already become common, with results, as we might expect, highly favorable to both master and pupil.

Mr Brougham, whose sagacity no scheme of utility escapes,

and for whose philanthropic spirit no effort or plan for doing good, is too humble, recommends that artisans working in the same room, and in occupations not too noisy, should keep one of their number reading, while the rest are employed. The expense might be defrayed by a little additional effort of the men; or a boy, or girl might be engaged for the purpose, at a very slight cost. The suggestion seems to me particularly useful for us. Are there not in our country, many hundreds of shoemakers' and other shops, which, by the aid of a little encouragement, and a judicious supply of books, may be converted into schools of mental and moral improvement, without diminishing either industry or profits?

The subject of *books* and *apparatus* may properly be considered in this connexion. No one can doubt, that ready access to suitable books, is one of the most important auxiliaries to this cause. But to secure continued attention to them, it is not enough that books should be accessible. Of this, the fate of many a parish and social library, dispersed, or sold at auction, is ample proof. Some permanently exciting cause is needed,—and the want, is, we trust, to be supplied by the exercises and influence of Lyceums. Under a new impulse, the old and languid associations may be revived, and libraries now independent of each other, and accomplishing but little, may be united and made effective. The subject of books will call for particular attention and greater efforts, where no public collections yet exist. It has been suggested, as likely to be of beneficial tendency, to allow the members of book-clubs to name books to the amount of their subscription. Small neighbourhood associations have been found highly advantageous. Books and periodicals are procured and pass from house to house, at a slight annual expense to each individual. By suitable arrangements between different neighbourhoods, or between the respective classes of a Lyceum, the *circulating* system, so popular in Scotland, might be successfully applied. Such little and cheap itinerant libraries, travelling round from village to village, or from school to school, soiled and worn as they may be,—how much more usefully and more honorably employed, than many a splendid collection, reposing in guarded alcoves, and upon inaccessible shelves!

The aid afforded to *scientific* studies and lectures by suitable apparatus, render it an important object of attention. A few societies, whose means are ample, may command, in this respect, whatever they please, and will do well to import articles and models of finished workmanship, for the benefit of our own artists. But in a great majority of cases, expensive apparatus is out of the question. Fortunately, we have good reason to believe that the demand will create the supply. By due attention to simplicity and economy, much has already been done. Many valuable instruments may now be obtained, at a charge so moderate as to be beyond the reach of but few. It is not, probably, new to most of you, that for about thirty dollars each, sets of pneumatic apparatus may be obtained in this place, by which may be illustrated satisfactorily, all the principles that can be shown by the corresponding articles in a college cabinet,—among which the air-pump alone used to cost several hundred dollars. Similar results may be anticipated in other branches. But, without waiting for these, how many illustrative articles of cheap construction may be furnished anywhere, by the aid of a little ingenuity. This is particularly the case in mechanical philosophy, in electricity, and in chemistry generally. Need I allude, in confirmation, to the memorable examples of Scheele, Priestley, and Black, or to the famous thermometer and phials, which, in the hands of Watt, led to the developement of important principles, by the application of which he was enabled to construct a machine, that now spins and weaves the clothing of half the world?

It is not improbable that there has existed in some of our smaller communities, unnecessary discouragement in regard to this matter. They have not been aware how easily many of those useful helps might be procured, nor yet how much might be accomplished without them. Let them be disabused of this mistake.

You will indulge me in a few remarks, in regard to the *branches of knowledge*, to which the Lyceum may, or ought to be made a means of directing public attention. Hitherto, as lectures have been the most common method of instruction, the sciences, to which the mode is perhaps best adapted, have been the most frequent topics. The alluring nature of many of these, the visible and tangible forms in which they may be exhibited, their practical bearings, their direct and intimate connexion with improvement in the arts, and the comforts of life, are circumstances that very naturally account for the attention they have received. And I believe that the desired impulse can be given so well in no other way. I would say nothing to discourage the continued or ever increased cultivation of a department of learning, which combines, in so high a degree, utility and pleasure. I am confident, however, that few candid and careful observers of the times, will deny that there is a prevailing inclination in favor of mere physical science, calculated to give it undue elevation on the scale of knowledge. On the many evidences of this fact, I cannot dwell; but it will be in point for me to say, that I have noticed in some of the journals of the day, not without apprehensions of their injurious influence, more then one statement of the objects of a Lyceum, which seemed to recognise the importance of no science, but that which relates to matter. A society, formed for the diffusion of knowledge, surely cannot fulfil its high destiny, if it fall in with this practical tendency of our age. Indeed, it cannot fulfil it, unless it exert a counteracting influence, by giving to other equally or more important branches their due estimation. Let those, who possess the ability and taste, employ every timely occasion and all judicious methods, to promote in the community, the cultivation of those improving and ennobling studies, mental and moral philosophy. I need not remind you how many expedients to accomplish this, will present themselves to a mind anxious to be useful, and ingenious in doing good. History and biography, embodying, under the interesting form of narrative and fact, so many abstract truths, and presenting impressive examples of vice and virtue, will be found valuable auxiliaries in this undertaking.

A knowledge of the great principles of general politics and political economy, is a matter of so evident and deep concernment to the citizens of a free country, that it deserves an ample share of regard, and can hardly fail to secure it.

The claims and value of mere literature, and of poetry in particular, will not perhaps be so readily allowed. The tentative and comparative character of these studies; their total want of that demonstrative quality, which is the grand essential with mere practical men; their connexion with the imagination, a power that often misleads; and their having little to do with the gains, motives, and pleasures of a mere material life,—are reasons that sufficiently account for their being often undervalued, and sometimes condemned. From their very nature, their effects are gradual and internal; displayed, not in additions to the visible comforts of our physical existence, but in refining and elevating the unseen principle within—in the nameless graces and elevating virtues of private and social life. Their power, if there be truth in history, or reliance may be placed on individual testimony, is sufficient materially to influence personal, and social, and even national character and happiness.

> 'Oh deem not, mid this worldly strife,
> An idle art the poet brings;
> Let high Philosophy control,
> And sages calm the stream of life;—
> 'T is he refines its fountain springs,
> The nobler passions of the soul.'

I shall not attempt to prescribe the methods, by which these subjects can be recommended to public attention; if the importance of the object be appreciated, the ways and means will certainly be devised. On this topic, I will add only one consideration more. If the study of the Greek and Roman classics is justly recommended to scholars, as the best preservative against a vitiated taste and style, then should the friends of popular education neither forget, nor suffer to be forgotten, those chaste models of English prose literature, which come nearest to the tried standards of ancient genius. And, for even stronger reasons, should they endeavour to bring again into favor and fashion, the deep, rich, sententious strains of an earlier muse, the manly and labored productions of those great poets, who fortunately, perhaps, for their lasting fame, lived before our *gilded* age.

I come now to a brief enumeration of the advantages, which may reasonably be anticipated, from this new, but already wide-spread effort to diffuse useful intelligence. And here I am met by the fundamental objection of those, who believe that no advantage will result, but on the contrary, much evil; who think it wrong to dispel the ignorance of men, compelled to toil for a subsistence, and comprising by far the greater proportion of the whole community, lest you unsettle their views in regard to the relations of life, making them ambitious, discontented, and consequently less happy. Without adverting to other arguments, of which there is certainly no deficiency, I should be willing to test the validity of this objection by a simple appeal to facts. Will you compare two families in humble life,—the specimen may readily be found,—similarly situated in their outward circumstances, but differing widely in their mental condition? One of them is decently educated, and accustomed to habits of reading and reflection,—the other, grossly ignorant. Will you find the latter family more industrious, peaceful, happy, or virtuous, than their less illiterate neighbours? Compare, again, two countries, in one of which the blessings of education are secured to all by custom or law, while in the other they are the privilege only of a few. Or, contrast two different periods of the same country. In England, for instance, there are now probably a hundred respectably educated persons to every ten a century ago.

Now, can many doubt the result of such comparisons as these? If, however, that result, disappointing our expectations and hopes, should prove, beyond a doubt, that the advantage is, and has been, on the side of ignorance, I see no alternative but to give up the point, and confess that we are upon the wrong track; that the boasted march of mind and spread of knowledge, so far as man's best interests are concerned, are, after all, but retrograde movements. With our benevolent objector, who doubtless desires the greatest good of the greatest number, let us welcome back those good old times, when the bliss of ignorance was universal and undisturbed. Let us crush every effort to teach men, generally, any other duty than that of unconditional submission. Let the paper mills, the type foundries, and the printing houses be destroyed; and, to complete the work, collect from every corner of the globe, those books, which, in uncounted millions, are now diffusing the miseries of intelligence, set fire to them, and let the light of their funeral pyre be the last which they shed on the world.

But a more numerous and more reasonable class, feel indifferent or hostile to the project, not because they disapprove of its object, but because they have doubts of its practicability, or fear its perversion. It must be allowed that there is room for such apprehensions. Like many other benevolent and promising schemes, this may prove one of ephemeral duration; or like others, again, it may be wrested to injurious and unworthy purposes. But what is the natural inference from this concession, if it be not the obligation, vastly increased, of those, with whom, for the present, it rests to say, whether this institution shall either go down, or be abused? Let the men of education, wealth, and leisure, in our land, catch but a tythe of the zeal, wisdom, and perseverance, which have won for Pestalozzi and Fellenberg, a fame pure as the snows, and durable as the granite of their own Alps, and this work *must* go on, it *will* succeed.

The characteristics and probable advantages of these associations, I cannot better express, than in the summary language of one of our jurists.* 'They are recommended by their simplicity, by their economy, by their social bearings, by their practical tendencies, by their moral influences, by their accordance with our republican institutions, and by their tendency to excite and direct to worthy objects a noble spirit of inquiry. They appear to be adapted to all circumstances, to all times, and to all states of society among us. They recognise no place and no community among us, where intellect exists, in which it is not the duty and the privilege of its possessors to adopt measures by which intellect may be improved. To the parent as well as to the child, to the master as well as to the apprentice, to the man of gray hairs as well as to the sprightly youth, to him who earns his bread in the sweat of his face, as well as to him who fares sumptuously every day, they offer sources, facilities, motives, and inducements for social, intellectual, and moral exercises and enjoyments. If generally established, and faithfully conducted, they will shed abroad the dignity of science, while they carry the success of business into every farm-house and work-shop. They will convert the family, the social circle, and even the tea-table and fire-side, into schools of mutual improvement, and scenes of the purest and highest enjoyment.'

To these considerations, let me add, that Lyceums, if successful, promise to be effectual auxiliaries to the cause of youthful education, to that of temperance, and to morality generally. They may be welcomed as well adapted to remove, not only aristocratic, but vulgar prejudices. They can hardly fail to soften the asperities of political and religious parties. They have a direct tendency to elevate the tone of politics and legislation.

Viewing the institution as a component part of the great system of education, may it not become the solid wall of a well-proportioned fabric, of which infant schools are the deep and sure foundation? Or, to extend a figure which has already been applied, while *these* are Hercules in his rocking-shield,

* Judge Williams.

crushing the serpents that have hitherto infested the cradle of infancy,—*that* is the hero in his manly strength, grasping the club that is to free society of its more formidable monsters.

Amid so many feverish excitements and factious struggles for honors and office, will not our countrymen more generally learn, that there is a nobler kind of power, with which every man may invest himself, and of which no man can be deprived. Let them remember that the power, which knowledge gives, is not only the best counterpoise to numerical and moneyed strength, but the best consolation for the loss of it. Instead of indulging in jealousy and discontent, while we witness the growing disproportion of different regions, and the encroaching dispositions of some stronger party,—let us endeavour to diffuse through the whole community, those treasures of the mind, which are better than commerce or manufactures, than canals or rail-roads, than political influence or golden gains. As members, neither of state, section, nor union, be it so much our ambition, to draw a bow of 'Ulyssean greatness,' as to be found with those, who are striving for the fairer palm of Ulyssean wisdom.

MR NEWMAN'S LECTURE.

LECTURE VI.

ON
A PRACTICAL METHOD
OF TEACHING RHETORIC.

BY SAMUEL P. NEWMAN,
PROFESSOR OF RHETORIC AND ORATORY, AND LECTURER ON CIVIL
POLITY AND POLITICAL ECONOMY, IN BOWDOIN COLLEGE.

By the indulgence of your Committee I am permitted to offer you my views on a Practical Method of Teaching Rhetoric. These views, I will premise, are the result of some years' experience as an instructer, and of that reflection on the subject, to which I have been more particularly led, in an attempt to furnish an elementary treatise for the use of my pupils. It will be my endeavour to convey them to you in a manner as plain and didactic as within my power.

With the impression, that in proposing a subject to me your Committee had more particularly in view that part of the art which is called composition, and in this sense the word rhetoric is often used, I now proceed to point out a 'practical method of instruction' in this department of study.

And here it is necessary that I bring distinctly before your view the several advantages proposed to be attained by the study of rhetoric. This is important, since the most direct and sure way of obtaining these advantages, must be the best practical method of studying rhetoric. They are as follows;—

1. Some acquaintance with the philosophy of rhetoric.

2. The cultivation of the taste, and, in connexion, the exercise of the imagination.

3. Skill in the use of language.

4. Skill in literary criticism.

5. The formation of a good style.

I shall, therefore, in discussing the proposed subject, direct your attention to these several particulars in succession.

What, then, is the best practical method of giving the student some acquaintance with the philosophy of rhetoric? This is our first inquiry.

By the philosophy of rhetoric, I here refer to those principles in the science of the philosophy of mind, and in the philosophy of language, on which are founded those conclusions and directions which are applicable to literary criticism, and to the formation of style. Obviously, then, it may be answered, that an acquaintance with the science of intellectual philosophy, and with the philosophy of language, should precede the study of rhetoric. Hence, no doubt, Milton and others assign to this branch of study the last place in a course of education. As before closing my lecture, I shall offer some remarks on the proper time of studying rhetoric, I here omit the discussion of this topic. It is known to all, that the prevalent opinion and practice are different from those recommended by Milton; so that our inquiry should be, what is the best practical method of acquainting the young with the philosophy of rhetoric—those whose minds are not accustomed to philosophical investigations, and who are ignorant of those sciences on which the art of rhetoric is founded.

I answer, that, while the attention should be directed to but few principles, and those most essential in a practical view, instruction should be imparted principally by familiar, talking lectures. A text-book, if one is used, should contain but a mere outline,—some general principles plainly stated and well illustrated.

Here I would more fully state, what I mean by familiar, talking lectures. Suppose I wish to make the student understand what I mean by taste, and in so doing, I have occasion to speak of the judgment, sensibility, imagination, emotions of beauty and sublimity. Now, should I attempt to effect my purpose by a definition, or an extended technical explanation of these terms, there would be little reason to hope for success. I would rather refer him directly to the operations of his own mind, point out to him instances where he forms a judgment, where his sensibility is excited, his imagination called into exercise, and emotions of beauty and sublimity kindled up in his own soul. It is true, he may not, after this, be able to give me an exact definition of these faculties and intellectual operations, but he has learned what is meant by the proposed terms; and when I have occasion to use them afterwards, I have no fears of not being understood.

That instruction in this part of rhetoric is attended with difficulty, no one will deny. The subjects themselves are intricate; hard to be understood, and still harder to explain, especially to those whose minds are immature and unaccustomed to philosophical reasonings. Here, then, is room for much ingenuity in the instructer; and without a skilful effort on his part, the efforts of the pupil will be of little avail. Above all things, let not the mockery of set questions and set answers be practised, in teaching what pertains to the philosophy of rhetoric.

After all, it must be allowed, that with the most skilful instructer, and the best text-book, young students will obtain but imperfect ideas in what pertains to the philosophy of rhetoric. Still, what is thus imperfectly acquired, will be of importance to them as opening some interesting fields of thought, which, with strengthened powers, they may afterwards explore; and further, as aiding them in better understanding the nature of the rules and directions founded on these important and somewhat intricate principles.

I have stated as a second object to be attained by the study of rhetoric, the cultivation of a literary taste, and, in connexion, the exercise of the imagination.

My remarks on this head may be better understood, should I state concisely in what sense I use the phrase *literary taste*. I would define it, then, as the ability to judge of whatever attempts are made in literary productions to excite emotions of beauty and sublimity, founded on past experience. The man of cultivated literary taste, carries in his own mind a standard of taste, that conforms to the general standard of taste, which is but the agreeing voice of all ages and nations—the voice of nature. The decisions which he makes, are decisions not to be reversed; for they rest on unfailing, unchanging principles. He knows, too, in the highest and fullest sense, the pleasures of literature.

To aid them in the cultivation of literary taste, as thus explained; to make familiar to the mind the established, unvarying principles, found in this part of the constitution of things; to open to it these rich and high sources of enjoyment, is one important object of instruction in rhetoric, and our second inquiry relates to the best practical method in which this purpose can be effected.

The cultivation of a literary taste must evidently depend principally on a familiarity with those productions, which are esteemed models of excellence in literature. In this respect, there is a close analogy to the cultivation of taste in painting, or in any of the fine arts. We may also learn something on this subject, from the course pursued by painters in the improvement of their taste. They visit the most celebrated galleries, and seek for models of excellence in their art; and these they make the objects of close, long-continued and patient study. They inquire what there is to excite admiration in these paintings, and dwell on their different prominent beauties, and in this way cultivate and improve their tastes. Now it is in the same way that a literary taste is to be cultivated. And that the student may skilfully use his models of excellence in literature, and unite with his observation of them the application of those principles on which they depend, he needs the assistance of an instructer.

In stating the details of the course here recommended, I remark, that, by the aid of a text-book prepared with reference to the proposed method of instruction, the student may have brought to his view examples of those instances, where there is most frequent occasion for the exercise of literary taste. I here refer to what are termed the ornaments of style. In connexion with those examples, the nature of whatever in literary production comes under the cognizance of literary taste, may be explained. The different ornaments of style may be pointed out to his notice, and he may be led fully to see why attempts of this kind are in some instances successful, and in other instances fail.

When the examples thus cited, and the comments upon them, have become familiar to the student, let his attention next be directed to finding examples in English writers, which may exhibit similar ornaments of style, and in the examination of which, there is opportunity for the application of the same principles. Here it is that important aid may be rendered by the instructer, since, in conducting these inquiries and forming his decisions, the student needs both guidance and confirmation.

To make myself fully understood, I will here illustrate my remarks. Suppose that a student finds in his text-book the following comparison from the writings of Locke;—

'The minds of the aged are like the tombs to which they are approaching; where, though the brass and the marble remain, yet the inscriptions are effaced by time, and the imagery has mouldered away.'

This comparison, he is told, is *naturally suggested;* and in connexion with the example, the meaning of this phrase is fully explained to him. And not only is he made to see what is meant by a comparison's being naturally suggested, but to feel, that, in the absence of this trait, the pleasure to be derived from it, as exciting an emotion of taste, would be impaired. Let the student now be directed to bring forward from any author, instances of comparison, which are in the same manner naturally suggested; and in this way let him become familiar with the principle stated, and with its application. In the same manner, by directing the attention in succession to the different traits in the various ornaments of style, and illustrating, in connexion with examples, the various principles on which these attempts to excite emotions of taste are founded, the pupil is led to a full acquaintance with this part of rhetoric. He is enabled at once, when reading the productions of any author, to perceive the beauties of style and to classify and arrange them;—in other words, he acquires a good literary taste.

But there is another point, connected with this part of my subject, to which I will for a moment direct your attention. I refer to the exercise thus given to the imagination. In our courses of study, we have discipline for the memory, the reasoning powers in their various forms, and the invention. But no regard is paid to the exercise and improvement of the imagination. And this, not because this faculty of the mind is useless, or because it admits not of being strengthened and improved by exercise. The impression is, that there is no method which can be adopted for the attainment of this end. Now I would ask, if, by the course here recommended, the imagination will not be called into exercise, and strengthened? These attempts to excite emotions of taste are addressed to the imagination, they are understood by the imagination; and it is a just inference, that the plan of study I have now recommended, will furnish a salutary discipline to the imagination.

Of the favorable tendency of the method of instruction, I can, from my own experience as an instructer, speak with some confidence. I have ever found, that my pupils engage in this part of their rhetorical course with interest. They get new views of the nature of style, are led to notice their susceptibilities of emotions, of which before they have been unmindful. They also become conscious of their own powers of imagination, and learn something of the nature and offices of this faculty; and with these views and this consciousness, they find that a new source of pleasure is opened to them. Thus they both derive important aid in becoming writers themselves, and are prepared to read with increased interest the writings of others.

Before concluding my remarks on this head, let me say, that what is here recommended, is perfectly practicable. It is an employment, which any student with common powers of mind may pursue; and it requires, on the part of the instructer, only that degree of literary taste, which every one professing to teach rhetoric should possess.

I may be permitted, also, in this connexion, to speak of rhetoric as an appropriate branch of female education. It is well known, that the female mind is highly imaginative, and at the same time strongly susceptible of emotions of taste. There are then peculiar reasons, why the attention of those thus constituted, should be directed where the imagination may receive guidance and assistance in its flights, and the susceptibility of sublime and beautiful emotions be cherished and improved; in other words, where a good taste may be formed.

Should we look, too, to one prominent object of female education, we shall be led to the same result; for I may say, that, since in literature are opened new and rich sources of high enjoyment to the mind, whatever tends to the improvement of the taste, and to excite a relish for literary pleasures, must, at the same time, increase the ability of contributing to the enjoyments of the fireside and the social circle.

The third object proposed to be obtained by the study of rhetoric, is skill in the use of language. Here I refer both to the choice of words, so far as purity and propriety are concerned, and to the construction of sentences.

Instruction in this part of rhetoric should be conducted with reference to two points,—to acquaint the student with the nature and principles of verbal criticism, and further to lead him to beware of those faults in construction, to which he is most liable.

The former of these appertains to the philosophy of rhetoric, and is included under my first head; but I here offer an additional remark. It was stated, when speaking of giving instruction on the philosophy of rhetoric, that difficulties attend this part of the course. These difficulties exist but in a slight degree, when exhibiting what is connected with the philosophy of language. Here is such abundant opportunity for illustration, and examples are so easily adduced, that every principle may without difficulty be made perfectly intelligible. Neither is this part of the study uninteresting to students. Curiosity is fully awake to whatever pertains to the nature of language, and to the rules that govern its use. And here I may be permitted to mention a work, which, in what pertains to this part of rhetoric, I regard as of the highest authority. I refer to Campbell's Philosophy of Rhetoric,—the ingenious, elaborate production of the Quinctilian of English literature.

To lead the student to beware of those faults in construction which are of most common occurrence, the other object in view in this part of the course, must evidently be effected by adducing examples of these faults. From the nature of the case, the endless forms of correct construction cannot be stated. On the obvious principle, then, that where one has erred, another will be liable to leave the right way, we direct the attention to these wanderings, and connect with such instances the cautions they naturally suggest. The object here in view may be accomplished for the most part by the text-book. All that is incumbent on the instructer, is, to lead the pupil fully to see what in every example adduced the failure is, and how it is to be remedied. This part of a text-book does not require to be dwelt upon in the recitation room. It is rather a part to be referred to by the student, when, hesitating as to the construction of sentences, he needs guidance and assistance.

I mention in the fourth place, as an object to be obtained by the study of rhetoric, skill in literary criticism.

Under this head, I include whatever pertains more particularly to style, its nature and diversities, as seen in the writings of different individuals, and in different classes of literary productions. Our inquiry is, What can be done by the instructer most efficiently, to aid the pupil in acquiring skill in literary criticism, as thus explained?

Style has been happily defined by Buffon as 'the man himself.' If I wish to become acquainted with any individual, I seek an introduction to him; I endeavour to learn from personal observation the peculiar traits in his character. I may, indeed, from the description of a third person, receive some general and perhaps just impressions respecting this individual; but all this, though it might prepare the way for my better understanding his peculiarities when in his presence, would alone make me but imperfectly acquainted with him.

The same holds true, if I wish to become acquainted with the peculiarities of those of different nations. You might describe to me the national traits of the French, and of the Spanish; but a visit to those countries, and familiarity with their inhabitants, would be of far more avail in learning their national traits of character.

This illustration suggests the best practical method of giving instruction in what relates to literary criticism. A text-book, or an instructer, may describe with accuracy and fulness the peculiarities of style, as they are seen in the writings of different individuals, or found in different classes of literary productions. But this is not enough. That the student may clearly discern these characteristic traits, and understand their nature, and the causes on which they depend, his attention must be directed to these writings. He must in some good degree become familiar with them, and thus learn wherein they differ, and what there is in each to approve or condemn.

It may be thought, that to bring to the view of the student in this manner the peculiarities of different styles, may require too much time and labor. But, with the aid of a text-book, much of the work may be performed by the student himself. What is most necessary on the part of the instructer, is, to direct the attention to specimens of different styles, and in some few instances to point out characteristic traits. The student, with this aid, will soon acquire sufficient knowledge and skill to apply the remarks found in the text-book himself.

This leads me to remark generally on the importance of reading good authors in connexion with rhetorical studies. This part of education is, I fear, in most of our schools and colleges, too much neglected. From his inability to judge of the merits of writers, the student needs guidance in selecting those which may be most useful to him, and this guidance the instructer should feel it is incumbent on him to supply. To read over occasionally with the pupil some choice specimens of style, may also be of essential advantage. To learn how to read, is no easy acquisition. Of course, I refer, not to the pronunciation of the words, or the inflections of the voice, but to the quick and true apprehension of the meaning, and a susceptibility to the beauties of style.

In this connexion, too, the student may be taught the true nature of literary criticism. It looks not for faults. It cherishes not a censorious, captious spirit. Its eye is directed after what is excellent and praiseworthy; after what may inform the mind, give grateful exercise to the imagination, and refinement to the taste. And when it discerns excellences of a high order, as if dazzled with what is bright and imposing, it sees not minute and unimportant defects. It is indeed nearly allied to that charity which is kind, and which, where she discovers what is truly worthy of her regard, throws her mantle of forgiveness over a multitude of sins.

I proceed now to notice the last mentioned advantage proposed to be obtained by the study of rhetoric. I refer to the formation of style.

This part of a rhetorical course of instruction is not particularly connected with the use of a text-book, further than that it furnishes opportunities for the application of principles and rules, which are there found. The aid furnished by an instructer, is principally in the correction of attempts in composition, with such general guidance and advice, as the intellectual habits and peculiarities of the individual may require. I offer, therefore, on this head, merely a few practical suggestions.

1. It is highly important, that the attention of the student, in his first attempts, should be directed to the management of his subject. I would require of him to exhibit a plan, or skeleton, stating the precise object he has in view, the divisions he proposes to make with reference to this point, and the manner in which he designs to enlarge on each head. In this way, he will not only be aided in forming habits of methodically arranging his thoughts, but will be led to adopt the easiest and most direct method of proceeding, in writing on any subject.

2. I have ever found, that, so far as the construction of sentences is concerned, and here I refer both to the division of a paragraph into sentences and to the phrases and forms of expression,—I remark, that, in relation to this part of the work of composition, I have ever found, that students derive important aid from translating select passages from the writings of good authors in other languages. Every one knows, that in this way a command of language is acquired. And I would extend the meaning of the phrase, so as to include, not only that *copia verborum*, and that power of nice discrimination in the use of words, which are generally understood to be implied by it, but also the right arrangement of words, and the correct construction of sentences. Other things being equal, he who, during the first six months in which the attention is directed to composition, should devote half of his efforts to the writing of translation, would, I doubt not, be in advance of him, all whose exertions had been employed in the work of composition.

3. I would further recommend a familiar mode of correcting the first attempts of the student. If practicable, the instructer may with advantage read over with the pupil his production, and alone with him freely comment upon its defects and ex-

cellences. While in this way needed encouragement is given, the attention of the student is directed to that point where there is most need of improvement. Besides, it not unfrequently happens, that the efforts of the student have taken some wrong direction. He has some erroneous impressions as to the nature of style, or as to the manner in which a good style may be formed. It may be that he is laboring too much on the choice and arrangement of his words, or the construction of his sentences; or, assigning undue importance to the ornaments of style, he may be seeking principally after what is figurative, and the elegances of expression; or, again, with false notions of what is original and forcible, he may be striving after what is sententious and striking. Sometimes, too, there exists a fastidiousness of taste, which is detrimental. The student is kept from doing anything, because he is unable to do better than he can do. In other instances, there is an injurious propensity to imitation. The student has fixed upon some writer as his model, and, servilely copying his master, his own native powers are neglected. Now in all these instances, the advice of the instructer may be of essential benefit.

One general remark, is all that I have to offer further on this head. It should ever be impressed on the student, that, in forming a style, he is to acquire a manner of writing, to some extent, peculiarly his own, and which is to be the index of his modes of thinking—the developement of his intellectual traits and feelings. It is the office of the instructer to facilitate the accomplishment of this important end, both by wisely directing the efforts of his pupil, and by removing every obstacle in his way.

I have now completed the remarks which I have to offer in connexion with the division of my subject. A few others, suggested by what has been brought forward, are all that I have to subjoin.

1. The impression, that the study of rhetoric is but of little practical advantage, which has to some extent prevailed, is an

erroneous impression. An acquaintance with the philosophy of rhetoric, the cultivation of the taste, the exercise of the imagination, skill in the use of language and in literary criticism, and the formation of a good style, are certainly important objects. It has also been shown, as I hope, that a skilful instructer, and a text-book adapted to the proposed method of instruction, may effect much in aiding the student to make these acquisitions.

That rhetoric, taught as it often is, does not prove of much practical advantage to the student, must indeed be allowed. And what can be expected from merely committing to memory a rhetorical catechism?

Hudibras' satirical couplet is too true, as the art is thus taught.

> 'For all a rhetorician's rules
> Teach nothing but to name his tools.'

The fact is, that the great secret of making the study of this art of practical advantage, is to direct the attention to examples and illustrations. Thus pursued, the study is of advantage. Otherwise, the prejudices which have existed on the subject, are but too well founded.

But there are other causes, to which the prejudices of which I here speak, are in part to be referred. Both those who have taught, and those who have studied this art, have not had in view, with sufficient distinctness, the different purposes which it aims to accomplish. The impression which generally prevails, is, that the only object of the study of rhetoric is the acquisition of a good style; and because this accomplishment is not immediately acquired, or does not unfailingly follow as a consequence from the study of rhetoric, it is thought a part of education of but little value.

In pointing out to you several advantages to be obtained by the study of rhetoric, I have, I trust, in part removed the impression on which this prejudice is founded. And I remark further, that while the formation of a good style, is one important object, which this study is designed to advance, the study of rhetoric alone will never effect this important result. Let the mind but be directed for a moment to what is meant by style, as already stated in this lecture, and it will be seen, that it is something depending on the intellectual habits and acquisitions generally,—a consummation of all that is effected by the discipline of the powers and the various attainments in knowledge. To expect, then, that the acquisition of a good style will necessarily follow from a course of rhetorical study, is to expect more than rhetoric professes to confer.

And in this connexion I remark that too much is wont to be expected generally from rhetorical studies. Quinctilian professed to take the child *ab incunabulis*, and to train it up for the forum. But in the division of labor, which has obtained in more advanced states of society, the designs of rhetoric are far more limited. She does not profess to inspire genius, to strengthen the intellect, and store the mind with knowledge. It is her office, as has been already stated, to guide the efforts of the improved mind, to cherish its susceptibilities of pleasurable emotions, and to arrange and display its stores of knowledge.

Let, then, just impressions exist as to the nature and design of rhetorical studies, and the prejudices, of which I have spoken, will pass away.

Another erroneous impression which exists on this subject, is, that the rules of rhetoric are restraints on genius, fetters to confine and limit the free action of the soaring powers of the human intellect. He who regards them must be content to 'dwell in decencies forever,' and never can exhibit that originality and vigor of thought and expression, which are indications of a superior mind.

I would ask those who have such views, to consider, for a moment, the origin and design of these rules. So far as they are founded on conventional agreement, which is the case in respect to all rules which relate to the use of language, they must exist, and be observed, whether found in systems of rhetoric or not. They are restraints to genius no further than the use of imperfect means for the expression of the thoughts and conceptions of the mind, are restraints; and while man is compelled to use symbols for the conveyance of his thoughts, such restraints must exist.

Those rules which belong to literary taste, rest, it is true, on a different basis, but still on one which has solidity and fixedness. They are not, as they are sometimes supposed to be, the *a priori* decisions of men, who have assumed to themselves unauthorised power. Derived as they are from those writings, which, in different ages and nations, have been objects of admiration, they are in consonance with the general feelings of men—with what is found in the constitution of the human mind. The loftiest genius, untaught, may conform to them; it cannot with impunity transgress them.

It may be further added, that the restraints which leave room for the genius of an Irving and a Scott, will not keep down those who make the complaint we are considering, from rising to any height, to which it is safe for them to venture.

But if the prejudice we are considering, be without just foundation, it must still be allowed, that there is some ground for it, looking at our old systems of rhetoric. This art we know was cultivated with great assiduity, both in Greece and in Rome, and among the literary relics of those ancient times, are standard rhetorical works of high authority. Now it has been too far the case, that our modern systems have been based on these ancient standard works. What is required by a difference of language, and the different intellectual habits, and other peculiarities of communities so widely removed from each other, has not been kept sufficiently in view. As illustrations of this remark, I will just refer to the long chapter in some of our systems of rhetoric, on harmony of sentences,—a subject of importance in a transpositive language, but far otherwise, as requiring rules and directions for its attainment, in our own. I mention also the explanations and directions respecting the different parts of a discourse,—

the introduction, proposition, narration, confirmation, confutation, and peroration, all of which, with our modes of thinking and reasoning, are but of little value. And it is from directing the attention to these useless parts of rhetoric, that the prejudice we are considering has arisen. I readily grant, that such rules are restraints, and unnecessary, injurious restraints, on genius; at the same time, I assert, that what remains, after these parts have been omitted, is highly important and useful.

Another prejudice, which rhetoric in company with her sister branches is called to encounter, is, that she has to do with mere words,—those words which we are told are the 'daughters of earth, while things are the sons of heaven.' This objection to the study of rhetoric, which, indeed, is not always, or most frequently, made by those who are most familiar with these sons of heaven, has influence on many minds. There is, in fact, a feeling of pride, which is nourished by its indulgence. To answer it, however, is easy. No one asserts, that mere words, however well chosen and marshalled, however harmonious and flowing, are objects worthy the attention of thinking, reflecting men. Neither is there, on the other hand, any question, that *thoughts* alone, however valuable, would be of but little use to the world at large, without that clearness and power of expression, which it is the province of rhetoric to furnish; so that, continuing the illustration, we might ask, what would be the worth of these vaunted sons of heaven, without the daughters of earth to make them known, and adorn them?

In concluding my remarks on this head, I would say, let rhetoric be taught in the manner recommended in this lecture; let there be distinctly in the mind the several advantages proposed to be attained by this study, without too high raised expectations of immediate and necessary benefits; let the nature of the rules and principles it inculcates be fully understood, and I have no fear that it will continue to be regarded as a study of little practical advantage.

Let me next, for a moment, direct your attention to the qualifications of a competent instructer in rhetoric.

1. He should possess some knowledge of intellectual philosophy. The art of rhetoric, like other arts, is founded on science of mind. It is from a knowledge of what is in man, of the constitution of the human mind, its susceptibilities of emotion, and the various influences it feels, that the skilful writer is enabled to address himself with success to his readers, and subject them to his power. And further, many of the rules of rhetoric, based as they are on principles unfolded in the science of mind, are but aids for the effecting of this purpose. How absolutely necessary, then, that he who attempts to explain and illustrate these rules, and to assist in cultivating the taste and forming the style, should possess some knowledge of that science whose principles are thus applied.

2. An instructer in rhetoric should possess some acquaintance with the most prominent writings in his native language. Familiarity with good writers will evidently prove highly serviceable in illustrating the rules and principles, which he has occasion to bring to the notice of his pupils. With this familiarity, also, will most probably be associated some skill in literary criticism, and some refinement of the taste, both of which are highly conducive to the success of an instructer.

I further add, what indeed is not confined to this branch of study, that he who attempts to instruct in rhetoric, should possess an aptness to teach. As we have seen, there are parts of the art which are difficult, hard to be understood, and requiring much explanation and illustration, on the part of the instructer. But on this head, I will not further enlarge, lest I seem unduly to magnify my office, and at the same time to condemn myself. Let it however be remembered, that not every one who has read a work on rhetoric, and who can ask questions out of a book, is fitted to instruct in this department of study.

Permit me next to offer one remark on the most suitable time for studying rhetoric.

There is some difficulty in determining the most suitable period for this branch of study. To comprehend in any good degree the philosophy of rhetoric, or to become skilful in literary criticism, requires maturity of mind. Hence, there seems a propriety in deferring the study till late in the course. Again, the student needs the aid which the study of this art affords, in the formation of his style, and its favorable influence on his literary taste; and these are reasons for placing rhetoric earlier in the course.

There are two ways in which this difficulty may be obviated. The attention may first be directed to some parts of rhetoric, particularly to what refers to the cultivation of the taste and to skill in the use of language, leaving to a later period what requires more maturity of mind. Another mode, and that which I am more disposed to recommend, is, to adopt a mean as to the time of studying rhetoric,—late enough to have the mind come to the work with a good degree of maturity, and early enough to derive benefit both to the taste and the style. I am more inclined to recommend the latter mode, because I do not approve of very early attempts in writing. I speak on this point from my own observation. Students in the college with which I am connected, begin to write themes the last term in the Sophomore year, having devoted their attention, during two preceding terms, to translations. At this time, a student has maturity of mind enough to 'look a subject into shape;' and till he can do this, my own opinion is, that he should not attempt to write. All the benefit to be derived from earlier attempts, relates to ease of expression, and this may better be acquired by translation. Those who attempt to write when very young, almost invariably acquire habits of desultory thinking. They learn to write without connexion or point, and thus all the ease of expression acquired, is dearly paid for. I much prefer, that a student should never have attempted the work of composition, than that he should have become desultory in his habits of thought. In the one case, all that is required, is to form good habits; in the other, bad habits are to be broken up, before right ones can be formed.

Before closing, I will advert to an objection, which has been sometimes urged against the method of instruction which has now been recommended. It is thought to be too difficult, to require too much effort.

To this objection I answer, that from the nature of this branch of knowledge, some difficulties must attend its pursuit. Who, without effort, can hope to look into the human breast, and to discern those hidden springs of action, those trembling chords of emotion, to which the eloquent writer must address himself? Who can expect to acquire skill in the use of language, and refinement of taste, without labor? Where is the able writer, who has not made himself such by his own unwearied exertions?

> '————Nil sine magno
> Vita labore dedit mortalibus.'

But there is another view. It should be no objection to a course of study, that it requires effort, that it tasks the mind and calls for the vigorous exertion of its powers. For one, I confess myself in a measure skeptical as to the value of those improvements in education, which remove all difficulties out of the way, which, if they do not open a royal road to knowledge, make a smooth and a level one, and sometimes burden the traveller with help as he goes on his way. I am by no means persuaded, that these facilities are in the end to advance our scholars farther in their course. The higher you ascend the hill, the steeper and the rougher is the way; and it is only the strong muscle, and the sturdy step of him, who knows what it is to toil and to struggle, that can mount these steeps, and move onwards unimpeded by these roughnesses. I might here ask, what made our fathers what they were, and how comes it to pass, that there were giants in those days? But this topic belongs to others, and I dismiss it, with the objection which has led me to remark upon it, believing that the latter requires no further notice.

Gentlemen, if what I have now said has tended to increase the definiteness of your views as to the objects to be obtained by the study of rhetoric; and especially, if any suggestions have been offered, which may aid those who teach in becoming more useful to those who are taught this art, my design is accomplished.

MR GRUND'S LECTURE.

LECTURE VII.

ON

GEOMETRY AND ALGEBRA,

AS

ELEMENTARY BRANCHES OF EDUCATION.

BY F. J. GRUND.

Science and arts are useful, only in proportion as they contribute to our happiness, either by providing the means of our physical comfort, or by ennobling human nature and increasing the number and intensity of our intellectual enjoyments. Education is the appropriate means of securing these. I shall be justified, therefore, when, in speaking of the two principal branches of mathematical knowledge, algebra and geometry, I first dwell on the general purposes of education, in order to determine the rank which mathematical sciences ought to hold in early instruction, and the bearing which they have on the developement of intellect, and the formation of character.

Education has, at all times, held a distinguished place among the acknowledged interests of civilized nations. It has been successively the subject of thought and research with the most eminent philosophers of antiquity. Statesmen and reformers of empires have bestowed upon it their utmost cares, and legislators secured and perpetuated its progress by laws. We have seen it keep pace with the political developement of nations; here cramped, chilled, and oppressed, by tyranny and despotism, bearing all the marks and deformities of a gothic age; whilst, on the other hand, we have seen it share and extend the blessings of liberal governments. But education is not only a national cause; it is the cause of humanity, of mankind;—the continuance and progress of civilization depend upon it. No one can be indifferent as to its advancement; for there is none, who is not, at least indirectly, interested in its success.

The truth of these remarks has at no period been felt more strongly than in this; at no time has the call for improvements in education been so general. The increased number of literary institutions in England, France, and Germany, the introduction of Sabbath schools, the number of periodicals, solely devoted to the purposes of education, the efforts of philanthropic societies in almost every part of the civilized world, the patient labors of Badesow, Resewitz, Campe, Salzman, Olivier, Schulz, and Pestalozzi, bear ample testimony to this assertion. Yet there is no country, and perhaps no community, in which this demand for popular education is so loud, so unanimous, as in this; because there is none, whose political welfare, nay, whose very existence, is so intimately connected with its progress. The system of free schools throughout this State, the institution of the Latin and High Schools in this city, the Mechanics' Institute, the Society for the Promotion of Useful Knowledge, finally, the formation of Lyceums in almost every part of the New-England States, are strong proofs of the vigilance of the people, as to moral and intellectual improvement.

Much, however, is yet left to be done, and great caution is to be used, lest the general call for popular and practical instruction, should defeat its very object.

In the minds of perhaps the majority of persons, education still consists in the acquiring of certain facilties for particular purposes in life. But this does not deserve the name of education. A system of instruction adapted merely to *this purpose*, enslaves and degrades human nature. It reduces men to machines, by bringing up workmen for a manufactory. Let us, for a moment, consider the errors into which it leads.

The mind of the child is considered a mere receptacle, which is to be *stored* with knowledge. Its pliability is abused into a mechanical and spiritless routine. Neither the individuality nor the peculiar structure of his mind, not even his age, is taken into consideration. His mental faculties are not roused to action; the mind does not operate upon itself; for, in *receiving* knowledge, the pupil is merely passive. Principles are pronounced dogmatically, and are heaped upon each other without plan or system. Children the most unlike in capacity, are put together in the same class, and have to learn, each day, a fixed portion of one science or another; and the test of their acquirements is a verbal recitation from a book. The memory is charged with the crudest and most heterogeneous conceptions, without allowing the mind the least respite to assort and adjust them, much less the time which it needs to reflect upon them, in order to convert them into part of its own substance. Thus, from the first moment the boy goes to school, until the young man leaves college, he is harassed and haunted with the variety and unreasonable number of studies he is obliged to pursue, without spirit or inclination; and it is indeed a wonder if his mental powers are not in this way prostrated or destroyed.

A bounteous Providence seems to bestow the same parental care upon the preservation of intellect, which it does upon the continuance of certain species in the animal and vegetable kingdoms, where, notwithstanding the ravages of those who feed upon them, and the devastations committed by the fury of the elements, the prodigious number of seeds prevents the race from becoming extinct.

Many men can trace the developement of their minds to the time they left college, or the hot vapor baths of inferior institutions of learning. This is the period of the emancipation of their minds. They are now for the first time, perhaps, permitted to look round, and view calmly the immense territory of science, which lies as yet unexplored before them. They are now allowed to take their own standing, and to strike out a plan for their self-education. Many a happy thought that lay dormant, or was oppressed by the burthen of other studies, for which the student had neither taste nor talent, quickens now into life. One idea gives birth to another. They soon accumulate, and give the mind a tenor which lasts through life; and it is not unfrequent to see men acquire more information from one year's self-discipline, than from all the instruction they had in schools. Men whose talents, while at school, were considered little above mediocrity, when circumstances call forth their energies, develope, sometimes, powers of mind, which confound those who are acquainted with them, and of which they themselves were unconscious, because they were degraded in their own estimation, and the mechanism of their education, leaving no room for individual efforts, gave them no stimulus to mental action.

Is, then, the object of education to leave to circumstances to raise the edifice of which the corner-stone ought to be laid in early childhood? How many adults can command the leisure which is necessary for a course of thorough self-discipline? Most young men, immediately after leaving school or college, emerge into active life; their minds are engrossed with business; their thoughts become rivetted on interest and gain, as the means of procuring to them physical comfort, the want of which is, in all countries, and at all times, felt more strongly than that of intellectual riches. Physical wants have an immediate bearing upon our own happiness, and impair that of those who depend upon us. They are therefore more pressing, and not so likely to be lost sight of, as the culture of our minds. Are we, then, to leave to *men* to atone for the faults of their early education? Is it to be left to the man of business to root out the excrescences and to correct the misconceptions of his mind? In how many cases can mature age divest itself of prejudices imbibed in infancy? When does it entirely overcome the enslaving mechanism to which it has been accustomed in early life? Thus, in providing for a livelihood, the *mind* becomes crippled and deformed, and whilst, what is so natural to the human breast, men are greedy in the pursuit of pleasure, the greatest of all, the only lasting one, that of *intellectual enjoyment*, is irrecoverably lost to them.

These are the consequences of a mechanical, spiritless method of instruction, which, without elevating the mind, without exciting it to thought and reflection, leaves the noblest faculties of the soul uncultivated, whilst, by forcing the child into a premature activity of inferior powers, it impairs even its physical energies, and perverts and distorts human nature.

Great improvements have undoubtedly been made in education within the last twentyfive years, and among the happiest ones are those for which we are indebted to Pestalozzi. But his system remains yet to be fully understood and operated upon. The belief is yet too common among parents and teachers, that education consists in *receiving* certain principles and maxims, and in becoming conversant with such sciences, as it is supposed will be useful in after life. The term, *practical* education, has been misconstrued into the acquirement of such branches of learning only, as the pupil, when grown up, is likely to have an immediate call for; and by *useful* knowledge is meant that which can be *turned to some account*. This is undoubtedly the reason, why, in almost every branch of learning, authors have started up to condense and contract science, and to give, in a neat duodecimo, the researches and labors of ages. This is by some deemed a great advantage; but it is, in fact, a serious evil. Such treatises may be admirably adapted to men of business, who have neither the leisure nor the patience which is necessary to become proficients in science, and whose object it is, merely to get acquainted with a few principles, or, perhaps, a bare abstract of them, in order to apply them to trade or to the mechanic arts; but, for the education of children, such books are totally unfit. Besides the general tendency which they have to make learners superficial, they are deficient in other respects. In treating of a science in a cursory manner, it is impossible to preserve that gradual transition from one principle to another, which constitutes the chief merit of all elementary instruction.

In addition to these remarks it may be observed that most authors attempt to make their works as complete as possible. Nothing essential, therefore, is omitted in them. They contain as many propositions and rules as the most complete treatises on the same sciences, and the natural consequence is, that such works become crowded, and instead of smoothing the road to knowledge, they merely bring the obstacles nearer together. Such books may be very useful to men, who, after having gone through a regular course of studies, wish to have a book of reference for those principles which are of immediate application in practice. But a cursory *treatise* on a science is not a proper *introduction* to it. An introduction to any kind of knowledge, is to prepare the mind for the reception of either more complicated or more abstract truths, by making it familiar with the plainest and simplest ones. A great deal depends on awakening a taste for learning, and on treating it in such a way as not to harass or fatigue the mind. If the subject is *completed*, the work is no longer an introduction; it takes the place of a full treatise, which is put into the hands of the pupil, instead of a more extended and thorough work. Thus, instead of *removing* difficulties, their *number* only is decreased, by diminishing the quantity of knowledge which is imparted.

In early education it does not matter how *far* the child goes in a particular science; but merely how *understandingly* it goes to work—how far the acquaintance with new principles contributes to draw out its mind. The '*method*' of instruction is vastly more important than the number of things and principles the child becomes acquainted with. It is, in this respect, with the sciences, as it is with the fine arts. A pupil profits more by drawing a few well selected copies from eminent masters, than by copying a thousand indifferent pieces.

The method of instruction must be such as to enable the pupil to acquire knowledge and facility by his own individual exertion; for 'nothing is ours but what we acquire ourselves.' Less depends on the shortness of the way, than on its security. Neither is the mass of knowledge so important as the manner in which it is acquired, in order to render the pupil morally healthful and self-dependent. This is the spirit of Pestalozzi's method, whose principle it is to start, in education, from the most elementary points of all human knowledge, to generate the germ of it in the child's own mind, and to strengthen and mature it, by regular, systematic activity. Not the reading, writing, ciphering, drawing, &c, but the exercising and developing of the child's powers, through the medium of these, ought, according to his idea, to be the principal object of all elementary instruction. Pestalozzi's method evidently aims at making the child independent of its teacher, by bringing it to think and act from principles to which it became sensible by the force of its own application. This intellectual education is analagous to the physical developement of the child. It is consequently more negative and preventive, than positive or dogmatical. Like a watchful nurse, he would prevent the child from falling, and yet give it full scope for the exercise of its own strength, by trying to walk by itself. This is the only rational influence which the teacher ought to exercise over his pupils. Education consists only in the natural influence of adults on children, in order to develope their mental and physical faculties to such a degree as to enable them to advance toward perfection of their own accord.

Having thus spoken of the purposes of education in general, let us turn our attention to the importance of mathematical studies in early instruction, and the influence they have on mind and character.

'Mathematics,' in the words of an English reviewer, 'are a high and important branch of study. They are a science closely concerned in the investigation of abstract truth, requiring intensity of attention, accuracy of research, acuteness of application, and severity of judgment.

'They are intimately connected with the most useful arts, and with the sublimest speculations, with those inventions which give man power over the world in which he is placed, and with those discoveries which elevate him to the knowledge of contemplating the worlds beyond and around him.'

But neither the sublimity of mathematics, nor their utility in almost every stage of life, is the principal reason for which they ought to be made a regular branch of study in common schools. It is because there is no other science so admirably calculated to draw out the thinking faculties of children, and therefore none which forwards so effectually the purposes of elementary instruction. It is on this account, Pestalozzi, and all modern reformers of education, have devoted so much of their attention to arithmetic and geometry. These two studies, when pursued in the proper manner, go hand in hand, and form the very ground-work of an intellectual education. They are almost the only branches taught at schools, which call upon the pupil's judgment, prompt his mind to thought and reflection, and teach him to reason from given things to things unknown. They lead the pupil to institute comparisons, and to determine the relations which things bear to each other. Thus exercising every faculty of his mind, he acquires a habit of close attention, and strengthens and confirms his mental energies by concentrating them, and bringing all to bear upon the same point. With this regard it may be said, that mathematics facilitate every other study. The mind which is once to a certain degree developed, and which has acquired the habit of thinking and reasoning, can easily apply the same powers to other branches of knowledge. Whatever study the pupil may now undertake, is entered upon more systematically. He is now accustomed to investigate for himself. H has not the same dependence on authority, for in his previous study none has been assumed; nor does he lay so much stress on the conceptions of others, until they are made his own by a fair appeal to his understanding.

But if the study of mathematics is really to produce these happy effects, it must be commenced early. Not that I mean, that children ought to be made mathematicians. This would be absurd. I admit that there are certain theorems and propositions, both in geometry and algebra, which require great power of combination and abstraction, and a skill in analyzing, such as children cannot be supposed to possess. I will go still farther, I will say that there are certain branches of the pure mathematics, which puzzle even the minds of adults; and there are others, which it seems are almost inaccessible to ordinary capacities. But among these are certainly neither the elements of geometry nor algebra, which are by far the most useful branches, whilst some of those which I have alluded to, are but of little application either in practical life, or even in the natural sciences. They are the province of the amateur and the scholar, and enter rarely even the sacred halls of a college.

It is the peculiar property of geometry to be adapted to every gradation of capacity. Children from six to ten years of age, may be as much benefited by mathematical instruction, as people advanced in life,—only the *method* of instruction, the style and arrangement of the text-books, and, above all, the object which the teacher has in view in communicating knowledge, must vary according to the age and capacity of the pupils.

In instructing pupils of a mature age, due attention must be paid to the mechanism of the science, as the means of acquiring facility of calculation. In teaching children, this consideration must entirely vanish, when compared with the object of forwarding the general purposes of education. Mechanism in all early instruction is fatal, even when a proper explanation has gone before. For whilst the mind is abandoning itself to the security of the road, it remains inactive, and is likely to relapse; but when it is once, to a certain degree, developed, nothing is to be apprehended from a moderate share of mechanical operations. They are then indispensable; they afford the mind a sort of intellectual *recess*; and while the pupil is still at work, he may gather strength for renewed mental exertion.

I have said that the study of mathematics ought to be commenced early. By this I mean that the mathematical method should be acquired in childhood. Besides the reasons which I have already alleged in favor of this principle, there are others no less important and deserving of consideration. It is with the faculties of the mind as it is with those of the body. If you would see a man in full possession of his physical energies, having a perfect command over his limbs and muscles, you must let him begin to exercise them at an early period, lest they should become obtuse and inflexible. The same is the case with the mind. The habit of attention, the power of abstraction, and of bringing the mind for a length of time to bear upon the same subject, and, above all, that strength which will sustain intellectual labor without fatigue, must be acquired early, or they will never be our own. Genius may break through, and strike out its own way, but the greater part will remain far behind mediocrity.

It might be objected, that the mind may be cultivated by other studies, not less important than mathematics. To this I would answer that most studies pursued in schools are more or less matter of memory. Spelling, geography, grammar and even history, as taught to boys, require little reflection or individual effort. Independently of this consideration, it may be observed, that there are certain branches of mathematical knowledge, which are requisite for the common purposes of life. These boys are obliged to render themselves familiar with, during the short period in which they are at school, and if they do not begin when young, so as to have the time to acquire them in a rational manner, they abandon themselves to a mechanical routine, and consider mathematics as witchcraft or a talisman, by which they may obtain the answer to certain questions, by proceeding according to rules. Instances of this kind we see every day, though, in exoneration of the teacher it must be said, that it is impossible to impart a competent knowledge of any science, in the short time which they are allowed to devote to it.

The question has frequently been asked, Of what use is the study of algebra and geometry to those who do not wish to make a profession of it? The answer is contained in what I have said of their influence on the developement and growth of the mind. I would add only that it is the peculiar characteristic of the mathematical sciences to adapt themselves to all conditions, and to be useful, whatever the extent to which they may be carried. An acquaintance with only a few principles in other sciences is rarely beneficial, and may often prove a serious injury. In mathematics, the smallest number of principles is complete in itself, and affords satisfaction. It is not the reading of a tale of which you judge by the end; it is like the study of history, every page of which is crowded with useful instruction, in which the philosopher perceives a wise connexion, which enables him from the statistics of the day to foretell the history of future ages.

So far I have been speaking of the positive advantages of the study of mathematics; but it is not less to be recommended as a preventive against frivolous reading and a premature developement of the imagination. It gives the mind a solid cast, and a depth of reflection, which does not suffer it to delight in the easy and dangerous plays of fancy. The love of truth and investigation will lead it into the vast domains of the natural sciences, and strengthen and elevate it, by the principles of a sound philosophy.

Before entering on the method of teaching algebra and geometry, I deem it necessary to speak of the prevailing system of instruction, in which the study of algebra takes the precedence of geometry. This must be considered an inversion of the natural order in which the different branches of mathematics ought to follow each other.

Geometry is of all mathematical knowledge the easiest of comprehension; it being the least abstract, and the most capable of being represented to the mind through the medium of the senses. It is in this respect even easier than arithmetic, and there is no reason, why it should not be made as common a branch of education, and be taught as early as spelling or grammar. I certainly do not mean to put Euclid or Legendre into the hands of children; but that the first principles of geometry are really capable of being presented in a manner which shall render them a proper study even for children in primary schools, has been happily illustrated by Pestalozzi and many of his pupils.

Lacroix, in his essay on instruction, speaks of mathematics, as that kind of knowledge, which is founded on the smallest number of conceptions, but *upon* those which are oftenest repeated; which lead to the idea of number and space. These ideas enter the mind at so early a period, that none can recollect when and how they are acquired; and such is their similitude, that there is no reason for beginning the education of the child with the consequences of the one sooner than with those of the other. But the applications of the numerical calculus being more frequent, the habit of beginning with the science of numbers or arithmetic, has prevailed.

The same argument cannot be offered with regard to algebra, for though it is a study of unbounded utility, including, in the widest sense of the word, the whole cycle of mathematical sciences; and though by means of its symbols it is capable of representing the elements of all speculative knowledge, yet, with regard to the common purposes of life, and particularly the mechanic arts, it is less useful than geometry. An acquaintance with this science is indispensable to the draftsman, the architect, the mason, the carpenter, and to most practical men, whilst the study of algebra holds out stronger inducements to the analyzer and the adept in science.

The same inference may be drawn from the history of mathematics. Geometry was cultivated before any other branch of the exact sciences. We can trace it back to the cradle of civilization, to India and Egypt; arithmetic and algebra are comparatively a *modern* invention. The former was but little known among the Greeks, and the latter was not cultivated until the sixteenth century. The six books of Diophantes,* which have come down to us, contain but indefinite problems. Besides, he adopted no scientific method of representing quantities; and from that period till 1494, no author on that science is known. The writings of the Arabians Ben-Musa and Thebit-Ben Corah, in the ninth century, exist only in manuscript, and are scattered in the Bodleian and other libraries of England, and in that of the Escurial in Spain. Great efforts were made in the sixteenth century by men like Luccas Pacciolo, Michel Stiefel, Scipio Ferreo, Tartaglia, Cardanus and Bombelli; but the known quantities were yet represented by numbers, and the unknown ones by signs. It was reserved for Francis Vieta to introduce the first scientific notation, and to represent known and unknown quantities by letters. One of the most useful parts of algebra, the invention of Logarithms, is but of the seventeenth century; for in Stifelius' Arithmetica Integra, geometric and arithmetic series are merely compared without any interpolation; and it is only since Newton and Leibnitz that algebra has been brought into a regular system. Thus the most perfect treatise on geometry, Euclid's Elements, preceded the regular study of algebra nearly twentythree centuries.

No plausible reason can be assigned for this astonishing difference, except that geometrical truth is in its very nature more simple and therefore easier perceived. It does not require the same intensity of speculation as algebra; it needs no symbols to represent to the mind its object; for this is plainly set before us, and we are in many cases prompted to ask, why does

---

* These six books were found in the 6th century, in the library of the Vatican, in Rome.

this need a demonstration? and it is because geometry is more intimately connected with practical life; the call for it is more general, its object is everywhere,—here, and in the spheres beyond us.

In almost every case where algebra is studied before geometry, it is not carried beyond the solution of a quadratic or the developement of a surd. There the pupil is obliged to stop, and begin geometry. But no sooner does he venture himself upon trigonometry, than he perceives he has not sufficient facility of algebraic calculation. He is now put into a new and more extended treatise on algebra, and has to spend another year, before he is able to complete the elements of a college course. But these checks weary his patience, diminish his zeal for the study, and discourage his hope of success. How much better would it be, to begin geometry as soon as the first principles of arithmetic are properly understood. The mind would then acquire sufficient strength to digest at once a full treatise on algebra. Its march would be more secure, and its progress less interrupted by changes of study.

Let us imitate the example of the best writers on geometry, all of whom exclude algebraic reasoning from the body of their works, in order to render them an introduction to a course of mathematical studies. The analytic method may be that of invention; but it is not the way to teach, particularly younger pupils. All education is necessarily synthetic. Its principles are to be adapted to the state of the mind, and cannot wholly be deduced from a general view of the sciences.

I am now to speak of the method of *teaching* algebra and geometry. This flows naturally from the science itself, and from the object which both teacher and pupil have in view. For this purpose, we would in the first place recommend to every instructer, first to make himself perfectly familiar with the knowledge he is to communicate, before he enters upon the duties of his profession. This may be called a bare truism; it is nevertheless a *truth* which cannot be too often repeated. The great and rapid advancements, which have lately been made in the common system of instruction, enable every man, no matter of what qualification, to teach, not only one, but all branches of education; like a village physician, who is accustomed to be summoned to cases of all descriptions, and treats a fever with the same ease as he applies a blister, extracts a tooth, or amputates a limb.

Our text-books have lately arrived at such perfection as to render explanations and lectures from the instructer altogether superfluous, if he is only a *disciplinarian*, and watches over the *good behaviour* of his pupils. From the head-quarters of his school-room he then directs the different evolutions of their minds, and sees that they go through their exercises with punctuality and precision; or, he acts the part of an overseer, whilst the slaves are doomed to search for the diamonds from amid the dust, and, after washing and cleansing them, deliver them up at a recitation. These are carefully collected and treasured up, and at the end of the year they are neatly set, and not without a good deal of foil, *exhibited*, for the double purpose of inviting purchasers, and stimulating others to similar exertions.

As long as such a system exists, mathematics may as well be entirely struck out from the course of studies pursued in schools. If the mind is not to be *benefited*, why should it be *fatigued* and *mal-treated*. Perhaps it will some time or other take up this study of its own accord, perhaps make proficiency in it by its own power and activity, if we do not stifle and disgust it, at the outset, with the very name of mathematical truth, by the spiritless manner in which it is presented.

It is an idle assertion that mathematics are dry and unpalatable. Whatever is perfectly understood, never excites disrelish. Why is it that, in the schools taught after the plan of Pestalozzi, mathematics are a favorite study with the young? It is because the pupils understand what they are learning; they are not hurried into new propositions before they are perfectly familiar with the preceding ones; their minds are opened by gentle degrees; the road to knowledge is rendered smooth and the ascent gradual, to make the journey both easy and pleasant.

In this manner, the first principles of geometry ought to be taught. Nothing must be advanced in a positive manner. The mind of the *pupil* is to be the principal operator; it must instruct, convince, and confute *itself;* and when it arrives at some important truth or result, it must be through its own powers. It ought not even to perceive that it has been guided thither.

While in class, the pupils ought to be at the most perfect ease; they ought to be permitted to ask explanations, whenever they have not been able fully to comprehend the instructer; and he ought to encourage their curiosity by the most familiar treatment that is compatible with his own dignity; for in proportion as a science is supposed to be difficult, the manner of teaching it ought to be engaging and cheerful.

To captivate the attention of the pupils, inductive interrogation is advisable; because it is the most natural way of teaching, and best adapted to the faculties of the young. Thus, queries may be substituted instead of rigid propositions; for what is lost by them in brevity and precision, is gained in easiness and familiarity of style.

One plan of teaching geometry, which may be suggested as useful, is the following. Teach not more than *one* proposition or query in a day. This the pupils can bring themselves to understand with ease, and without neglecting their other studies. But let it be explained in as many different ways as possible, in order to suit their different capacities. The pupils should then draw the figure on their slates, or on the board, and be directed to vary and change it, for the sake of studying the relative position of its different parts, and to enter more fully upon the spirit of the query. At the end of each lesson one or two questions may be proposed for the pupils to think and reflect upon until the next day. This will excite their curiosity, make the study more interesting, and stimulate them to individual efforts. The pupils ought not to commit any proposition or query to memory, in order to recite it by rote; they ought to understand its *meaning*, and be obliged to give it in their *own* words. The same course is to be pursued with regard to demonstrations and problems. If the teacher uses a book, he should not be satisfied with the explanations contained in it. The best book on any science needs much aid from the instructer. The latter ought to illustrate the different principles of the science he is to teach, by familiar conversation, with his pupils; for if all his instruction is a mere paraphrase of the book, how can he interest them, or command their attention?

Instruction given in this way will occupy more time; but it will be more agreeable to the pupils, and insure more effectually success in teaching. The progress of the learner will be slow, but every step of it will be well secured; their minds will never be satiated, but by that means they will feel a constant desire to learn more; they will not, at the age of fifteen or sixteen, think themselves mathematicians; but the road to improvement will be left open to them, and they will feel that they need improvement; they will not wait until necessity calls forth their energies,—they will advance of their own accord, and scorn the assistance of others.

It would lead me too far to enter, here, upon the different parts of geometry, and the order in which they are to follow each other, in a regular course of instruction. Most authors are, in this respect, at variance with each other, and it is for the instructer to decide, which system agrees best with his plan of teaching. I would only point out two errors committed even by the best writers on mathematics. I mean the attempt to prove rigidly the theory of parallel lines, and the measure of the circle. The former is deemed impossible by the best geometers. The theory of parallel lines has baffled the efforts of the most eminent mathematicians, and will probably forever remain imperfect, on account of the imperfect definition of a straight line. Even Lagrange followed the example of Euclid by taking for granted, that through one point only *one* line can be drawn parallel to another. Why then torment the pupils with useless attempts to prove what is self-evident? The same remark applies to the definition of a circle as a polygon of an infinite number of sides. Definitions do not rid us of difficulties which are inherent in the substance of things. Making a curve line consist of an infinite number of points, does not make it differ from the possible definition of a straight line; and we have as yet no exact ratio between the diameter and the circumference of a circle. But it is at once plain and evident to every mind, that by continuing to inscribe regular polygons of double the number of sides, the perimeters of these polygons will finally *approximate* to the circumference; the rigorous form of reasoning can, in this case, only vitiate the mind, by presenting an exceptionable principle, as perfectly satisfactory.

What I have said of the method of teaching *geometry*, applies in a great measure also to *algebra*. I will therefore confine myself to a few remarks.

It is a common practice among many instructers, to let their pupils go through a treatise on algebra, without proposing to them any additional problems, either to exercise their skill in analyzing, or to give them facility of calculation. A similar course is pursued even in colleges, and the consequence is, that most students, when venturing themselves upon the calculus or even on an inferior branch of analysis, meet with insurmountable obstacles. Problems, which lead to simple equations of the first and second degrees, are found in many elementary works on algebra; but those which involve more intricate analytical processes are hardly ever met with in *text*-books. With justice have English mathematicians charged French writers with abundance of theory and want of examples; but it is not less true that the greater portion of English authors contain principally examples, and hardly any theory, which is equally to be deprecated. Those authors, says Lacroix, in his essay on instruction, have neglected to give the *spirit* of the mathematical method; the pupils may learn from them the *mechanism* of the algebraic calculus, but they will not comprehend its philosophy, without which algebra is nothing but a trade, destitute of all interest to men of thought and reflection.

But there is a way of uniting both the English and the French method, by taking the text of a French writer,—for instance, that of Lacroix, which is generally used in American colleges,—and supplying the want of examples with the aid of books written solely for that purpose. The algebraic problems of Bland and Meier Hirsch are admirably calculated for younger students. Those of Meier Hirsch have been lately translated into English, and may be considered superior to Bland's, on account of the vast number of analytic processes they contain. Among these, the problems on the radical calculus, afford the best means of initiating the learner into finite analysis.*

For the purpose of studying analytic geometry, the works of Biot and Boucharlat may be used. The former treats his subject more in the abstract. Boucharlat, in his theory of curves, adheres more strictly to the geometric method, and abounds with useful and interesting problems. He was a pupil of Lagrange, and his works are dedicated to, and met with the approbation of his illustrious teacher.

When the student has acquired the necessary facility of algebraic calculation, and is sufficiently acquainted with analytic geometry, then, and no sooner, ought he to undertake the study of the differential calculus. Lacroix, Boucharlat and Tobias Meyer are the most comprehensive authors on this branch of the pure mathematics; and an intimate acquaintance with either of them, will enable the student to read the gigantic works of La Place, as presented to us in the invaluable translation of Dr Bowditch. The notes of the translator, which occupy nearly as much space as the body of the work itself,

---

* A new translation of these problems, adapted to the use of the American student, is now in press, and will soon be published by Carter, Hendee and Babcock, Boston.

offer far greater facilities to the American student, than the original does to the French. Whilst a much longer course of preparatory studies, and years of application are necessary, to read single chapters of the Mécanique Céleste, all difficulties seem to be removed, and the road levelled everywhere by the indefatigable labors of the American translator.

But it is not for me, in this lecture, to point out the road, which the scholar must take to become a *proficient* in science: my object has been to show how the study of mathematics may be made easy and agreeable to *beginners*. If the hints which I have now thrown out should in any degree contribute to promote the study of a science which has hitherto been too much neglected, I shall be amply rewarded for the pains I may have taken to present them in this form.

MR OLIVER'S LECTURE.

LECTURE VIII.

ON
THE ADVANTAGES AND DEFECTS
OF THE
MONITORIAL SYSTEM;

WITH SOME SUGGESTIONS, SHOWING IN WHAT PARTICULARS IT MAY
BE SAFELY ADOPTED INTO OUR SCHOOLS.

BY HENRY K. OLIVER,
OF SALEM, MASS.

'Δος πȣ στω και την γην κινησω.'

'GIVE me a place whereon I may stand, and I will raise the world,' said the mighty prince of ancient mathematicians, as the great truths of mechanical science flashed across his mind. In later days, and from a land where learning once held imperial sway, though now, over her widely extended plains, ignorance and barbarism are brooding in deepest intellectual midnight, there has been heard a voice, bearing to us, my friends, who are actively engaged in the great business of education, and to all, who feel a proper interest in its promotion, sounds of the deepest import. 'Give me a handful of pupils to-day, and I will give you as many teachers to-morrow, as you want.' This was a saying very frequently used by the celebrated Dr Bell, the well-known founder of the Madras, or Monitorial System of Instruction. The verification of an assertion like this, would evince in him, who should so make it good, the possession of even greater power than Archimedes would have displayed, had he found a place whence he might have shaken the world from her deep and strongly laid foundations. For he, who should, with such rapidity, create the means whereby to accomplish so noble an end, would possess himself of a host of intellectual levers, (if I may be allowed the use of such an expression,) which should exert an influence to move the world, which not all the strivings of folly and of prejudice, would be able to withstand. The cry that 'the schoolmaster is abroad,' would have been uttered long before it fell from the lips of Brougham, and the wide plains which the siroc blast of ignorance had scorched and withered into a wilderness and a desert place, would have blossomed like the rose, and been strewed with the rich and life-giving fruits of the tree of heaven-born science. But unfortunately for so fair a speculation and 'a consummation so devoutly to be wished,' we fear that the inefficiency of the means and the feebleness of the levers, will render many of the efforts to move the world of ignorance almost, if not entirely, futile.

It has fallen to my lot, my respected friends, to address you, upon 'the advantages and defects of the monitorial system of instruction,' and to endeavour to show how far it may be safely adopted into our schools.

I shall take up the subject in the order here laid down, and shall give you the results of my own observation and study, referring you neither to individuals nor to books, for corroboration of any assertions which may be made. I am induced to take this course, because I have thought, that when a subject like the present is proposed, in the particular manner which the phraseology of ours seems to indicate, it is as frequently expected, that the writer should advance his own opinions, as that he should collate and publish those of other people. There is this advantage attendant upon the former course of procedure, that the opinions advanced will be received as the opinions of a single individual, and so far only, entitled to consideration. While, if the latter be pursued, the magic of great names, and, of high-sounding authorities, may be apt to exert a controlling influence, and sometimes even an illimitable sway over many minds, and to compel them to yield that assent, and, perhaps, that entire submission, which they would never concede to individual assertion. The latter course may restrain, and even effectually check, our own freedom of opinion, while the former leaves it to act unbound and unembarrassed. Permit me to importune your candid hearing and judgment, and allow me to express my regrets that the subject has not fallen to the disposal of abler and more experienced hands.

The advantages which the monitorial system of instruction possesses over the ordinary method, are the following:—

1. It provides, by the same means, and within the same amount of time, for the tuition of a far greater number of pupils.

2. In consequence of such a provision, there results a very considerable economy of time.

3. In a school, where this system is adopted, every individual is kept in constant employment.

4. A fourth advantage, and one resulting from the preceding, is, that by this method, the disrelish and irksomeness on the part of scholars to school employments, are lessened in no inconsiderable measure.

5. The monitorial system of instruction removes from the teacher much of the wearisome tediousness consequent upon long-continued efforts in teaching the ordinary and more mechanical branches of learning, and enables him to introduce his pupils, or at least some portion of them, to more advanced and important studies, than he would be able to do if his attention and services were constantly required for the instruction of each individual pupil.

These five points, it is believed, are the principal ones, upon which the advocates for the system of mutual instruction found their claims for the preference. Some of them are of the greatest importance, and are fairly entitled to the highest consideration.

18*

We shall proceed to speak of each of them more particularly.

1. The monitorial system, by the same means, and within the same amount of time, provides for the tuition of a far greater number of pupils, than are taught by the ordinary method.

It has been found that by the use of monitors, or assistant teachers in miniature, one principal instructer may conduct the studies of two hundred and fifty, or three hundred boys, thus performing the duties of at least five teachers. In many places, particularly in crowded cities and in extensive manufacturing districts, such an advantage is of incalculable importance. The amount of time usually allotted to children in such situations, for obtaining some acquaintance with the simpler elements of knowledge, is extremely limited, and this small portion ought to be most constantly occupied and sedulously improved. In such cases, the system under consideration, as it affords the means of obtaining the greater amount of instruction in the smaller portion of time, though that instruction is from the nature of the case quite superficial, possesses unquestionable claims for the preference. This application of the system, and this alone, it is believed, was that contemplated by the originator or originators of it. At any rate, it is certainly the case, that it was originally applied to the children of the lower classes in crowded cities, for the laudable purpose of affording them, what they had never before been blessed with, some small portion of instruction; which instruction, from the peculiar exigency of the case, was necessarily imparted with a prudent economy both of time and of money. Where but little instruction, therefore, can be communicated, and that little, sparing as it is, must be given in an extremely limited portion of time, we know of no better method of procedure, than that of adopting the system under consideration.

2. The method of mutual instruction insures no inconsiderable economy of time.

In a school of one hundred and fifty members, taught by

the customary method, the actual amount of time during which each scholar is entitled to the personal attention of his teacher, is precisely two minutes and two-fifths. Were there two instructers, he would be entitled to the double of this portion. Now let us suppose the school to be conducted on the monitorial system, and that there is employed one instructer, who has under him two divisions of monitors, each consisting of twenty persons. We will suppose the instructer to be constantly occupied with these two divisions in alternate order, and that the division not under immediate instruction is employed in the tuition of subdivisions of pupils. The twenty individuals around the teacher will receive, in the course of the customary six hours of daily school time, eighteen minutes of personal instruction, and the members of the subdivisions under the care of monitors will receive, (being reduced in numbers, by the deduction of the monitors, to one hundred and ten,) sixtyfive minutes and a half of monitorial teaching, equivalent perhaps, in point of value, to the eighteen minutes of teaching given by the presiding monitor, the master, to his division. On this supposition, which will show, fairly enough, the usual routine of a monitorial school, each scholar receives nine times as much instruction as he would do in an ordinary case. Nor are the monitors, when actually employed in teaching, losing or wasting time; for we are undoubtedly all well aware, that there is no better method of learning and securing the knowledge of any particular branch of study, than, after acquiring some little acquaintance with it, to be diligently engaged in teaching it. So that it has been rightly said, that the best way to learn is to teach. It is a most lamentable fact, that in all our common schools, there is (not because of any fault of the teacher, but from the very defects of the common school system), a most profuse and shameful waste of time. This lavishness of the best and most precious of Heaven's gifts, and doubly precious to the growing mind, exists mostly in that part of the scholars who are at their desks apart from the teacher, and who ought to be employed in preparing an assigned exercise for recitation. Yet they, from that unfortunate peculiarity of human nature which tempts us to prefer ease to labor, suffer themselves to be employed only so long, as will suffice for the preparation of, in most instances, a defective and miserable recitation. There they sit, as even the most unobserving spectator of our ordinary schools cannot but notice, wasting the priceless energies of mind and of body, and acquiring habits of inattention and of idleness, the most miserable influence of which, not the lapse of years, nor the utmost labor of maturer days, can ever wholly eradicate. To so unfortunate a profuseness of time, we contend that any employment, even the most unsatisfactory, is preferable. Let it not be said that we require too much of the young, that we would keep them too constantly employed, that we would unwisely strain their youthful powers in the accomplishment of impossibilities. The time apportioned to school exercises is sparing enough; and the residue of the day, and the frequent recurrence of vacations and of holidays, give them the most ample opportunities for relaxation. But it may be said,—'*Arcum nec semper tendit Apollo.*' True. But he never unbent it when in the fury of the chase. He never relaxed the keenness of his aim, till the prey was prostrate at his feet.

3. A third advantage is, that, in a school where this system is adopted, every individual is kept in constant employment.

No one, as we have already observed, who is even but partially acquainted with the state of our schools under the ordinary management, can avoid observing, how very great a portion of the customary school hours is wasted in absolute idleness. Let us suppose an instance of a teacher having the supervision and instruction of a school of forty members, who are divided into four classes. These four classes, we will suppose, are to recite in regular rotation, commencing with the lowest. While this class is employed with the teacher, the other three classes are, or ought to be, engaged in the preparation of a lesson. Now it is usually the case, that the lessons assigned to lads, do not, or, from their fault, will not, occupy them more than three quarters of an hour, or at the most, an entire hour. The class reciting will, perhaps, occupy about the same amount of time; and when the teacher shall have finished with them, there are the three other classes, each and all, prepared to recite at the same time. Now but a single one can be attended to, and the other two must and do sit absolutely unoccupied. Nay, so far as the discipline of the school, and their own benefit is concerned, they are worse than idle, since they will be sure to resort to some mischievous expedients to kill the monster Time, till their turn for recitation comes round. But where the monitorial system, or something equivalent or better, is adopted, no such difficulties can occur, because, as it in truth ought always to be the case, recitation occupies more of school time, than study. We have supposed what we believe to be a favorable instance, in the selection of a school of forty members. And if so much time be there worse than wasted, what shall we say of one which contains from one hundred and fifty, to two hundred scholars? These last numbers give the usual amount committed to the charge of a single teacher in all our large towns; and we hazard nothing in making the assertion, that of this large number, one half are unemployed, so far as the acquisition of knowledge is concerned, more than one half of their time. Nay, even in the very best regulated schools, where but a single master is employed in the instruction of any considerable number of pupils, and without any assistance from them, this evil exists in a most alarming measure.

We conceive this difficulty to be the grand and most discouraging obstacle to the advancement of our common schools. We believe that they will never awake from the sluggishness under which so many of them lie buried, until this palsying incubus, which broods over and withers their best energies, be shaken from them. We believe that they will never take and maintain that rank, which their numberless friends most earnestly desire them to do, until the constant employment of every individual, and the unsparing occupation of every moment of time, be universally prevalent. In our opinion, this feature of the monitorial system is above all praise; and the sooner it is found to exist, in some shape or other, in every school in the country, the sooner will their best interests be promoted. What teacher is there among us all, who has not felt a glow of satisfaction and even of delight, when, on surveying his little kingdom, he has found every individual sedulously and profitably and constantly employed? Who is there among us all, who does not esteem such moments among the very proudest of his professional career?

There is another point gained by the use of monitors, which we mention here, because connected with the subject of frequent recitation. There can scarcely be found a parent, who is not only willing, but even desirous, that his children should have some employment connected with school-exercises, out of the ordinary limits of school-hours. This is particularly the case in the winter season, when the days are short, and school-time is contracted into the narrow bounds of five hours, and the evenings are of protracted length, and, on the part of children, mostly unoccupied. Lessons prepared out of school can, where the monitorial system is adopted, be recited as soon as school commences, and can *all* be recited and simultaneously, and the whole work may be accomplished in less than an hour. But where the old method prevails, the more lessons there are learned, the worse it is for the learner, so far as recitation, which is the very life-blood and soul of school-time, is concerned.

4. The fourth advantage which we would mention, although they all seem to be so intimately connected, that they might be easily enumerated under a single division, is, that the influence of this constant employment fairly and effectually removes the disrelish and irksomeness on the part of scholars and of teachers, attendant upon the ordinary method of instruction.

We all know that when we are constantly and busily employed, time flies as upon noiseless and unheeded wings. There is no instructer from whom the fleeting hours do not pass away too rapidly; and many a one is there, if his school be exclusively conducted on the ordinary system, who has many a time found that his narrow portion of time is all elapsed, and his work is but half done. How readily and how heartily might such an one exclaim, were his dactyls handy,

> Hei mihi! nunc quid agam? nimium celeri pede fugit
> Hora———

Now by this constant employment, which is a characteristic feature of the system of mutual instruction, the same effects are produced in the removal of fatigue and irksomeness from the bodies and minds of scholars. And it is from them that we should be particularly anxious to remove every feeling and every impression that may be, in the least degree, unfavorable to the employments of the school-room. Make that a spot to which they will delight to resort; make it, in deed and in truth, a '*ludus literarius,*' and you will remove the chief obstacles in the way of your success as an instructer.

5. The fifth and last point which we shall mention, in which the monitorial system has an advantage, is, that it exempts the teacher from much of the wearisome tediousness consequent upon long-continued efforts in teaching the ordinary and more mechanical branches of learning, and enables him to introduce his pupils, or, at least, some portion of them, to more advanced and important studies, than he would be able to do, if his attention and services were constantly needed for the instruction of each individual scholar.

The zealous and the ambitious instructer, the man who is in love with the profession, for of such a man alone can success be predicated, will never rest satisfied that his school is as good as his neighbour's; that he teaches well, and that his pupils learn well, certain assigned, and therefore expected, branches of study; or, in other words, that it does not move in a retrograde direction, or that it is merely stationary. Περι τȣ Θεμιστοκλεους λέγεται, ὡς καθευδειν αυτον ουκ εώη το τȣ Μιλτιάδȣ τροπαιον.' * * 'Of Themistocles it is said, that the trophies of Miltiades would not let him sleep.' Now, will it not be the case with the ambitious in every vocation—will it not be the case with the ambitious teacher, that the laurels of his brethren of the same calling will excite in his bosom, not the evil canker-worm of envy, but a generous, an open, a manly spirit of emulation, whose well-disciplined efforts shall benefit himself, his profession, and the world? Will not his motto be 'Onward, and onward still?' Will he not be unwilling to move, all his life long, in one unvarying beaten track, to perform forever a stale, and, to himself, a profitless round of tedious duties, destitute alike of interest and of novelty? We believe that he will. We believe that the history of his school will be distinguished by those periods of time, at which some farther progress has been made in an assigned course of study, or some new department of learning has been introduced. Now, how can so desirable an end be so effectually accomplished, as when he can avail himself of the services of a great number of assistants? To accomplish it thoroughly and satisfactorily, his assistants ought, indeed, to be adult teachers, and of sufficient acquirements and experience. But since, in ordinary cases, the possession of such adult teachers is next to an impossibility, let him make the nearest practicable approximation he can to the benefits which their aid would secure, by making use of such helps as a selection from his best scholars will afford him; or, in other words, by adopting some feature of the method of mutual instruction.

We do not mean that the progress of his school, to which we have alluded, shall be made at the sacrifice of thorough instruction, or that his school shall *appear* merely to have got over a greater than ordinary amount of study; though, as we shall hereafter show, we apprehend these to be the rocks upon which every monitorial school, in the strict meaning of the name, will eventually be wrecked. But it is very evident, that by the employment of a greater number of teachers, a greater amount of time is called into service, and, of course, a greater amount of labor performed. The best and surest way, however, to attain to the proper perform ance of this labor, is to employ, as we have already hinted, a greater number of adult and experienced teachers than is done in ordinary cases. But if this cannot be done (and that it cannot, will always be true, so long as the public are opposed to the disbursement of a larger amount than is paid, at the present moment, for the instruction of public schools, and teachers are found who are willing to work at the public's prices), if this cannot be done, we say, let the teacher make use of the best means and the best assistance within his reach; that is, let him train up the most intelligent, and the farthest advanced portion of his pupils to the business of teaching.

We have now done with the consideration of the advantages resulting from the system of mutual instruction. We have stated them, we believe, fairly and candidly, and have stated all, which are entitled to much praise. We now proceed to show its defects. These we shall endeavour to lay down in the order of their relative magnitude.

We object to the monitorial system,

1. Because no school can be conducted upon it, separably from great noise and confusion.

2. Because it is next to an impossibility to procure monitors, who will prove, in every particular, faithful and adequate to the duties expected of them.

3. Because, in a school conducted upon this system, the principal instructer cannot be sufficiently well acquainted with the particular merits and failings of each individual pupil.

4. Because we believe its legitimate tendency is to make anything but thorough scholars, and to introduce into all, excepting the more mechanical parts of knowledge, a degree of superficialness and inaccuracy highly prejudicial to the best interests of sound learning.

Of these we proceed to speak, also, more at large.

1. And in the first place, we object to the monitorial system,

because we believe no school can be conducted upon it, separably from noise and confusion.

No one who has ever visited a monitorial school, can be otherwise than aware, that this objection is founded upon what is strictly true. From the very nature of the case, noise and confusion, and those of no ordinary palpability, are absolutely inherent in the system. They were born with it, and have 'grown with its growth, and have strengthened with its strength.' In all monitorial schools, a very large portion of the scholars, and sometimes all of them, are called into simultaneous recitation. This cannot occasion anything else, than a confused uproar of exclamation, and a motley medley of vociferations. From the immediate contiguity in which many, and, in fact, we may say all, the reciting classes are placed, and from the circumstance, that usually all of them are performing their exercises within the limits of a single room, it cannot but follow, that one set of reciters should continually interrupt and confuse those in their immediate proximity, particularly if they are reciting a different lesson. And so far as the interest of the learner is concerned, it is, in some particular cases, even worse, if the adjacent divisions are reciting the same lesson. For then, if there happen to be a dull scholar in No. 1, he has only to listen to and repeat the words of his comrade in the neighbouring No. 2, who has been blessed with a better head, and has acquired closer habits of application than himself. To this doffing the dunce and donning the wise one, to this literary smuggling, we have more than once been the amused witness. Again, if one half of the members of the school are reciting, and the other half are endeavouring to study, how can it be, that the noise and din of the reciters should have any other effect than to render the attempts of those who are required to be employed in study, really and truly nothing but attempts, and those attempts the most abortive and futile? Who can apply himself undistractedly to study, with confusion and noise echoing around his head? What scholar can comprehend the meaning of a difficult passage in a classic writer, or investigate successfully a complicated and slippery formula in the mathematics, when one half of the little world of his fellow pupils are vociferating their lessons at the very top of their vocal powers? *Aurora musis amica,* and not more so from her freshness and beauty, than from the calming influence, and soothing nature of her noiseless hours.

2. Our second objection to this system is, that it is next to an impossibility to procure Monitors, who will prove, in every particular, faithful and adequate to the duties expected of them.

To instruct in any given branch of knowledge, thoroughly and successfully, requires something more than even the greatest familiarity with the particular text book which may have been adopted for that branch. If this were not the case, there would be no necessity that the individual, whose design it may have become, to qualify himself for the business of instruction, should go into an extensive and laborious course of reading and of study. He would be necessitated, merely, to drill himself to perfection in a certain set of books, and to have at convenient readiness a certain set of questions appended and chained down to a certain set of answers, and he would be armed and equipped for the pedagogical warfare. Now we maintain that this will not answer. We maintain that every teacher, to perform his duties faithfully and successfully, should be a person of studious habits, of extensive reading, and of very considerable acquisitions in every branch of learning, which has any relation to the particular course of study, adopted for the school into which it may be his fortune to be thrown. We do not mean that a man to teach arithmetic successfully should be extensively learned in the Latin and the Greek languages; or that he, whose province it may be, to teach history or geography, should be profoundly versed in mathematical learning. But, in the former case, he will be far more likely to be successful, and certainly he will perform his labors with more satisfaction to himself, if he possess a good knowledge of the ordinary branches of the mathematics; and in the latter case, it is indispensable that he be familiar with the general history of the world, and even more than familiar with the particular history of individual countries. Now, that a mere child, or a mere school-boy (for they are the monitors), should possess this knowledge, is by no means to be expected; and that they should perform the duties of teaching these branches of study, with a desired success, is as little to be expected. We are willing, indeed to make some exception, with regard to teaching, or rather superintending, the performance of the merely mechanical parts of arithmetical or other science. But in the other instance adduced, we cannot see how any exception can be made. How many subjects, but cursorily or darkly hinted at in our little compends of history, can the well-informed teacher fully and satisfactorily elucidate! How much interest can he call forth from his youthful auditory, by entering at large into the narration of some important and interesting subject, which the limited nature of the text-book has allowed to be but incidentally mentioned! How much light will a good knowledge of mathematics enable him to throw upon many of the rules and investigations of common arithmetic! For there are, as we all know, very many problems given for solution in our ordinary arithmetical treatises, which can only be demonstrated and understood, by a reference to some principles of algebra or of geometry. Now, can we expect all these elucidations, desirable as they are, from the mouth of a common monitor to his fellow pupils? Most assuredly not. For so far as monitorial recitation goes, it is solely and purely mechanical, and altogether restricted to the prescribed text book, or to an answer printed down in the books, and numbered to accord with a certain question. We know that the difficulty is still greater in those schools in which instruction in the ancient and modern languages is given by monitors. To make a young person familiar with the principles and the pronunciation of a language, even of his own, requires a long continued and persevering course of instruction. Of the Greek, Latin and French languages, this is particularly true. To pronounce either of the former correctly, requires a perfect familiarity with the quantity of every word in the language, and this familiarity is not acquired in one, two, or even three years. Of the difficulties in acquiring a correct pronunciation of the latter, we are all aware, and we are all as well aware of the great difficulty of acquiring the language from any other mouth than from that of a native teacher. How then can a common school monitor impart satisfactory instruction in these two instances? We have been witnesses to the vain attempt. We have heard reiterated errors in the pronunciation of both the former languages pass entirely unheeded and uncorrected by the presiding monitor. We will not distract your ears by repeating what these errors were. Let it suffice, merely to say, that they were terrific enough to make the bones of Porson rattle beneath the incumbent ground, and to frighten the manes of Bentley into annihilation. We do not think that any blame can, in the instance to which we allude, attach itself to the monitor himself. For his sin was the sin of ignorance. He was but little better informed upon the subject than the individuals over whose recitation he was presiding. He had, indeed, received instruction in advance of his division, and intruction of a very good quality; but it is useless to expect faultlessness and a perfect readiness in every particular, on the part of persons of so little experience as lads at school must necessarily possess. It may be said that the head-master himself was injudicious in his selection. In reply to this, we would say, that we believe that the best selection was made, which the nature of the case permitted. The fault was neither in the teacher nor in the monitor, but was then, and is now, absolutely inherent in the system itself. For that system directs us to place reliance upon those resources from which it is perfectly impossible that good and sufficient support should be obtained. Years of study, and the most extensive reading, and the most perfect familiarity with any language, ancient or modern, are, in our opinion, necessary, nay, indispensable, if a man would teach it thoroughly and satisfactorily.

3. Our third objection is founded upon a belief that in a school conducted upon the monitorial system, the principal instructer cannot be sufficiently well acquainted with the particular merits and failings of each individual pupil.

This acquaintance we esteem to be of the very highest importance. He is not at home in his school-room, nor does he know the materials with which he is to labor, who is not perfectly familiar with the disposition, talents, and acquirements, of every individual in it. He must be unable to designate the good and the bad, the industrious and the indolent, the gentle and the stubborn, the incorrigible and the yielding. He cannot praise and promote the one, and judiciously punish or degrade the other, because he does not sufficiently know them. The power to understand and to discriminate should be in the teacher almost an innate capacity. He who is destitute of this capacity, or who neglects to cultivate and to improve it to the highest degree of excellence, is culpable in the extreme. And it is equally unfortunate for him, if the peculiar constitution and organization of his establishment put the means of acquiring this knowledge beyond his reach. Now that this is the case in monitorial schools, we are fully persuaded. The great distance at which many of the pupils, not under the immediate supervision and instruction of the principal teacher, are necessarily kept, from the circumstance of their being disciplined and taught by the intervention of others, renders it impossible that the case should be otherwise.

4. Our fourth and final objection to this system is, that we believe its legitimate tendency is to make anything but thorough scholars, and to introduce into all, excepting the more mechanical departments of knowledge, a degree of superficialness and of inaccuracy highly prejudicial to the best interests of sound learning.

Were there no other objection to be brought against the monitorial system, as a whole,—let me be distinctly understood, this alone would possess power enough to overthrow almost every argument which could be adduced in its favor. It is not our object here to enter into any disquisition upon the importance of a deep and thorough knowledge of whatever branch of learning we undertake to become acquainted with. The praises of sound learning have often and even recently been uttered in your ears, and we will not repeat the thrice-told, though still delightful tale. In your own bosoms, if there live there, as we most sincerely hope there does, that richly merited veneration for profound and unyielding investigation, to whatever department of learning it may be directed, in your own bosoms, these praises must have found a responsive voice.

'Drink deep, or taste not the Piërian spring,' is a line of peerless merit, and fraught with the wisest counsel; counsel of more than ordinary value in these degenerated days of surface and of skimming, the prevailing genius of which is, we fear, becoming more and more averse to that uncompromising toil and patient labor, which can alone fast bind the bays and the laurels around the scholar's brow. We hold it to be self-evident, that no man is fairly entitled to the meed of sound classical scholarship, unless he be deeply versed in the grammatical principles of ancient language, unless he be extensively acquainted with the splendid productions of ancient learning, and unless he be almost a worshipper of every letter in every name which beautifies the long list of the genius and intellect of classic days. Nor would we award to him the merit of mathematical skill, who is not as familiar with every department of that heaven-born science, as with the sounds of his native tongue. We expect not to find, in every age and in every land, the immortal names of a Porson and a Bentley, of a La Place and a Bowditch. No, the world has not worth enough to be blessed with them, and science hardly a depth beyond the reach of their researches. But when such giant intellects are found, let no diminution be made from their just praises. Let us not forget them, and fall into the miserable fashion of the day, of heaping indiscriminate laudings upon a mushroom growth of what are called profound scholars, yet whose claims and whose very appellation will prove as ephemeral as their own existence. Now, we ask, is it the influence of the system under consideration, to bring forward scholars like those whose names we have adduced? Is it the influence of this system to foster, to encourage, or even to awaken their love for science, their unsatisfying thirst for the deepest waters of the fountains of learning? We believe it is not. We believe that it is directly the reverse. Is it to be expected, is it reasonable to hope, we do not say from the nature of *things*, but from the nature and habits of young people, that they will exert themselves to the utmost point of the requisite diligence and investigation, to possess themselves perfectly of a certain prescribed portion, suppose of some classic author, if they are assured in their own minds, that this portion will not be required of them, and strictly required, by one, whose knowledge in the matter is infinitely superior to their own, and whose authority to require it is commensurate with his knowledge? If studying the writings of the prince of epic poets, will they sedulously investigate the multiplied and endless changes in the form of his words? Will they, with critical acumen, learn thoroughly to distinguish the interminable variety of his dialects? Will they make themselves competent to point out the Attic and the Doric, or even the more common Ionic forms? We believe they will not. We believe they will reason (as even many older individuals would do, except when spurred on by some more than ordinary incitement), that they need not fret themselves, and labor, and toil, and *dig*, as they call it, to obtain all this familiarity with their author, because they are sure that he, to whose share it will fall to examine them, knows but little, if any, more about the matter, than they themselves do. Is not such reasoning perfectly consonant with the principles of human nature? Do we not see its operations in the every day business of our schools and of our lives? Here, then, is the great peril. Here then, in our belief, is the grand difficulty and defect in the whole system of monitorial instruction. It will make deficient, defective and superficial scholars, an evil most sincerely to be deprecated, as the canker-worm and destruction of all sound learning. Will all the strivings, will all the counsel, will even the very utmost authority of the principal teacher, prevent entirely so ruinous a result? We fear not. So great is the waywardness, so chainless and powerful the aversion to studious efforts in many, if not in most young people, that all his labor and his counsel will pass by them 'like the idle wind.' We are sensible that all scholars are not equally opposed to application. We are sensible that there are many, of whose very nature, labor and sedulous application seem to be a constituent part; many who would labor and learn in the very worst school the imagination of man ever conceived of.

> 'Some trees will thrive, in spite of arid soil;
> Some hold their stately fo.m, 'midst raging tempest's toil.'

But not so of all. And even for the security and stability of the good principles and firmly fixed habits of the most diligent scholars, we should have some fears, amidst the general recklessness and indolence which surround them.

We come now, at length, to the consideration of the last topic alluded to in the heading of our remarks, which is, 'to show how far the system of Mutual Instruction may be safely adopted into our schools.' We confess that we should prefer leaving the entire subject here, after having stated the advantages and defects of the system, permitting each one to form an opinion for himself. It is a point to be dealt with, with the extremest wariness and prudence. That the prevailing system of school management has defects, and those, too, of the most palpable and mischievous nature, is an assertion as incontrovertible as truth itself. And it is equally undeniable, that an entire, thorough and radical change, of some kind or another is loudly demanded. If the monitorial system will cure these defects, without introducing others equally glaring and mischievous, if it will place our schools upon the long and ardently desired footing of preeminence and of excellence, the sooner it is universally introduced, the better. But, as we have seen, this system, as well as the ordinary one, has certain essential and inherent defects. As we have seen, also, it possesses some very eminent points of excellence. This being the case, it would seem as though the voice of prudence would direct us to separate the chaff from the wheat; to adopt what is good, so far as the nature of our school system will permit, while at the same time we retain whatever is meritorious in the old, and to reject whatever is bad and therefore mischievous, from them both. *In medio tutissimus ibis*, is a motto of the soundest prudence, and as applicable to the case in discussion as to the numerous others, to which it has been so frequently applied. The course, then, which we believe might be followed with entire safety, and even with absolute benefit, would be to adopt into all our schools, those points in the monitorial system, which, possessing in themselves universally acknowledged excellence, have, at the same time, the desired power of effectually remedying several of the greatest defects in our common system. That we may be more precisely understood, we proceed to be more particular. We have already stated in the former part of these remarks, that there is a very great portion of time, in a school conducted upon the ordinary method, which is spent in the most unprofitable idleness. We have observed, also, that this failing was not consequent upon any fault of the teacher (for the faithful teacher is constantly employed), but because of the utter impossibility of his giving his attention to more than one set of scholars at a time. Now, in cases like this, and where the number of scholars is greater than can be kept in unremitted occupation by the solitary teacher, let him make use of what is infinitely preferable to a wasteful lavishness of time, the monitorial system. Let him select some prominent individuals from a superior class, and appoint them to superintend some useful exercises to be carried forward simultaneously by a whole class. These exercises should be such, however, as have been previously explained and taught by the presiding master, and of the correct conclusion of which there cannot a doubt arise. Let them be, perhaps, in arithmetic, in algebra, in written translations from Latin or Greek into English, or from English into Latin or Greek, when the monitors can have the assistance of printed keys. We have practised upon this method with great advantage both to pupils and to monitors. As the particular course pursued has sometimes been thought worthy of a passing inquiry, we will, by your permission, enter into an explanation.

Let there be provided a set of black-boards, of such a number as the convenience of the school-room and the necessities of the school may require, each board being about forty inches by thirty. Let them be arranged in a convenient part of the room, at about three feet apart, standing contiguous to the wall, and at right angles with it, and parallel to each other. We have always made use of twentyfour. This number may be enlarged or diminished, to conform to the number of pupils who may be required to use them. When the pupils are stationed at them, each has a separate board, the size and position of which, together with the vigilance of the teacher or monitor, prevent his seeing the work upon the board next before him. To every three boards there is appointed a monitor of supervision, who is selected from among the best scholars in the class. Over the whole, there is placed a presiding monitor, who is always selected from the highest class in school, and who, consequently, has been over the whole course of instruction over which he is directed to preside.* At these boards, are performed numerous exercises in translations; all exercises in arithmetic and algebra; all those in the practical parts of geometry and trigonometry; and many in the demonstrative parts of the latter sciences; each pupil being required to draw the figure, and to write out the demon-

---

* Whenever the occupations of the teacher of the school will permit, let him be the presiding monitor. He will find this method of teaching and reciting, particularly in the mathematics, the best that can be devised.

stration. It is to be understood, also, that all these exercises are performed by the pupils, entirely without the aid of their text-books, excepting in very extraordinary cases. They are, of course, never allowed to use them, nor even to carry them from their seats to the boards, when about to recite demonstrations in geometry and trigonometry. In long and complicated questions in arithmetic and algebra, they are sometimes favored with them. But in ordinary cases, the presiding monitor alone holds the book, and announces the question for solution. Each scholar then takes the data, as he hears them given out, and afterwards completes the operation. The monitors of supervision, also, are required to perform all questions, upon slates held in their hands, and to exhibit them to the presiding monitor. They afterwards inspect the work of the three individuals, committed to their charge, and report, if right or wrong, to the presiding monitor. It is the chief excellence of this application of the monitorial system, and this particular manner of using the black-board, that each and every question, is performed by each and every scholar. And the circumstance of his being unprovided with a book, from which to copy his formulas, or to obtain his rules, and the fact that he cannot possibly get assistance from any other one than himself, render it certain that he must become, in some greater or less degree, familiar with the subjects to which his attention is directed.

There are very many useful purposes to which a set of blackboards like these, may be applied, all of which the circumstances of the school and the matured judgment of the experienced teacher will point out to him. He may also, with advantage to his pupils, adopt the monitorial system in cases of reviewing a lesson which has been already recited to himself in geography, spelling, and in the more simple and mechanical parts of knowledge, as has been already remarked.

But we do not feel willing to say to any, 'Adopt the system of mutual instruction in full, since it is the very best that has been ever devised.' For we should then be saying what we cannot bring ourselves to believe. What then is the course, or the system, which as a whole may be safely and advantageously introduced into our schools? We will briefly explain our views on this subject, and then bring out remarks to a close. In the first place, we believe that the most beneficial course which can be followed, is, that the number of scholars in our public schools should be lessened, or that the number of teachers should be increased. Of the two alternatives we should prefer the latter, and have come to the belief that a method somewhat similar to that recently adopted for the management of the Boston public schools, would prove satisfactory and beneficial. Taat is to say, in the regular organization of a school we would give as assistants to the principal teacher, one, or two, or more adults, and as many younger assistants as the exigences of the school would require. These latter should be persons who had been regularly *through the whole course of instruction in the same school in which they were appointed to teach*, and under the tuition of the same teacher, whose helps they were appointed to be. If we were to take our choice between a half dozen such young teachers, and one or even two ushers, we should infinitely prefer the former, even at a greater expense. But that they may be obtained at a less, is unquestionably true; and of their becoming very competent and skilful, we have not the least doubt, particularly if kept in employ for three or four successive years. Such persons, by thus serving an apprenticeship at the business of instruction, in the positive necessity of which we have the fullest belief, would become infinitely better qualified for the profession than any of our young men, fresh and green from the embrace of Alma Mater. We would be understood as meaning that they should pursue a systematic course of instruction and of study, aside from their regular and daily service as teachers, and that these studies should be directed with a view to the particular situation in which they might be expected to teach. Such an experiment has been made, and has resulted in entire success; and we can see no reason why

MR WOODBRIDGE'S LECTURE.

LECTURE IX.

ON

VOCAL MUSIC

AS

A BRANCH OF COMMON EDUCATION.

BY WILLIAM C. WOODBRIDGE.

In the United States, vocal music was usually regarded as one of the luxuries of education, until the establishment of Sunday Schools rendered it more general. During a visit to the continent of Europe, the speaker was surprised to find it almost a universal acquisition, and in several countries a branch of the national system of education. He became convinced of the importance and practicability of making it a part of our common education, and one of our manly amusements, and was led to resolve on bringing the subject before his countrymen.

The first point to be gained was to introduce a simple, rational method of instruction, which should render it *practicable*, instead of that mysterious and mechanical plan, which is generally adopted; and the second, to supply the species of music adapted to children, which should be simple, without being infantile, and elevated, without becoming artificial or unintelligible.

Both these objects have been effected in many parts of Germany and Switzerland. Music is regularly taught, both in theory and practice, and has become the delight of childhood, the amusement of youth, and the cordial of age. He resolved to do all which his ignorance of the science would permit for extending the same benefits to our own country, by bringing from abroad the music and the system of Switzerland, in the hope of finding persons able and willing to attempt a work which he deemed of no small importance to our national character and interests. Such individuals he has found: he has placed all these materials in their hands, and hopes soon to see the essential works before the public.

But another object still remains to be accomplished—to awaken public interest, and inspire public confidence; and this he fears will be the most difficult task. It was the reluctance to lose an occasion so favorable as the present, which induced him to accept the invitation to deliver this address, amidst the pressure of peculiar circumstances, which allow him no opportunity of doing justice to the subject.* It was the desire to convince others of the importance and the practicability of giving instruction to children in music, and thus to obtain coadjutors in the cause, and if possible to persuade every teacher to endeavour to introduce it into his school, and every parent to provide the necessary means of instruction for his children.

It is the same motive also, and not the desire of exciting the admiration of the audience or the vanity of the performers, which has induced him to invite a juvenile choir to exhibit to you some specimens of the music he has referred to; and he knows not how he can better win his way to your indulgent feelings, than by calling on them to aid him with one of these simple melodies.

* He has to regret that a train of similar circumstances, combined with ill health, oblige him to send it for publication, almost in the same imperfect form in which it was delivered.

THE MORNING CALL. C. M.

2. Brother, wake!
Hark! the cheerful lark is singing,
And the hills and dales are ringing
  With her joyful hymn.

3. Sister, wake!
Everything is now reviving—

Every one around is striving,
  In some new pursuit.

4. All awake!
See! the sun with splendor beaming,
O'er the distant waters streaming,
  Pours his glorious light.

The Creator seems to have formed an immediate connexion between the ear and the heart. Every feeling expresses itself by a tone, and every tone awakens again the feeling from which it sprung. Hence children and passionate persons increase their sorrow or their anger by cries, or heighten their joys by shouts.* Hence the instinctive huzzas of a joyous crowd; and hence we may trace the origin of vocal music. The feelings of the more passionate produced a succession of varying sounds. The ears of the more sensitive perceived these variations, and their skill was employed to imitate them, in order to awaken anew the same feelings, in connexion with the rude recitation of traditional history, or the more refined melody of the poetic tales of Bards or Troubadours. They roused to war, and soothed to peace—they kindled anger, and awakened joy, and calmed the paroxysms of sorrow and passion—and the influence of David's harp, and the effects of songs in the battles of the barbarous Germans, and the melting power of the sweet *Ranz des Vaches* on the Swiss soldier, would seem to indicate that the tale of Orpheus is but half a fable.

> ' When Music, heavenly maid, was young,
> While yet in early Greece she sung,
> The passions oft to hear her shell,
> Thronged around her magic cell,
> Exulting, trembling, raging, fainting,
> Possessed beyond the muse's painting.'

But whether it be owing to the deteriorating character which Buffon ascribes to the new continent, or to the withering influence of our rude and variable climate, or to the inhospitable treatment she has received, this well nigh fairest of the muses has lost her power of fascination on this side the Atlantic. Her voice has become harsh and dissonant; her

---

* I cannot omit, on such an occasion, the important maxims suggested in educating ourselves and others. He who governs his voice, will find it easier to govern his feelings; and he who allows himself to use habitually the tones of passion, will increase its strength.

palsied head moves in unequal time; her lyre, notwithstanding every effort of a few distinguished masters to keep it in tune, has lost half its cords, and more than half its harmony; and her trembling hand wanders among the few remaining strings, without regularity or force.

We listen, we criticise, and sometimes we are delighted with music; but how seldom do we feel what the melody is designed to express! Whether it be in the solemn service, or the social circle, it is too often retained, like some old servant, from mere habit, and is generally heard with listless indifference, or positive uneasiness, even by ears that are not tortured with its jarring notes. It sometimes excites a smile, when it is intended to call forth a tear; and its joyous notes are too often only a discordant clamor of voices. Could we but divest it of the artificial character which a false taste has given it, and bring it back to its native simplicity; could we but employ the voice of childhood in its execution, and gradually train up the whole community to join in harmonious chorus, we might then hope to restore to music its pristine beauty, and its soul-subduing power. It might again soothe to rest the sons of sorrow. It might assist in subduing to peace the unsated cravings of the lust for gold, the devouring rage of ambition, and the ferocious spirit of party that infest our lands—more unsparing, more desolating in their ravages, than the wild beasts that were subdued by the harp of Orpheus. It might do much to calm the demoniac passions, and overcome the grovelling propensities which follow in their train. It might assist in elevating our hearts to the Author of our being, and invigorate us in our progress toward heaven, and give us many a foretaste of its joys on earth.

The *immediate object* to be accomplished by making vocal music a branch of common education, is, to cultivate one of the faculties which our Creator, in his wisdom, has seen fit to bestow upon us. To neglect it, is to imply that it was unnecessary—that it is useless. It is to treat a noble gift in a manner which in any other case would be considered as disrespectful and ungrateful.

But the *ultimate objects* are those for which it is obvious this gift was bestowed. The first and highest is to unite with our fellow Christians in expressing our gratitude and love to our heavenly Father. In doing this, we rouse and excite our own devotional feelings, and stir up each other to new life in the worship of God. For these purposes, God himself commanded the use of music in the Israelitish church. Indeed, he has written this law on the hearts of men. Scarcely a temple, or a service, has ever existed, except in Mohammedan countries, in which music did not occupy an important place.

In this view, the subject is of great importance. The defects in our church music are felt as well as admitted; and no thorough improvement can be made without acting on the rising generation. 'In order to produce its proper effects,' as an able writer on music observes, 'it must not be a mere tickling of the ear, in order to effect through that medium the susceptible nerves, and never reach the heart. We have degraded it by making it a mere instrument of gratifying the senses.' We must elevate it, by employing it as one of the wings of devotion, in union with poetry, its sister art.

But it is highly useful as a means of refreshing the weary mind, and is perhaps the only employment which leaves the intellect in complete repose. On this account it is peculiarly important to literary men. A distinguished professor of the island of Sicily, on hearing the sad tale of the influence of study on our literary men, asked me, 'What amusements have your literary men in America?' As you will readily imagine, I was only able to answer—*None*. He expressed his astonishment, and added, 'No wonder they are sick, and die of study.' He informed me that he spent a stated portion of the day in recreations, of which instrumental and vocal music were an essential part, and thought he could not live without the relief which they gave his mind.

Vocal music is also very useful, by its direct effect on the constitution. It was the opinion of Dr Rush that young ladies especially, who by the custom of society are debarred from many kinds of salubrious exercise, should cultivate singing, not only as an accomplishment, but as a means of preserving health. He particularly insists that it should never be neglected in the education of females; and states that besides its salutary operation in enabling them to soothe the cares of domestic life, and quiet sorrow by the united assistance of the sound and sentiment of a properly chosen song, it has a still more direct and important effect. 'I here introduce a fact,' he remarks, 'which has been suggested to me by my profession, and that is, that the exercise of the organs of the breast by singing, contributes very much to defend them from those diseases to which the climate and other causes expose them. The Germans are seldom afflicted with consumptions, nor have I ever known but one instance of spitting blood among them. This I believe is in part occasioned by the strength which their lungs acquire by exercising them frequently in vocal music; for this constitutes an essential branch of their education. The music master of our academy has furnished me with an observation still more in favor of this opinion. He informed me that he had known several instances of persons who were strongly disposed to consumption, who were restored to health by the exercise of their lungs in singing.'

As the mere expression and excitement of cheerfulness, music is a precious gift of God; and it should be used as a means of enjoyment, that it may lead us on to devotion. The ear as well as the eye is made the inlet of pleasure, that we may first enjoy it, and then, by learning its value, be made thankful to Him who bestows it. The late President Dwight observed, 'The great end of God in the creation is to make men happy, and he that makes a little child happier for half an hour, is so far a fellow-worker with God.' Could music be introduced into common schools, would it not make many little hearts leap with joy? For this purpose, the words and the music must be of the proper character; and I would beg my young friends to present you with a specimen of the hymns of this kind employed in Germany and Switzerland,— the mere expression of childish pleasure.

THE GARDEN.

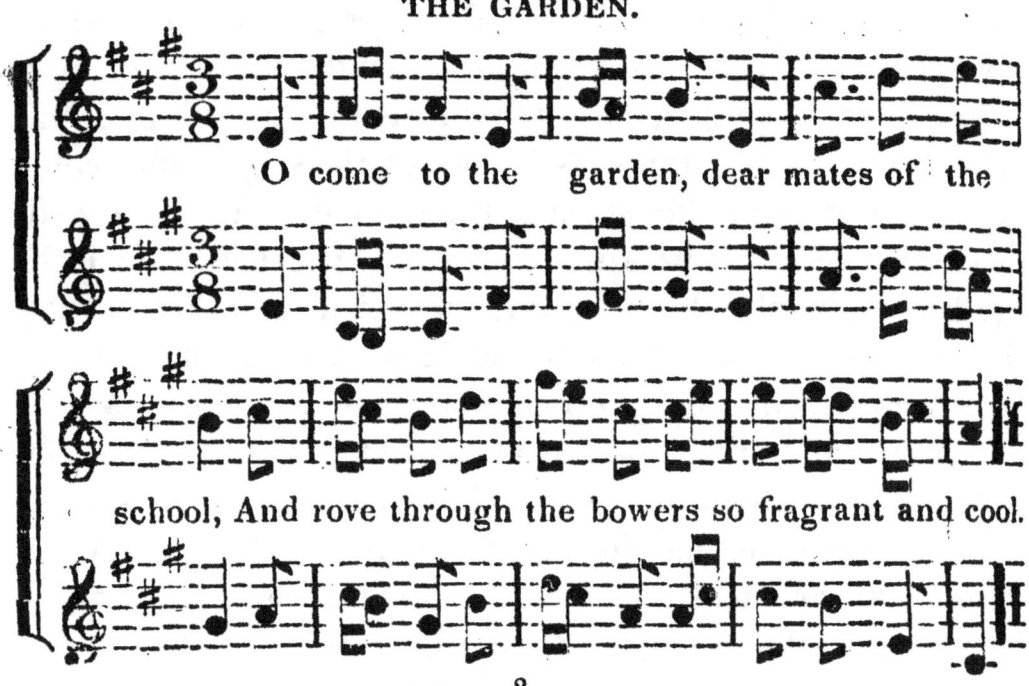

O come to the garden, dear mates of the school, And rove through the bowers so fragrant and cool.

2.
We'll gather the lily and jessamine fair,
And twine them with roses to garland our hair.

3.
We'll cull all the sweets to make a bouquet
To give to our teacher this warm summer day.

4.
Then hie to our school-room, with joy and with glee,
And sing our sweet ballads, so happy are we.

Could we furnish children with the means of amusement which songs like this would afford, I think it is obvious that we should divert them from others of doubtful or injurious character. Could we give our young men such a means of excitement, by music appropriate to their age and feelings, we should diminish the temptation of resorting to stimulating liquors or other questionable means of producing cheerfulness. I have known and visited a village in Switzerland, where a set of drinking, disorderly young men were led, by the cultivation of music among them, to an entire reformation, which was regarded with as much surprise as the change in regard to temperance in our own country. I have seen them, when they met at a public house, resort to this method of raising their spirits, instead of drinking, and spend their time in singing songs and hymns, adapted to improve the mind and elevate the heart, instead of the profane or indecent conversation, or noisy clamor which is generally heard on such occasions.

But music also has an effect which cannot be doubted in softening and elevating the character. It diminishes the strength of the passions, by keeping them, for a time at least, in a state of inaction. It counteracts them, by producing the opposite and softer feelings. On this subject allow me to quote the opinion of Luther, whose well known skill as a composer of music, no less than his character as a great reformer, must give weight to his opinion.

'I ought now to speak,' says he, ' of the utility of this noble art, which is indeed so great, that no one, however learned he may be, can give a satisfactory account of it. This one thing I can declare (of which I am convinced by experience also,) that according to the sacred Word of God, no art deserves so much celebrity and praise as music; inasmuch as it has a mighty control over every movement of the human heart, and often governs and restrains mankind, as their Lord. Stringed instruments and the lower animals utter *sounds* merely, and are incapable of language. Man, however, was endowed with the powers of *speech*, that he might be able to speak and sing the praise of God at the same time, and thus magnify his goodness and grace by the combined efforts of both.— When natural music, however, is highly cultivated and polished, then we ascertain, for the first time, in part, (for it never can be fully understood,) and with astonishment, the great and perfect wisdom of God, displayed in this curious art. Wherefore, I recommend it to every man, particularly to youth, and hereby admonish them duly to love, honor, and esteem this precious, useful, and cheerful gift of God; the knowledge and diligent use of which, will, at all times, drive off evil thoughts, and diminish the effect of evil society and vices.'

So universal and essential was a knowledge of it at that

time among teachers, that Luther observes, 'It is necessary that this art be taught in schools. A schoolmaster must be able to sing, or else I will not *look upon him.* The youth must always be accustomed to this art, for it makes good and virtuous people.'

Plato says, 'Bodily exercise is the sister of pure and simple music; and as exercise imparts health to the body, so music imparts the power of self-government to the soul.' In accordance with this sentiment, I am convinced that it has no small influence on school discipline. I was struck with the superior order and kindly aspect of the German schools in comparison with our own, and ascribed it not a little to the cultivation of music in them. Those who unite in singing with their fellows and their master, will be more disposed to be kind to the one, and obedient to the other.

In addition to this, the study of music, from its very nature, cultivates the habits of order, and obedience, and union. All must follow a precise rule. All must act together, and move in obedience to a leader; and the habit acquired in one part of our pursuits necessarily affects others.

But we cannot give music its full influence without combining it with words. It has in this way been made the handmaid of vice, and the companion of depravity, and its influence has been fearful. It should be converted to a better use. 'Let me make the ballads of a nation, and you may make their laws,' said one who was well acquainted with human nature. The maxim is one of obvious soundness. The law is but seen in shadow, and its threatenings heard as distant thunder. Even the pulpit brings forth its instructions only weekly; and the preacher often writes upon a sand beach, from which the returning tides of the business of the week speedily efface almost every vestige of his instructions. But the ballad is fixed in the memory by the association of rhyme and sound: it is constantly brought home to the heart by the sweet influence of melody; and while the law is out of view and the sermon forgotten, it repeats and reiterates its expressions until it penetrates the hardest heart, and fastens itself in its strongest feelings. Let us but have hundreds of hymns, not merely sacred, but *moral, social,* and *national,* which shall convey elevated sentiments and stimulate to noble acts, and we send forth so many little messengers of good, which can penetrate even through the walls of a castle, and be conveyed on the wings of the wind to every quarter of the globe. Some of the best European airs have been found by travellers transported to the centre of Africa.

Especially will this be the case, if these songs are associated with familiar objects and events. The Germans have hymns for children and youth, on the Rising Sun, the Morning Star, Harvest, a Storm, a Forest, &c., which are recalled every time the objects are seen, and thus all nature is made vocal.*

A specimen of this class of songs, will best show you their tendency.

THE RISING SUN.

*The pupils of the agricultural school at Hofwyl, on returning from their labors at night, saw the evening star rising, and immediately, with one accord, struck up the appropriate song. Such occurrences are frequent, and during my residence at Hofwyl, I have often heard them going to their work before day, uniting, in chorus, in a morning hymn or a harvest song.

the rising sun.

2 With grateful hearts and voices,
  We hail thy kindly rays;
All nature now rejoices,
  And sings thy Maker's praise.

3 O shed thy radiance o'er us,
  And cheer each youthful mind;
Like thee our Lord is glorious,
  Like thee our God is kind.

But many, who are ready to admit the pleasure and the profit to be derived from vocal music, suppose that they can never be extended to the mass of the community. We are met on the threshold with the objection, that this branch of education must be reserved for those who have what is termed a 'natural ear' and a 'natural voice,' and that only a few persons can distinguish musical sounds, and imitate them accurately.

If the grounds of this opinion are demanded, we are presented with a greater or less number of individuals in society, who tell us they cannot distinguish one sound or one tune from another—that they know not whether notes are high or low; accordant or discordant; and that they cannot imitate any of them.

The first difficulty sometimes arises from not understanding the terms employed. Sounds, like colors, cannot be described in words. They must be taught by examples, patiently repeated and carefully attended to, until the ear is familiar with them; and gradually extended, as its powers of discrimination are increased. I have known cases in which persons who said they could not distinguish one note from another, have found no difficulty in doing it, as soon as a few notes had been sounded before them, and the use of the appropriate terms had been illustrated.

But, in addition to this, the examples taken are not fair ones. They are of persons whose ear and vocal organs have been formed to certain habits so long, that they cannot be supposed to be so susceptible or flexible as they once were. Read a portion of French or German to the same individuals, and see if they can distinguish the similar words and sounds at once. Call upon them to pronounce the nasal and guttural sounds of these languages; or require a foreigner to pronounce our own language, and it requires no second sight to determine that they would not succeed better than in music. Is this an evidence that they have not a natural ear or a natural voice for German, or French, or English? Surely not. Why then apply this reasoning to music? Indeed, the argument would be more applicable to language, so far as experience extends. Who ever heard of an individual who spent whole days, for several years together, in singing, who did not find an ear for it? But we have few examples of men who pronounce a foreign language without obvious errors, even after years of study or of residence in a country where they speak it incessantly. Until we are presented with individuals who were taught music as they were taught language, from their childhood, and who still cannot distinguish or imitate musical sounds, there is no good reason for admitting that any considerable number of persons are naturally destitute of an ear for music.

I do not mean to deny that there are defects of hearing of every degree, from absolute deafness, to mere dulness of hearing, which renders it difficult to perceive nice distinctions, and so on to a perfect state of the organ; nor that some individuals may have a natural rigidness or other defect of the muscles and cartilages of the mouth and throat, as others have in their limbs. Nor have I any doubt that great natural differences exist as to the degree of accuracy in imitating musical sounds, as they do in the distinctness of articulation and the correctness of reading, in those whose organs are not obviously defective. But I am satisfied from the testimony of those who have had extensive means of observation and experiment, both in this country and in Europe, as teachers of music, as well as by an obvious course of reasoning, that these cases are almost as few in number as those of the lame, and the deaf and dumb. Vehrli, the remarkable teacher of the agricultural school in the institution of Fellenberg, assured me that among several hundred poor neglected children confided to his care, he had found only two whom he could not teach to sing.

Pfeiffer, the author of the Pestalozzian system of instruction in music, informed me, that he had found not more than one or two in ten, who could not be taught to sing. The same opinion was expressed by most of the practical teachers I met with in Europe. The few I found of another opinion, were men whose exquisite sensibility of ear and of nerves, rendered the discord of a learner's notes a species of torture, and who therefore could not exercise the patience necessary to go through an elementary course, except with very apt scholars. The same difficulty would probably have arisen, if they had attempted to teach their own language to a foreigner. Several of the most experienced teachers of music in our own country have assured me that the result of their experience was the same. One who has taught four thousand pupils, and enjoys much reputation as an instructer, assured me, that although he found the same variety in these organs as in others, he never found an individual who could not be taught to sing.

But we shall find substantial reasons for believing this true, arising from the nature of vocal music. It consists of a succession of vocal sounds, some of which are long and others short, some slow and others quick, some high and others low. Now what else is speech? Speech also has high and low sounds, slow and quick, and long and short; and these variations have been reduced to a system of surprising accuracy. Chapman, in his Rhythmical Grammar, and Rush and Barber, in their works, have pointed out very clearly the musical intervals, which are necessary in order to speak and read correctly and intelligibly. They have shown that in order to ask a question, the voice usually rises a third, or three tones; that when the question is more earnest, or asked with surprise, the tone is a fifth higher than usual; and that when the earnestness is still greater, the voice rises eight tones; and that these intervals are to a considerable extent uniform. The answer falls in the same manner. The rapidity and force with which we speak, obviously vary with the state of our feelings. In short, a very little examination will show us that our speaking is in effect a kind of singing. This, indeed, is the great obstacle which a foreigner has to encounter in learning our language—and the want of it is that which we term a foreign accent. It is evident, then, that every man who understands the difference between the mode of pronouncing a question and an answer, and between a common question and an earnest one, can distinguish a high note from a low, and can even tell the difference between a third and a fifth. He must, therefore, so far, have a musical ear.

The ordinary tones of voice are in the major key. The tones of distress, or the whine of a beggar, are in the minor key. If he can *distinguish* these, he proves that he has, to this extent at least, a musical ear. If he can *imitate* all these various sounds, I know not how we can deny him a musical voice. In short, he who can discriminate the variations of speech, can distinguish musical sounds. He who has learned to *speak correctly*, may learn to *sing*.

We cannot omit noticing a topic which properly belongs to another lecture,—that practice in music will be the best preparation and aid for the formation of good readers and good speakers, and that he who does not understand something of musical tones, and has not habituated his organs to the sudden and precise variations which they require, cannot understand perfectly the modern rules of elocution, nor enjoy the full benefit of the excellent instructions we now have in this art.

In regard to all the efforts yet made among us, to ascertain how large a portion of the community can be taught vocal music, the experiments have been desultory in their character, short in their duration, and generally conducted by unskilful hands. Nothing then can be inferred from them against a new experiment, at a period when the habits of the body and mind are not fixed. But the complete answer to all doubts on this point is furnished by the fact, that wherever the experiment has been made at the proper age, and in the proper manner, it has been successful.

I have already stated that it forms a part of common school education throughout Germany and Switzerland. In the improved schools, it is deemed no more difficult, and no more remarkable to read and write music, than language. I have also quoted the opinion of Luther, as to its importance. Allow me to add the opinion of distinguished men of the same countries, both in regard to the importance, and the practicability of teaching it to all.

Niemeyer, one of the most celebrated writers on education in Prussia, observes ;—' The organs of speech are improved by singing; the ear is formed and rendered more acute, and the well known power of music, even upon savages, proves that we should least of all neglect a branch of instruction which exerts so important an influence in softening the passions, in elevating the social and finer feelings, in aiding the moral cultivation, and cherishing the spirit of devotion.'

Schwartz, one of the surviving fathers of education in Germany, remarks ;—' In the cultivation of the ear, we have a means of cultivating the harmony of the soul and the purity of the heart, and of promoting heavenly love and spiritual life, which will probably not be fully appreciated for a long time to come.'

Denzel, a veteran of this cause, who has been enployed in organizing the school system of two of the German States, observes ;—' The formation of the voice is too important, and the influence of vocal music on the mind and heart too great, to permit us to dispense with it in common schools. It is no longer doubted that it ought to constitute a branch of study, in every institution for elementary education.'

Harnisch, a distinguished educator of Prussia, quotes the following remark from Richter;—'We cannot imagine a complete education of man without music. It is the gymnastic of the affections;' and adds, 'Music and bodily exercise, in suitable connexion, are necessary to keep body and soul in health.'

Fellenberg observes;—'We have learned from experience how much musical exercises contribute, not merely to the pleasures of society, and to the formation of the taste (which often affords more assistance to human weakness, in resisting evil, than cold principles of morals,) but also to religious elevation, and the spirit of devotion.' Vehrli, the instructer of the agricultural school of Hofwyl, regards vocal music as of the highest importance; and observes, that he has uniformly found, that, in proportion as it was improved, the spirit of kindness and devotion among his pupils increased.

Pfeiffer and Nageli, the fellow laborers of Pestalozzi, and writing under his direction, express similar opinions in similar terms. An author who quotes them, observes;—'These authors have not only given an impulse to singing, but have pointed out the only true way of teaching it. Their efforts have not been fruitless; for music is already taught, both in our country and city schools, with the greatest success; and what has already been accomplished, in this respect, would, not long since, have been deemed impossible.'

But no more decisive evidence can be required than that of the government of Prussia, which has done more than most others in Europe for the improvement of common schools.

The following ordinance, extracted from the Prussian official Gazette, (Amts Blait,) Cologne, January 15, 1828, will show the light in which this subject is viewed by that government.

'Among the essential branches of education, which ought to be found in all common schools, and to which every teacher who undertakes the management of such schools, is in duty bound to attend, is instruction in singing. Its principal object in these schools, is to cultivate the feelings, and exert an influence in forming the habits, and strengthening the powers of the will, for which mere knowledge of itself is often altogether insufficient; hence it constitutes an essential part of *educating instruction*, and if constantly and correctly applied, renders the most unpolished nature capable of softer emotions, and subject to their influences. From its very nature, it accustoms pupils to conform to general rules, and to act in concert with others. It is far more sure of producing such an effect in youth, when the heart is very susceptible of impressions of this kind; and no importance should be attached to the assertion of many teachers and directors of schools, that we can by no means anticipate this influence upon such wild youths as are found in the country. In general, this belief originates entirely from old prejudices, from a want of proper experience, from a love of indolence, or from an inadequate knowledge of the course and method of instruction. Convinced of the certainty of the result, where the means are correctly employed, we shall not stop to consider such objections as appear to be grounded solely upon exceptions. On the other hand, we shall hold those teachers in particular esteem, who labor, in this subject, with suitable zeal and success, in the conscientious discharge of the duties of their calling. We expect also that these efforts, together with their results, will be particularly noticed in the Report of the School Directors.

'Having recommended this important object of primary instruction, (the immediate connexion of which with religious instruction no one can fail to perceive) to the zealous exertions of the teachers, and the careful attention of the directors of schools, and, at the same time, having urged the study of the best writers upon the subject, which, so far as they relate to school instruction, ought to be found in the libraries of every district,—we shall here bring forward one point, which demands a closer and more universal attention.

'If instruction in singing is to accomplish with certainty the objects proposed, it must be *long continued without interruption*, and, of course, it is indispensably necessary that a regular attendance be required during the continuance of the duties of the school, and enforced in the strongest manner.'

It is unnecessary to illustrate the contrast between the last remark and the usual desultory mode in which singing is taught.

But the experiment has been tried in this country also. The system was first introduced, in Hartford, Connecticut, during the present summer. Several juvenile choirs were trained in a few months to sing in a manner which surprised and delighted all who heard them, by their accuracy in time and tone of expression. It was introduced into the infant school in that place with equal success,* and a distinguished musician who visited it observed, in a letter on the subject, 'I entered upon the examination of the system with some prejudices; but the more I have examined it, the more I am convinced of its superiority over the common method, especially in the simple manner in which the principles of music are presented to the mind of the child. The pupils of the infant school which I visited, after a short period of instruction in rhythm (time) only, surpassed in accuracy of time our ordinary choirs of singing.'

The time allows but a very brief sketch of the mode of teaching music, to which I have referred.

The *inductive system* of instruction was introduced in Switzerland and Germany at the end of the last century by Pestalozzi, and has been adopted in this country, in reference to some subjects. Early in the present century it was applied to *music*, in the institution, and under the direction of Pestalozzi, by Pfeiffer and Nageli, who published a manual of instruction on these principles in 1810. This system has since

---

* Both these experiments were made with disinterested zeal by Mr Ives, now a teacher of music in Philadelphia. A manual of instruction by this gentleman will soon be published, to accompany the Juvenile Lyre, a collection of songs for children, chiefly translated from the works of the Swiss and German composers, prepared by Mr Lowell Mason, President of the Handel and Haydn Society of Boston.

been diffused throughout the central portions of Europe, under various forms, and is acknowledged, in its fundamental principles, to be the only true one. These principles are,—

1. To teach *sounds before signs;* to make the child sing before he learns the written notes, or their names.

2. *To lead him to observe* by hearing and imitating sounds, their resemblances and differences, their agreeable or disagreeable effect, *instead of explaining* these things to him: in short, to make him *active*, instead of *passive*, in learning.

3. *In teaching but one thing at a time. Rhythm, melody, expression,* are taught and practised separately, before the child is called to the difficult task of attending to all at once.

4. *In making them practise each step of each of these divisions, until they are masters of it, before passing to the next.* For example, crotchets must be perfectly familiar in practice, before learning quavers; four notes must be sounded without hesitation, before learning the octave; and the elements learned must be combined in every possible form, before learning new ones.

5. In giving the *principles and theory after practice*, and as an induction from it.

6. In *analyzing and practising the elements of articulate sound,* in order to apply them to music.

7. Another peculiarity, which is not, however, essential to the system, is, that the names of the notes correspond to those employed in instrumental music, and are derived from the letters with variations for flats and sharps; a method whose utility is questioned by some, but which is deemed very important by others.

It will perhaps be useful to describe the manner in which these principles are applied. Instead of presenting a confused collection of mysterious characters, to serve as the mere signals for certain efforts of the voice, the reason and connexion of which are never explained, and thus leaving the pupil the painful and humbling task of groping his way blindly in the steps of another, he is first called upon to utter a *single distinct sound*, and then a letter or word. He is told that the one is called a musical tone, for which the note is the sign; and the other an articulate sound, used in speaking, for which letters are the signs. He thus arrives at a simple conception of song, as distinguished from speech. He is then required to increase or diminish the length of the sound two fold or four fold, and learns the appropriate signs for notes of different length. He discovers the importance of some standard of length for these notes, in order that many voices may sound in unison. His attention is called to the manner in which measure is employed to regulate movement in threshing, hammering, marching, &c. He is requested to unite with his companions in marching around the room, in movements of the hands and feet, in pronouncing words and syllables; and is thus easily led to appreciate and to practise the beating of time, an operation usually so mechanical and disagreeable to the novice in music. He is brought, by experiment and example, to perceive the agreeable effect that may be produced by a series of monotonous sounds, from the mere variation of length and accent. This encourages him to that course of practice which is necessary to produce accuracy in measure, and prepares him to make the proper use of melodious sounds.

The next exercise of the pupil is to listen to sounds which differ in their pitch, to exercise his ear in discriminating between the higher and the lower, and then to imitate them. Several series of tones in succession are made in his hearing. He is called upon to decide which is most agreeable, and is gratified with the discovery that he has selected those of the octave, which forms the basis of music in every nation upon earth.

In order to apply the knowledge he has gained, he is now made familiar with the first half of the octave, and learns to understand and practise the combinations of which these sounds are susceptible, before he proceeds to the second half. A few experiments will teach him the agreeable variations which may be produced in these same sounds, by the aid of emphasis and swell, and to perceive how they may be adapted to the expression of different feelings.

He is next led to perceive the striking difference which may be produced by a slight variation in the interval between some of these notes, and to discover the plaintive character of the minor key, and the peculiar effects of the various scales.

Two notes are next sounded together in his hearing, and then many others in successive pairs. He is called upon to decide which combinations are agreeable and which are disagreeable, and learns, with surprise, that he is pleased with those which all nations have pronounced to be in accord, and that he dislikes those which all have declared to be discords.

At every stage of his progress, the pupil is taught how the variations of sound he is learning may be applied in rendering language more expressive, and poetry more interesting. But this part of the course is equally removed from the ordinary mechanical mode of merely attaching a word to a note, or the still more objectionable system of obliging children, before they can sing correctly, to repeat the solemn and touching sentiments of psalms and hymns, as mere exercises of voice, in every variety of discord, and without any attention to their meaning. The most simple and childlike language on common subjects is combined with the first notes learned. Words of a more interesting or poetic character are gradually introduced, as the child acquires the skill in music necessary to give them their proper tones and emphasis. Every stanza which he sings, must first be explained and understood. He must be taught to consider in what manner the words and notes must be uttered, in order to show the idea most clearly, and express the feeling most fully, and is thus led to discover the connexion between the ear and the heart. Above all, the explanations must be such as to awaken in him the feeling appropriate to the subject; and he must never be suffered to employ the language of devotion without being taught its full import, and called upon to use it with corresponding feelings.

From all these particulars, he learns, what is vastly more important to his future progress and independence of mind than any accomplishment, that music, like all other sciences, is a collection of facts, and of principles deduced from them, which it is completely in his power to observe, and to verify.

With a method like this, the rising generation may be prepared to occupy their hours of vacancy, to give delight to those around them, and to make the praise of God glorious; while their own views are enlarged, their capacities developed, and themselves trained to habits the most important, and feelings the most elevated.

MR JOHNSON'S LECTURE.

LECTURE X.

ON
THE IMPORTANCE OF LINEAR DRAWING,
AND ON THE METHODS OF
TEACHING THE ART
IN COMMON SCHOOLS AND OTHER SEMINARIES.

BY WALTER R. JOHNSON,
PRINCIPAL OF THE HIGH SCHOOL OF PHILADELPHIA, AND PROFESSOR OF MECHANICS AND NATURAL PHILOSOPHY IN THE FRANKLIN INSTITUTE.

THE second aphorism of Bacon's *Novum Organum* contains a maxim of practical wisdom to which instructers may profitably recur in conducting the arduous duties of their profession.

'The hand alone, unaided by tools and implements, and the understanding alone, if compelled to depend on its unassisted energies, will seldom accomplish any important purpose. The business of both *is* effected by appropriate *instruments* and *means*, the employment of which is not less necessary to the *mind* than to the *hand*.'

Among the *means* of mental culture, and scientific progress to which the great philosopher alludes, it often happens, that, what conduces to give skill in manual execution, contributes likewise, in no slight degree, to foster and develope the faculties of the mind.

While, therefore, mental power, moral feeling, delicate

taste, and correct knowledge, are the ends of instruction, the means of their attainment must be constantly and distinctly kept in view. It were vain to expect the fruit of that tree, from which we had lopped the supporting branches and stripped the sheltering leaves. Equally preposterous were the anticipations of intellectual vigor, where we had required no efforts at comparing, judging, reasoning; or, of moral sensibility, where example, admonition, habit, had not conjoined their salutary influence; or, of refined sensibility to the beauties and deformities of nature and of art, where no models of excellence had been exhibited, and no discriminating guide had pointed out peculiar beauties or warned us of peculiar imperfections; or, of accurate comprehension of facts and principles, where verbal expressions alone had been presented to the understanding, and no exhibitions of things had rendered their application familiar.

Among the primary means of effecting all these great ends of instruction, is the formation of a habit of accurate observation, with a view to obtain exact perceptions of things. And since the perceptions, especially of youth, are almost wholly founded on an examination of the forms and other sensible qualities of objects, it follows, that whatever renders these distinctly intelligible, and easily remembered, contributes, in an eminent degree, to promote the great aims of all rational instruction.

The delineation of objects by the art of design, is so obviously calculated to produce the effects just mentioned, that we ought perhaps to deem its neglect, in a course of education pretending to be based on philosophical views, to be matter of no slight astonishment.

It is generally admitted, that at an advanced period of education, when the art of composition has been learned, the description, in language, of scenes and objects, is a most useful exercise for impressing the distinctive peculiarities of the thing portrayed on the mind of him who describes it. We are in the habit of conceding, too, that the best mode to extend and confirm our knowledge of any branch of science, art or literature, is to become teachers in that branch, and thereby accustom ourselves to dwell on all the minute traces, as well as on the general outlines of the subject to be communicated. The world knows how far preferable is that knowledge of a subject, which has been gained from an intimacy with practical details, to that which has extended only to some general maxims and theoretical speculations; and how the man, who contents himself with the latter, is ever liable to erroneous deductions and mortifying exposures.

And can we doubt, that the same degree of devoted attention to give a *visible* expression of an object, the same anxious solicitude to render that expression exact, and the same detailed examination of parts, and combined views of the whole, would be as serviceable, in the formation of clear perceptions, as description, teaching, and familiar practice are, in producing *their* appropriate effects? It has often been said, with reference to the higher efforts of the fine arts, that the painter, statuary, and poet, see the works of Nature as they are beheld by no one else. And however we may suppose the expression to be figurative, in regard to the last, we may readily admit its literal application to the two former. The productions of the pencil, and of the chisel, doubtless demand a delicacy and discipline of the organ of sight, far beyond what is necessary for many other professions. To *artists*, therefore, the improvement of the eye is the *final purpose* of instruction in the elements of design, while as a branch of general education it is to be regarded principally as a *means* of improving the perceptive powers, and through them, the judgment, the memory, and the imagination.

Because the mind is that which gives power and dignity to man, because its culture and improvement is so worthy of the best efforts of genius, shall we, therefore, throw aside with disdain every *instrument* for improvement, which the bodily organs can furnish? Shall we reject, for example, the attainment of manual skill, merely on the ground, that the process is unintellectual, unbecoming the dignity of scholarship? As well bid the student forego the customary gratification of his appetite, because the practice is *unscholarly*. Lay a tariff on all importations to the stomach, and where will you find the literary assemblage, throughout the world,—from the Wistar party that makes glad the sons of Penn, to the civic jubilee that annually revisits in their cradle, and rejoices the hearts of the children of the Pilgrims,—from those intellectual working-men, who make reprisals round the table of a London bookseller, to those intellectual playing-men, who perpetrate such goodly puns round our Phibetian tables,—that will not, by most cogent arguments and examples, nullify your law?

It will occur to every mind, conversant with the intellectual nature of man, that the improvement of the perceptive powers, by the art of delineation, must necessarily involve strong, though pleasing, efforts of *attention* and *judgment*. Hence it becomes one of those engaging arts, which contribute to mature and perfect the higher faculties of the understanding, while it corrects and strengthens that power, on which all our knowledge of the external world is originally founded.

Far be it from me to recommend the substitution of any manual art or other exercise of sense, for the strenuous exertions of mind itself; but still farther be the thought of allowing any essential means for its early improvement to be disregarded or lightly esteemed.

We have thus far glanced at the benefits which result to the intellectual habits of the individual, from an early attention to the art of *delineation*.

But, however efficacious in improving the mind any branch of study may claim to be, its pretensions will scarcely be admitted by the public, unless it can advance some title to the character of direct utility. Tried by this standard, we have fortunately no ground to fear that the study in question will be found wanting either in interest or importance.

Turn to the numerous arts and trades, which are conversant with the exterior forms of matter, and which imply the necessity of frequent representations, and how multiplied will you find the uses, to which the art of drawing may, and must be applied! To say nothing of architecture, civil, military, and naval, observe only the growing interest in those branches of art connected with our internal improvements and national industry. For all these, what more necessary qualification, than the art of giving fair and accurate representations of the object to be executed? Plans of surveys, maps of towns, counties, states, and countries, sea-charts, and harbour and coast surveys, fall within the range of those operations in which drawing is absolutely indispensable. Consult the jeweller and the plate-worker, as to the utility of a ready pencil, in the prosecution of their respective callings. Go to the pattern-loft of the iron and brass founder, and observe the multifarious uses to which the able draftsman applies his skill. Have you occasion for an article of furniture of peculiar form, or of apparatus of certain proportions, from the glass-blower? He will demand of you, an accurate sketch of the creation which he is to bring out of his fervent chaos. Would the upholsterer consult and gratify the taste of his employers, in the furnishing and decorating of apartments? Then must he have it in his power, not only to follow some vague, general directions, but by combining and adapting, in his designs, the parts and proportions of ornamental work, give a foretaste of the pleasure which his completed performance will produce. The professed mechanician is ever busy with his drawing-board and pencil.

The artisan who produces our mathematical and philosophical instruments, understands full well the value of this art of linear description, and derives profit accordingly. The utility of the same ar t the pursuit of anatomy and the various branches of natural history, will be readily acknowledged by every student in those departments of science. What shall we say, then, of engraving, calico-printing, paper-staining, and the delicate ornamental work of porcelain manufactures? The growing art of lithography, in common with all those before mentioned, owes its success to the skilful hand and the discriminating eye of him who traces the design.

In alluding thus hastily to the practical uses of outline drawing, I have not attempted to exhibit the art as a mere accomplishment, and have not referred to its connexion with painting as a profession. That it may, and must, be made the basis of both, is too obvious to require elucidation. As taught in schools, it may be rendered subservient to attainments in those liberal pursuits; and the future ranks of our academies of fine arts may be supplied with recruits, from those who have laid the foundation of their fame on a thorough knowledge of the elements of drawing. This would unquestionably have spared to many an eminent artist, the pain and mortification of having produced only total failures, in many of his earliest attempts.

It must not, however, be forgotten, that, as a branch of public instruction, drawing will be chiefly valued in its connexion with the useful arts. The pride of having executed, by the aid of a superserviceable teacher, a few tolerable heads, or, perhaps, intolerable miniatures, is often the chief motive to exertion, among students in drawing. If an animal, or a bouquet have been added to the collection, the accomplished proficient is at the height of his or her complacency, and lays down the pencil, probably forever. Not so the student who pursues utility in a rational manner. What he executes is his own, and may be repeated either with or without a master, whenever occasion shall require. As reason and good sense have dictated his exertions, the same motives will urge him to extend and perfect his skill, when the affairs of life call for the exercise of his talents.

A single additional motive for cultivating the art of drawing, may suffice to be mentioned at present. In the general arrangement of the business of instruction, the art of reading precedes that of writing, and most persons may imagine this to be a necessary order of things. That it is not so, will appear from the fact, that, in the early stages of penmanship, the process is wholly imitative, and that except in name, the thing to be imitated is entirely different from anything which the scholar has learned by reading. In general, the form of the English written character is as different from the printed as the latter is from the written alphabet of the Greek or German. Besides, the method of teaching penmanship, by analysing the characters into certain elementary principles, and forming classes on the basis of similarity, reduces the operation to a pure imitation; and learning to write, therefore, is nothing more than learning a peculiar modification of linear drawing. Now we are not without experience to show that a neat and elegant chirography may be attained by those who have never learned to read. Many deaf and dumb persons might be cited, as instances of this truth. The connexion therefore between reading and penmanship, is chiefly imaginary. Progress in one neither advances nor retards the first steps of the other. Hence, any preparatory exercises suited to introduce the pupil to the art of penmanship, may be taken independently of his acquisitions in reading; and even the art of writing, itself, may, if deemed expedient, be made the means of teaching the alphabet.

When the drawing of lines, in general, both with and without the aid of instruments, their division, relative positions, and various modifications, together with the formation of plane figures, and the terms applied to these various matters, have been made practically familiar to the pupil, he may proceed to that peculiar modification of linear drawing, which is executed with a pen, with the advantage of an acquired steadiness of hand; a habit of forming beforehand a clear conception of the thing to be done; a power of applying close attention to the written pattern; a judgment to discern differences and detect imperfections, and some degree of taste in regard to neatness of execution. All these things are known to be essential, in the acquisition of a good chirography, and most of them are, in the prevailing system, left to be acquired simultaneously with the neat or elegant hand of which they ought to be the foundation. It is not surprising that when so many things are to be effected at once, some or all of them should be but half, or not at all, accomplished. Even ornamental penmanship, which may be shown, to be susceptible of the analytical method before mentioned, is sometimes forced upon the student in a mass, before any degree of taste, any boldness of movement, or any motions of design, have prepared the way for excellence.

The views just stated, which are the result of considerable observation, have been confirmed by the assurances of a distinguished teacher of penmanship, that the progress in writing, of pupils who have received good instructions in linear drawing, is generally far more satisfactory, than that of individuals who have enjoyed no such advantages. Systematic instruction in pencil drawing, must not, however, be confounded with any mere random mode of *marking* without any definite idea of the object; since the latter would contribute as little to a ready acquisition of skill in *pen-drawing* (a term which we may apply to the art of writing), as the same tentative process does, under the old school *régime*, when applied to penmanship itself.

As to the method of teaching the elements of drawing, a considerable diversity of opinion prevails, among those who have written on the subject. Rousseau maintains, that the pupil should, from the very first, draw only from natural objects, and *that* without the aid of a teacher. He would allow him to practise, what is so often done on walls, by the vulgar,—draw a man by representing each of the limbs by a single line, and the fingers thicker, perhaps, than the arms. He would trust to casual observations and reflections to correct these incongruities, and to repeated trials to bring the representations nearer and nearer to a resemblance of the original. He would accompany his pupil in this series of scribbling and daubing operations, and make himself appear almost or altogether as little of a proficient as the scholar. He would give no instructions but what seem to come from lucky thoughts, arising out of some obvious error in preceding attempts. To excite self-emulation in the students, he would preserve the whole series of awkward attempts, putting the earliest and the worst, into highly ornamented gilt and glazed frames, but making the glass less costly, and the frames more simple, just in proportion as the pieces became more meritorious, until at length the best drawing is hung up in plain black wood. 'So that, to be put into *gilding*, will,' says he, 'in the view of myself and my pupil, one day become a distinction proverbially contemptible; and we shall wonder at the vast number of persons who are willing to be so justly dealt with, as to be hung up in *gilt frames*.'

Madame de Genlis' method is in every respect opposite to that of Rousseau. She contends, that the pupil should for several years be furnished with a drawing-master, who might give practical lessons in his presence, while the only occupation of the scholar should consist in carefully observing the performance, and noticing the various errors intentionally introduced. Some portion of time is also to be employed in examining books of geometrical figures, and portfolios of drawing-patterns, in visiting collections and sales in the fine arts, and in tracing beauties, as well as detecting faults.

In this manner, that part of a student's time, which is allotted to drawing, is passed, until the age of fourteen, when, having acquired the necessary taste and discrimination, he is, for the first time, allowed to use the pencil himself. Dexterity and flexibility of hand, are supposed to follow almost spontaneously, after the course of critical training, already described. The rewards of diligence and ability in judging the teacher's performance, consisted, according to Madame de Genlis, of counters, toys, and the gratifying applause of the superintendent.

Both the methods just described, must for obvious reasons be limited to a small number of pupils, and cannot therefore be recommended, as part of a system of public instruction. A more simple and practical course, is, to commence by drawing simple, geometrical lines and figures, with a slate and pencil. And in this, some diversity of practice would be recommended by different authorities. While one would debar the scholar from the use of all instruments or other mechanical aids, compelling him to rely for correction, primarily on his own judgment, and ultimately on that of his teacher; another would allow the free use of a few simple instruments, to detect, with unerring certainty, every deviation from the intended effect.

When we reflect that children often pass several years of their lives, in learning to *see;* that when they feel sensible of an imperfection in their work, they may not be certain in what precise point it exists; that in correcting, by the eye alone, an error in one part, they may probably commit a greater in some other; that they are ever disposed to seek a *full assurance,* and ever dissatisfied with doubt and uncertainty,—we shall not hesitate to pronounce in favor of that method, which, while it requires a sedulous application of the eye and the judgment, and a certain degree of reliance on the perceptive powers, still places within reach of the scholar, the means of immediately deciding how far his judgment has been correct. The experience of several years has confirmed the deductions of reason in regard to this point of our subject, and led to the preparation, from a foreign language, of a small treatise* on the simplest elements of geometry, intended to furnish the preparatory lessons in drawing, and consisting entirely of problems to be performed and learned by the pupil, who is to execute every figure with the utmost exactness attainable either by his eye or his instruments. Every exercise, performed as a lesson in linear drawing, conveys also the definition of a *term,* or the

---

*The treatise above mentioned is entitled, 'First Lessons in Practical geometry; containing such Problems as are essentially necessary in exercising most of the Industrious Professions; intended for the Use of Students in Elementary Schools. Translated from the French of L. Gaultier. By Walter R. Johnson, Principal of the High School of Philadelphia.'

explanation of a process in practical geometry. A repetition of the geometrical course requiring greater reliance on the eye than at first, may generally be found profitable, chiefly for confirming the knowledge already acquired, but in part also for the purpose of varying and multiplying the exercises, at the discretion of the teacher. Having thus laid the foundation of his skill, the pupil proceeds to *linear drawing*, in the peculiar acceptation of the term, and executes his figures chiefly by the eye, with the aid of mechanical means for correction. In this stage of his progress, the slate and pencil continue to be used, but the patterns for imitation are taken from simple and familiar objects, actually drawn by the hand of a master on large paper, and mounted on *binders' boards*, as nearly as possible of the natural size, and with such distinctness as to be visible to the whole class. A proper classification of these models, enables the teacher to adapt the lesson to the attainments of his pupils. Instead of a pattern executed in the manner just described, the master sometimes draws the models in the presence of his class, on a black-board or colored wall, explaining the work, and pointing out the advantage of the particular succession of steps which he has adopted, and testing the accuracy of his work by large instruments when necessary. When the model, whether on paper or black-board, has thus been presented and explained to the class, each individual, being furnished with slate and pencil, proceeds to draw the same object of such a size as his slate will admit. The simplicity of the figures, will, in the first instance, be such, as to enable him to preserve the proportions. No measurements can now be made, since the figures are reduced in size; but the rule and compasses may be occasionally resorted to, for the purpose of deciding whether any particular part of the copy corresponds to the obvious requisitions of the pattern. When a graduated series of thirty or forty patterns has thus been executed, at as many successive lessons, and the teach has at each exercise examined, criticised, and recorded the merit of each scholar's performance, the whole may be repeated. But as some individuals will have made greater proficiency than others, a division of the class may now be expedient. While those who have made the greatest proficiency are allowed to draw the figures in a suitable drawing-book, in lead-pencil or crayon, with a view to permanent preservation, the second division repeat them in chalk on the black-board, on an enlarged scale; and the third and last class, having made the least advancement, are required to go over the whole series a second time with the slate and pencil. The simple rules of perspective are now to be explained as they severally occur. The next stage of the progress consists in drawing from separate patterns such figures as involve an acquaintance with perspective; as outlines of houses, landscapes, simple machines, and other inanimate objects.

The drawing of maps and charts may now be commenced. The delineation of parts of animated objects, such as the different human features and limbs, with the heads or whole forms of animals, may come in as the fourth series of exercises. The pleasure, which the pupil takes in this branch, will be found to rise with the increasing interest of the subjects embraced in his lessons. And if the collection of patterns be sufficiently extensive, some latitude may be allowed to his own taste, in regard to the nature of the subjects, and the order in which they shall be executed. But the judicious teacher will always exercise his own discretion, as to the limits within which the choice shall be confined.

The next step brings the pupil to draw directly from nature; that is, to make his copy immediately from a view of the object which it is to represent. The object itself may be either natural or artificial; the latter is however preferred for the first lessons in this series, for reasons similar to those which determined the selection of geometrical lines, as the first lessons on the slate. A few simple solids, not more than seven in number, are sufficient to afford examples of all the elementary forms of contour and shade; and by varying the number and relative positions of the different figures, an endless variety of groups may be produced, to exercise the skill and taste of the learner. When the teacher has formed a group with which he is particularly pleased, he may sometimes take a sketch to be preserved for future use, from which he can at once arrange the pieces in the order desired. The models are made perfectly white, in order to give full effect to the peculiar light in which they may be placed, and that no false positions may be imagined from the apparent situation of accidental lights and shades, and to avoid distracting the attention with too many things at the same time.

The multitude of different pictures, produced by varying the arrangement of these few geometrical solids, depends, in great measure, upon the relative positions, the distribution and contrast of light and shade, as well as upon the arrangement of the outlines.

The scholar is now prepared to combine sketches and shades, and may consequently employ himself upon any subject where only a moderate variety of figure is to be presented. Machines, apparatus, and furniture, may be the subjects of his early essays;—landscapes, into which animated figures are introduced, may follow;—heads in crayon, or full-length figures of convenient size, may succeed to these, and henceforward the exercises may take such a direction as the interests of the school, the convenience of the teacher, or the future pursuits of the individual scholar, may render expedient.

The interests of the school may sometimes demand, that a number of large drawings should be made from plates, which, on account of their expensiveness, cannot be in the hands of every member, but from which the teacher may desire to give his illustrations. Should instruction in agriculture be among the objects of the institution, the teacher in that department would find innumerable applications in representing implements of husbandry, the form and position of the necessary buildings, the relative situation of gardens, meadows, fields and woodlands, with the modes of hedging or fencing in *model farms;* the appearance and botanical characters of the vegetable kingdom; and the figures and peculiar *points* of domestic animals. Should instruction in natural history be attended to, in addition to the more obvious applications, we may observe, that the minute parts of creation may be drawn, of gigantic size, from an engraved plate, or from the screen of a solar microscope; if from the former, the scholar will not fail to avail himself of the aid of *proportional compasess*, to obtain a correct general outline.

I need hardly advert to the uses which may be made of this art by the professor in chemistry, natural philosophy and practical mechanics. However extensive may be their cabinets of apparatus, or their collections of working models, a vast proportion of what they would desire to explain, must, if they confine themselves to these alone, be left unexplained. Teachers in these departments, sometimes employ the black-board only; but the labors of a few scholars well instructed in drawing, may soon give permanency to those figures, which must otherwise be erased and afterwards repeated at every repetition of the course. In some cases, a very moderate share of improvement will enable the scholar, in pursuing this method, to render important services to his teacher.

Even in the classical departments of education, how much more clearness of conception, and how much higher satisfaction, would be derived, from illustrations of antiquity, made by the hand of a pupil and explained by the living voice of his teacher, to a class or a whole school, than are obtained from the solitary investigation of the student, which, on account of the forbidding aspect of the notes and dissertations contained in his text-books, often amounts to no investigation whatever. The number of text-books used in a classical school is generally very limited; so that it would commonly be no difficult matter to obtain a complete series of illustrations of the Greek and Latin courses. Of these the teacher might avail himself, presenting one or more at every lesson, and either giving the necessary explanations, or requiring them from the class. The latter method would stimulate to greater industry in studying the notes as well as the text of their class-books. An extensive practice in this department, employing large engravings and lithographic prints, has convinced me, that classical study may be rendered nearly as attractive by this species of demonstration, as any branch of physical science; especially, if the *means* of demonstration emanate from the skill and diligence of the pupils. A succession of classes might thus leave behind them permanent, visible, useful memorials of their diligence and assiduity in cultivating a taste for ancient learning, while they improved their skill in a most useful art. A large port-folio of drawings, adapted to each class book, bearing the proper references, and inscribed with the names of the respective students by whom they were produced, would, I apprehend, be a powerful auxiliary to the classical teacher, whatever might be his own learning or abilities.

But if neither the interests of the school, nor the convenience of the teacher, demands the exercise of the scholar's talents in drawing, it can seldom happen that his intended profession will be wholly unconnected with the applications of design; and therefore he can never feel at a loss for subjects tending to improve his skill, and to enlarge, or more deeply to impress, his knowledge of subjects in which he is individually concerned.

I have already referred to the connexion between drawing and penmanship, and will only mention in this place, that the plan which has been suggested by a writer on the subject, of performing both on the same or on opposite pages of the same book, may probably be found useful in exhibiting, at a view, the concurrent improvements in the two branches, and even when the drawing cannot, from its size, be admitted into the *copy-book*, it may not be amiss to cause the scholar to place a specimen of his writing on some part of the sheet. A degree of care will thus be induced, not always attainable in his ordinary writing lessons, and some improvement will not fail to be the result. The *first lessons*, consisting of small geometrical figures, may certainly be drawn in this manner, and the exercises in writing may consist of a copy of the problems and directions, whenever the improvement of the pupil in penmanship is sufficient for that purpose.

As to the *drawing materials* to be introduced into schools, especially for boys, I would recommend that they be confined principally to slate-pencils, lead-pencils, common crayons, and Indian ink, believing from experience, that the introduction of other *colors*, would, in most schools, be a source of more inconvenience than profit. The procuring and preparing for use, of suitable patterns, will probably present itself as a difficulty in the first introduction of this as a branch of school education; but this obstacle will soon disappear, if teachers and others manifest a disposition to cultivate the study. The presses of our engravers and lithographers, to say nothing of foreign sources, are sufficiently prolific, and might soon be induced to furnish abundant supplies. We have not seen that the calls of the public for improved school-books, were either tardily or sparingly answered; and there can be no reason to believe that those who work on stone, box-wood and copperplate, will be less vigilant for the public good, than their more numerous brethren of the type.

I have thus endeavoured to exhibit a practical view of the subject before us, noticing its connexions and tendencies in regard to intellectual improvement, its bearing on the useful arts and various occupations of life, its relation to another branch of early education of great practical importance, the methods in which its elements may be successfully communicated, and its usefulness in reacting on other departments of science and literature, throwing new light on the paths of learning and sensibly alleviating the pains of teaching.

The course of instruction now offered to the consideration of this assembly, claims not the merit of originating from a master of the art, who might be thought anxious to support a peculiar theory, or to further the extension of his particular practice. It is founded on no startling paradoxes or metaphysical subtleties. It offers to all classes, in all schools, a degree of practical skill, proportionate to the time, industry and talent devoted to its attainment. If but one step has been taken, the knowledge acquired is still not without its use in the business of life. If from any cause the career of the scholar be interrupted, he has not to indulge the useless regret, that for want of further instruction, all his past application is of no avail.

The circumstance just alluded to adapts this method to every class of public as well as of private institutions. The uses and applications of what is learned, to the *mind*, will keep pace with its uses and applications to the *purposes of life*, and to the business of instruction. The powers of conception, no less than the perceptive faculty, will be strengthened and improved. The taste will find abundant and profitable exercise, and a foundation will be laid for some discrimination in regard to the works of our meritorious—much neglected *artists*.

Note.—In the course of the lecture, a number of models and drawings, intended to exemplify the method described, were presented and explained. For several of these, the author takes pleasure in acknowledging his obligations to Mr William Mason, of Philadelphia; and to his pupils, under the instruction of that gentleman, for the remainder.

MR COLBURN'S LECTURE,

LECTURE XI.

ON THE
TEACHING OF ARITHMETIC.

BY WARREN COLBURN.

I HAVE been requested to address the Convention, on the subject of teaching arithmetic. I accepted the invitation with extreme diffidence, believing there would be many gentlemen present, much more competent to this task than myself. The subject is certainly an important one in every point of view; whether we consider its application to the affairs of life, or its effects as a discipline of the mind, or the time which is usually devoted to it.

With regard to its application, there are very few persons, either male or female, arrived at years of discretion, who have not occasions daily to make use of arithmetic, in some form or other, in the ordinary routine of business. And the person the most ready in calculation, is much the most likely to succeed in business of any kind. As our country becomes more thickly peopled, and competition in the various branches of business becomes greater, and farther progress is made in the arts, and new arts are discovered,—knowledge of all kinds is brought into requisition; and none more so than that of arithmetic, and the higher branches of mathematics, of which arithmetic is the foundation.

Arithmetic, when properly taught, is acknowledged by all to be very important as a discipline of the mind; so much so, that even if it had no practical application, which should render it valuable on its own account, it would still be well worth while to bestow a considerable portion of time on it for this purpose alone. This is a very important consideration, though a secondary one, compared with its practical utility.

The fact that the study of arithmetic is allowed to occupy so large a portion of time in all our schools, shows sufficiently the degree of importance attached to the subject by all classes of people. And that it does occupy so large a portion of time, is another very strong reason for attention to the mode of teaching it, that the time may be employed to the best advantage. As the demand for all kinds of knowledge is increasing, and new branches of learning are almost daily brought within the compass of the ordinary means of education; it becomes highly important, that those kinds, which require considerable labor for their acquirement, should be made to occupy as little time as may be consistently, without sacrificing the advantage of learning them well.

It may not seem improper here to introduce a few remarks concerning the relative advantages of the old and new systems of teaching arithmetic. For though most teachers, at the present time, prefer the new system, and the majority of the community are decidedly in favor of it; yet there are persons, and some whose opinions are entitled to high respect, who strongly object to the new system, and give a decided preference to the old. To such we ought at least to be able to give a reason why we prefer the new system.

For this we shall appeal to facts; they are stubborn things, and the side which they favor must prevail. It must be allowed by all, that previous to the introduction of the new system, fewer persons learned arithmetic than at present. At least, fewer made any considerable progress in it. Very few females pretended to study it at all, and the number of either sex, that advanced much beyond the four primary rules, was very inconsiderable. And the learner was very seldom found, who could give a satisfactory reason for any operation which he performed. The study of it used to be put off to a very late period. Scholars under twelve or thirteen years of age were not considered capable of learning it; and generally they were not capable. Many persons were obliged to leave school before they were old enough to commence the study of it.

At present, the study of arithmetic is very general with both sexes, and among all classes. It is taught to advantage even to the very youngest scholars in school, and made to fill a portion of time, which used to be left unoccupied. And most scholars now have a thorough knowledge of arithmetic at an earlier age than it used formerly to be commenced. And scholars, who cannot give a satisfactory reason for their operations, are now as rare as were formerly those who could.

But perhaps the advocate for the old system will say, I grant that it was a little more difficult, and on that very account it was a better exercise for the mind, and when it was learned, it was learned more thoroughly. But in this we shall again find the facts on our side. It cannot be pretended, that those who did not study it at all, had their minds exercised by it; nor can much more be claimed for those who pretended to learn it. In those two classes, we have seen, was comprehended a very large proportion of the scholars. And with regard to the remainder, a very little observation will show, that the advantage is in favor of the new system. I believe most teachers who have understood and taught well, the new system, will give it as their opinion, that most scholars who have studied arithmetic well, have learned more of other things, and learned them better, than they would have done, if they had not studied arithmetic at all, or had studied it the old way. And in this class of teachers, we shall find a great number, who have been successful both on the old and new systems. It will pass for no argument at all, at the present time, for a man, however well skilled in arithmetic he may be himself, to come forward and say, I have tried your system, and could not succeed with it at all; therefore it is good for nothing. The reply to such a one is, You have not taken the trouble to understand the system; therefore you have not given it a fair trial. And we are sure that a sufficient number of successful teachers on the new system can be produced to justify such an answer. Those who do not believe, that pupils taught by the new system, are as ready and expert in the use of figures, and in calculation generally, as those taught in the old way, have only to go into the best schools taught on the two systems, and examine for themselves. Unless they will do this, they will not be convinced; and if they do, we do not fear for the result.

We believe also that we have reason on our side, as well as facts. By the old system, the learner was presented with a rule which told him how to perform certain operations on figures, and when these were done, he would have the proper result. But no reason was given for a single step. His first application of his rule was on a set of abstract numbers, and so large that he could not reason on them, if he had been disposed to do so. And when he had got through, and obtained the result, he understood neither what it was, nor the use of it. Neither did he know that it was the proper result, but was obliged to rely wholly on the book, or more frequently on the teacher. As he began in the dark, so he continued; and the results of his calculation seemed to be obtained by some magical operation, rather than by the inductions of reason.

By the new system, the learner commences with practical examples, on which the numbers are so small that he can easily reason upon them. And the reference to sensible objects gives him an idea at once of the kind of result which he ought to produce, and suggests to him the method of proceeding necessary to obtain it. By this he is thrown immediately upon his own resources, and is compelled to exert his own powers. At the same time, he meets with no greater difficulty than he feels himself competent to overcome. In this way, every step is accompanied with complete demonstration. Every new example increases his powers and his confidence. And most scholars soon acquire such a habit of thinking and reasoning for themselves, that they will not be satisfied with anything, which they do not understand, in any of their studies.

Instead of studying rules in the book, the reason of which he does not understand, the scholar makes his own rules; and his rules are a generalization of his own reasoning, and in a way agreeable to his own associations.

We conclude, then, that the new system is preferable to the old. We now come to the question, What is the best mode of teaching the new system? This is a question frequently asked, and frequently discussed. In the way that the question is usually considered, it does not admit of an answer. It may be briefly stated to be his who teaches the best. But then it will be found to be the best only in his hands. For any other teacher, another method would be better; so that the method must be suited to the teacher; and the teacher again, to be successful, must adapt his method to the scholar. For, until mankind are all made to think alike, and act alike, and look alike, it will be worse than useless, it will be absolutely injurious, to endeavour to make them teach alike or learn alike: I mean in the detail. For there are a few general principles, some of which I shall endeavour by and by to explain, which are applicable to all, and must be attended to by all, who wish to be successful in teaching. The best method for any particular intructer, is that by which he can teach the best. It is that, which is suited to his particular mode of thinking, to his manners, to his temper, and disposition; and generally, also, it will be modified by the character of his school. So that if I am to give an instructer particular directions with regard to teaching, I must see him in his school, and see him teach. Then my instructions would not tend to change his manner, but to improve it, if it were faulty.

Teachers are very apt to pride themselves upon some plan, which they have discovered, for keeping up the attention of the scholars, or of directing their attention to some important point, or of making them remember certain things, or of explaining certain difficult subjects, or of exciting emulation among their pupils, and many other things of the like kind—which, they suppose, if it were generally known and adopted, would be a great improvement;—not being aware that the thing is peculiarly adapted to themselves, and to themselves only, and that if another person were to attempt the same thing he would fail. Many have felt so much confidence in improvements of this kind, mistaking a particular case in which they have been successful for a general principle, that they have been at the pains to prepare books, adapted to those particular modes, with the greatest expectations of success. But such books always fail of general success, not because the methods were not good and successful in the authors' hands, but because others cannot enter into the spirit of them. Such books, if they are not used in precisely the way that the authors intended, cannot be used at all.

By these remarks, however, I would by no means discourage any teacher from communicating his methods to others. On the contrary, I would encourage every one to do it, whatever his methods may be. For though others should not think proper to adopt them exactly, yet they may frequently draw hints from them to improve their own. And the very fact of a teacher's giving so much attention to his own methods, as to be able to explain them to others, will be very useful to himself, and often the cause of improvement in them. But no one should feel disappointed, because others do not adopt his plans; neither should he despise the plans of others, though he does not choose to adopt them himself.

Without giving any very particular directions with regard to modes of teaching, I will state a few general principles, that will apply to almost all modes; and whoever will pursue his own mode according to them, will teach successfully. Most of them are applicable to all other subjects, as well as to arithmetic. And if, in the course of the lectures, you may have heard them from others, or may hear them hereafter, which I dare say will be the case, they will not be injured by the repetition.

The first precept which I shall enjoin upon you, is, to teach but one thing at a time. This is a grand point in arithmetic, and in all other branches. Select the principle which you intend to teach the pupil, and apply yourself strictly and exclusively to that, until he is master of it. For as certainly as you endeavour to fix upon his mind two or more things at once, you distract his attention and blend the things together in his mind, so that he does not get a distinct idea of either; and neither of them will be learned well. In teaching any one point, therefore, all others should be kept entirely out of sight, except those which he already knows. These may be referred to at any time for illustration, or for showing the connexion. Be sure that the pupil is master of the principle before he is allowed to leave it, let it require what time it will, unless he becomes weary of it, and his mind gets confused; in which case, leave it entirely, for the present, and take it up afresh at some other time. If the learner is allowed to pass from one point to another, when the first is but partially learned, he soon acquires a habit of learning things imperfectly, which it is very difficult afterwards to break up. It begets habits of inattention, of thinking loosely and carelessly, and of not fixing anything in his mind as it should be. And if the teacher thinks to remedy this evil by constantly calling up those things, which have been poorly learned, he will find himself disappointed; for he will only confirm the habit, instead of curing it.

Almost every instructer succeeds in teaching some things, and almost every one partially fails in some things; that is, there are some things which he does not teach to his own satisfaction. If he will refer to them, he will perceive, that in those things in which he does succeed, his scholars are made thorough as they proceed; and that he is in the habit of seizing the important points, and keeping them distinct, both in his own mind, and in the minds of his pupils. But in those things in which he does not succeed, he lets them pass from step to step, without becoming perfect in any of them, and he is probably endeavouring to make up the deficiency by a constant repetition of the things, which they have so passed. With many teachers, English grammar would be a familiar illustration of the latter mode of proceeding. The old method of teaching grammar was very faulty in this respect. The learner was first required to commit the grammar to memory, without understanding it at all, or being expected to understand it. And then he was put to parsing all parts of speech at once. Of the success of that mode many of you, I dare say, are able to judge from experience in learning, if not in teaching by it. Many persons still find the subject a difficult one to teach, and the difficulty will generally be found to arise chiefly from the fault I have been speaking of; that is, of endeavouring to teach too many things at once.

In arithmetic, this difficulty does not happen exactly in the same way, though in this it is very likely to happen. In grammar, teachers frequently endeavour purposely to teach several things at once; but in arithmetic, they do not do it intentionally. They endeavour to teach only one thing at a time; but they are in too great haste to get along, and they do not make their scholars perfect in one thing, before they let them pass to another. Hence there is necessarily a reference to what is past, while what is past is still imperfectly understood, and the scholar is kept in continual confusion.

I repeat, therefore, Teach but one thing at a time, and be sure that that one thing be learned, before another is attempted. If by mistake the scholar is found to have passed some essential point without learning it, he should be put back to it again, and be made to learn it; but on no account should he try to learn it by reference. When such a case has taken place, the scholar will show it, by failing to get his lessons; by getting into difficulties too often, and requiring too many explanations. If it cannot readily be discovered what it is that he has neglected, he should be examined backward, until a place is found, where he meets with no difficulty, and then let him proceed from that. But it is by far the best way, that the scholar should be made thorough as he goes, and it is the only way to be successful. It is also the easiest and most expeditious.

By teaching one thing at a time, I would not be understood to mean, that the scholar should not study different subjects on the same day. It is necessary for most scholars to be attending to several subjects at the same time; for young persons cannot well be made to apply themselves to the same thing long at a time. A change therefore is necessary as a relief to the mind, and a judicious teacher will not keep his pupils upon any one exercise longer than he can keep their attention upon it.

Whatever subject you are teaching, keep this precept in view,—to teach only one point of it at once, and apply yourself strictly to that, until the learner is master of it, and then give him another. Be careful, in the selection, to choose the easiest first, and then the next easiest, and so on. And where one thing depends on another, make them follow each other as much as possible in the order of dependence. You cannot always decide, by your own judgment, what is the easiest. This must be discovered by trial on the scholars. It will often be found, that the thing which one scholar will learn the easiest first, will not be the same for another. Also, what is easiest with one teacher, will not always be so with another. Each teacher should satisfy himself, by experiment, what order he succeeds best with, and then pursue it as nearly as he can, varying only when the learner requires it. It is not always necessary to pursue the precise order of the text book. The order of the book should be followed in preference to any other, unless the teacher feels very sure that some other order succeeds better with him.

The learner should never be told directly how to perform

any operation in arithmetic. Much less should he have the operation performed for him. I know it is generally much easier for the teacher, when a scholar finds a question a little too difficult, and comes for assistance, either to solve the question for him, or tell him directly how to do it. In the old method this generally was done. Not unfrequently, the teacher took the question and solved it at home in the evening, if he could, and gave the scholar the solution the next day, to copy into his book. Now by this, generally no effect was produced on the scholar, except admiration of the *master's* skill in *ciphering*. He himself was none the wiser for it.

If the learner meets with a difficulty, the teacher, instead of telling him directly how to go on, should examine him, and endeavour to discover in what the difficulty consists; and then, if possible, remove it. Perhaps he does not fully understand the question. Then it should be explained to him. Perhaps it depends on some former principle, which he has learned, but does not readily call to mind. Then he should be put in mind of it. Perhaps it is a little too difficult. Then it should be simplified. This may be done by substituting smaller numbers, or by separating it into parts, and making a distinct question of each of the parts. Suppose the question were this: *If 8 men can do a piece of work in 12 days, how long would it take 15 men to do it?* It might be simplified by putting in smaller numbers, thus: *If 2 men can do a piece of work in 3 days, how long would it take 5 men to do it?* If this should still be found too difficult; say, *If 2 men can do a piece of work in 3 days, how long will it take 1 man to do it?* This being answered, say, *If 1 man will do it in 6 days, how long will it take 3 men to do it? In what time would 4 men do it? In what time would 5 men do it?* By degrees, in some such way as this, lead him to the original question. Some mode of this kind should always be practised; and by no means should the learner be told directly how to do it; for then the question is lost to him. For when the question is thus solved for him, he is perfectly satisfied with it, and he will give himself no farther trouble about the mode in which it is done.

When the learner begins to require assistance too often, it is an indication that something has not been learned thoroughly. He should then go back to some place, that he does perfectly understand, and review.

All illustrations should be given by practical examples having reference to sensible objects. Most people use the reverse of this principle, and think to simplify practical examples by means of abstract ones. For instance, if you propose to a child this simple question : *George had five cents, and his father gave him three more, how many had he then?* I have found that most persons think to simplify such practical examples, by putting them into an abstract form, and saying, *How many are five and three?* But this question is already in the simplest form that it can be. The only way that it can be made easier, is to put it in smaller numbers. If the child can count, this will hardly be necessary. No explanation more simple than the question itself can be given, and none is required. The reference to sensible objects, and to the action of giving, assists the mind of the child in thinking of it, and suggests immediately what operation he must perform; and he sets himself to calculate it. He has not yet learned what the sum of those two numbers is; he is therefore obliged to calculate it, in order to answer the question; and he will require some little time to do it. Most persons, when such a question is proposed, do not observe the process going on in the child's mind; but because he does not answer immediately, they think that he does not understand it, and they begin to assist him, as they suppose, and say, How many are five and three? Cannot you tell how many five and three are? Now this latter question is very much more difficult for the child, than the original one. Besides, the child would not probably perceive any connexion between them. He can very easily understand, and the question itself suggests it to him better than any explanation, that the five cents and three cents are to be counted together; but he does not easily perceive what the abstract numbers five and three have to do with it. This is a process of generalization, which it takes children some time to learn.

In all cases, then, especially in the early stages, it will be perplexing, and rather injurious, to refer the learner from a practical to an abstract question, for the purpose of explanation. And it is still worse to tell him the result, and not make him find it himself. If the question is sufficiently simple, he will solve it. And he should be allowed time to do it, and not be perplexed with questions or interruptions until he has done it. But if he does not solve the question, it will be because he does not fully comprehend it. And if he cannot be made to comprehend it, the question should be varied, either by varying the numbers, or the objects, or both, until a question is made that he can answer. One being found that he can answer, another should be made a little varied, and then another, and so on, till he is brought back to the one first proposed. It will be better that the question remain unanswered, than that the child be told the answer, or assisted in the operation, any farther than may be necessary to make him fully understand the question.

Some children, when a question is proposed, instead of thinking of it, and trying to solve it, will endeavour to guess at the result. This should be checked immediately.

It has often been asked whether the plates, which sometimes accompany Colburn's Intellectual Arithmetic, or anything else of a similar nature, are of any use to the learner? I think myself that they have very little effect upon his progress. At first, before he is familiar with the addition and multiplication tables, some kind of counters seem to be necessary; but it is not important what they are. The plates are very convenient, but I believe the fingers do about as well as anything. If the scholar is allowed any helps of this kind, he should be left to manage them entirely by himself, and in his own way. Any helps, by which the work is partly done for the scholar, are certainly injurious. It is by his own efforts, that a child is to learn, if he learns at all. The teacher cannot learn for him. Neither will he labor himself, if the teacher will endeavour to do the work for him. You might, with as much propriety, expect that his muscles would be strengthened by seeing others exercise in the gymnasium, as to expect a child's mind to be strengthened and improved, when the teacher does the work for him. The teacher may assist him in understanding the question, but not in the operation,—not even in arranging his counters; for to do this, is to do for him the most important part of the solution.

It is best that the learner should be exercised for some time in solving practical questions involving addition and multiplication, before he commits to memory the addition and multiplication tables. He should understand the use of them, and be able to make them, before he is required to learn them, and then he should be made to learn them thoroughly. It is not well for a child to commit anything to memory, that he does not understand, for he thereby acquires a habit of repeating it without attending to the sense; and it is more difficult to make him attend to the sense afterwards, when he repeats it, than if he had not seen it before. At least, this is generally the case. There may be exceptions. I might refer again to the subject of grammar, as furnishing the most familiar instance of this. For example, it is very easy for a scholar, when properly taught, to learn the distinction of cases in the pronouns. And yet I have had scholars, who had learned their grammar before they came under my care, so as to repeat it by heart, in parsing the word *him*, call it in the nominative case; and still persist in calling it so, after being required to decline it, five or six times in succession. Arithmetic, or any other subject, would furnish examples enough of the difficulty of making the scholars attend to the sense sufficiently to understand a rule or principle, when they have first committed it without understanding it. But grammar, perhaps, affords the most striking instances of it.

I shall now endeavour to explain a principle, which I consider to be a very important one. It is one less generally understood than any that I have mentioned, or shall mention. Many teachers have practised upon it very well without having particularly thought of it. Many of you, I presume, have both thought of it, and practised upon it. But there are many, who do not observe it, either in theory or practice. This principle depends on the association of ideas. I shall not enter here into a discussion of the principle of association. I leave it to the metaphysician to determine whether there are any general laws which regulate it or not. I shall confine myself to one simple matter of fact concerning it, and the practical consequences to be derived from it.

The fact is this, that two persons never have exactly the same associations of ideas. I mean, they never associate their ideas in exactly the same order. The consequence is, that no two persons think of the same proposition alike. Hence, a proposition expressed in certain terms, may be very clear and intelligible to one person, and very obscure or altogether unintelligible to another. And perhaps, with a very slight change of terms, the case would be entirely changed. It would be intelligible to the latter, and unintelligible to the former. An explanation, which is very clear and lucid to one, will often convey no idea at all to another. When a proposition is made for two persons to reason upon, they will often take it up and manage it very differently in their minds. When the subject is such as to admit of demonstration, as is the case with mathematics, they will generally come to the same conclusions. But on other subjects their conclusions will sometimes agree, and sometimes not.

There are several practical results to be derived from this. First, it is very important that a teacher should be able readily to trace, not only his own associations, but those of all his pupils, when he hears them recite their lessons. When a proposition or question is made to a scholar, he ought to be able to discover at once, whether the scholar understands it or not. If he does not understand it, the teacher should be able to discover the reason why, and then he can apply the remedy. This is to be done only by questioning the scholar, and tracing his associations, and finding what he is thinking about, and how he is thinking about it. Without doing this, the teacher is as likely to perplex the scholar, as to assist him by his explanations. And it is a very common thing to see scholars perplexed in this way.

Secondly, when the scholar does not understand the question or proposition, he should be allowed to reason upon it in his own way, and agreeably to his own associations. Whether his way is the best, or not, on the whole, it is the best way for him at first, and he ought by no means to be interrupted in it, or forced out of it. The judicious teacher will leave him to manage it entirely by himself, and in his own way, if he can. Or if he meets with a little difficulty, but is still in a way that will lead to a proper result, he will apply his aid so as to keep him in his own way. When the scholar has been through the process in his own way, he should be made to explain how he has done it; and if he has not proceeded by the best way, he should be led by degrees into the best way. Many teachers seem not to know that there is more than one way to do a thing, or think of a thing; and if they find a scholar pursuing a method different from their own, they suppose of course he must be wrong, and they check him at once, and endeavour to force him into their way, whether he understands it or not. If such teachers would have patience to listen to their scholars, and examine their operations, they would frequently discover very good ways that had never occurred to them before. Nothing is more discouraging to scholars, than to interrupt them, when they are proceeding by a method which they perfectly comprehend, and which they know to be right; and to endeavour to force them into one which they do not understand, and which is not agreeable to their way of thinking. And nothing gives scholars so much confidence in their own powers, and stimulates them so much to use their own efforts, as to allow them to pursue their own methods, and to encourage them in them.

It is very important for teachers to lead their scholars into the habit of attending to the process going on in their own minds, while solving questions; and of explaining how they solve them. Unless the teacher possesses the faculty of tracing the associations of others, he cannot make them do it effectually. But the teacher, who does possess this faculty perfectly, will get an explanation out of anybody that has any thoughts, and can be made to speak on the subject upon which he is questioned. He can take one of his scholars, or any other person, and make him trace out and explain a process of reasoning, which has passed in his mind, but of which he was not at all aware, and concerning which, if left to himself, he could give no account. He seems to have the thoughts of his scholars under his control. He will not only find out *what* they are thinking about, and *how* they are thinking of it, but he is able to turn their thoughts into almost any channel he pleases. And it is next to impossible for one person to direct the current of another's thoughts on any subject, unless he knows the channel in which they are already flowing.

This subject also suggests a hint with regard to making books, and especially those for children. The author should endeavour to instruct, by furnishing the learner with occasions for thinking, and exercising his own reasoning powers, and he should not endeavour to think and reason for him. It is often very well, that there should be a regular course of reasoning in the book on the subject taught; but the learner ought not to be compelled to pursue it, if it can possibly be avoided, until he has examined the subject and come to a conclusion in his own way. Then it is well for him to follow the reasoning of others, and see how they think of it.

I will now say a few words concerning recitations. They are of very great importance in instruction, in a great many points of view; and it is very essential that they be well conducted. They are the principal means, which the teacher has, to know what progress the scholars are making. It is chiefly at recitations that one scholar can compare himself with another; consequently they furnish the most effectual means of promoting emulation. They are an excellent exercise for the scholar, for forming the habit of expressing his ideas properly and readily. The scholar will be likely to learn his lesson more thoroughly, when he knows he shall be called upon to explain it. They give him an opportunity to discover whether he understands his subject fully or not, which he will not always be sure of, until he is called upon to give an account of it. Recitations in arithmetic, when properly conducted, produce a habit of quick and ready reckoning on the spur of the occasion, which can be produced in no other way, except in the business of life; and then only, when the business is of a kind to require constant practice. They are therefore a great help in preparing scholars for business.

Directions concerning recitations must be general. Each teacher must manage the detail of them in his own way.

In the first place, the scholar should be thoroughly prepared before he attempts to recite. No lessons should be received by the teacher, that are not well learned. If this is not insisted on, the scholar will soon become careless and inattentive.

It is best that the recitations, both in intellectual and written arithmetic, should be in classes, when practicable. It is best that they should be without the book, and that the scholar should perform the examples from hearing them read by the teacher. Questions that are put out to be solved at the recitation, should be solved at the recitation, and not answered from memory. The scholars should frequently be required to explain fully, and clearly, the steps by which they solve a question, and the reasons for them. Recitations should be conducted briskly, and not suffered to lag and become dull. The attention of every scholar should be kept on the subject, if possible, so that all shall hear everything that is said. For this, it is necessary that the questions pass round quickly, and that no scholar be allowed a longer time to think than is absolutely necessary. If the lesson is prepared as it should be, it will not take the scholar long to give his answer. It is not well to ask one scholar too many questions at a time; for by that, there is danger of losing the attention of the rest. It is a good plan, when practicable, so to manage the recitation, that every scholar shall endeavour to solve each question that is proposed for solution at the time of recitation. This may sometimes be done, by proposing the question without letting it be known who is to answer it, until all have had time to solve it; and then calling upon some one for the answer. No farther time should be allowed for the solution; but if the scholar so called on is not ready, the question should be immediately put to another in the same manner.

There is one point more which I shall urge, and it is one which I consider the most important of all. It is to make the scholars study. I can give no directions how to do it. Each teacher must do it in his own way, if he does it at all. He who succeeds in making his scholars study, will succeed in making them learn; whether he does it by punishing, or hiring, or persuading, or by exciting emulation, or by making the studies so interesting that they do it for the love of it. It is useless for me to say which will produce the best effects upon the scholars; each of you may judge of that for yourselves. But this I say, that he who makes his scholars study, will make them learn; and he who does not, will not make them learn much or well. There never has been found a royal road to learning of any kind, and I presume there never will be. Or if there should be, I may venture to say, that learning so obtained will not be worth the having. It is a law of our nature, and a wise one too, that nothing truly valuable can be obtained without labor. There are some facilities for learning at the present day, perhaps, which were not formerly known. These serve to render study less irksome, but they do not render it less necessary. They enable the scholar to obtain more knowledge with an equal quantity of labor, but they do not enable him to obtain any valuable knowledge without labor. If scholars were to learn wholly by the assistance of the teacher, without any efforts of their own, they would acquire habits of idleness and inactivity, which would be more injurious to them than their learning would be beneficial; and they would be little able to make any progress in learning after leaving school. But the scholar, who is made to apply himself closely, and to learn by his own efforts, acquires habits of diligence and perseverance which will be useful to him through life. And he learns (which is of more advantage than the immediate subject of his studies,) he learns how to learn by his own efforts, without the aid of a teacher.

I have now briefly noticed what I consider the essential points to be attended to in teaching arithmetic. Many of them, as I observed before, are not peculiar to arithmetic, but apply equally to all subjects. And I dare say you will hear some of them much more ably discussed during the course. But there are many essential points of a good instructer, that cannot be taught by lecture. This I will not undertake to describe. One point more, however, I will remark; that to teach a subject well, it is necessary for the teacher to understand it well himself, and to take an interest in it; otherwise he will not make it interesting to his scholars.

Allow me to close with a few remarks, expressing, though imperfectly, the interest I feel in the occasion that has brought us together. There have been, in every age, a few persons, who have felt the importance of the subject of education. But generally the numbers have been few. The business of teaching, except in great seminaries, has not been considered as one of the most honorable occupations, but rather degraded; so that few persons of talents would engage in it. Even in our own country and age, it has been too much the case, that persons with a little learning, and unwilling to work, and unfit for anything else, have turned schoolmasters, and have been encouraged in it. They have been encouraged in it, because the pay of school teachers, in most instances, has been just sufficient to obtain that class of persons, and no other but one, which, with few exceptions, is not much better. I mean such as engage in the business of teaching for a short time, in order to discharge a few debts, previous to entering on a profession.

But a new era, I trust, is now opened upon us. The community at large are beginning to feel the importance of the subject, and to show an interest in it. The fact of there being so many persons, both teachers and others, and many of them from distant parts of the country, collected here on this occasion, is a sufficient proof that the interest is neither small, nor confined to one section of the country. A few years ago it would have been impossible to assemble such a number of persons for such a purpose. It seems now to be generally agreed that the business of teaching ought to be considered as a profession; and that the persons engaging in it ought to be instructed expressly for it, as for a profession. And institutions are getting up for that purpose. Your assembling here in this way, for mutual instruction on this important subject, though it will not supply the place of regular institutions for it, will greatly promote the general object, and hasten on the period of their adoption. I rejoice, therefore, to see this meeting. Though at present engaged in a pursuit very different from yours, I cheerfully accepted the proposals to deliver a lecture before you; not because I felt that I could do the subject justice, but because I was glad of the opportunity of contributing my mite, however small, to the promotion of so great a cause. I hope, therefore, that you will improve the opportunity you now have of receiving and communicating information, and that you will lay the foundation of a great work, of which not only your own immediate neighbourhoods, but our country at large, and not our country only, but the whole world, shall feel the influence.

MR FELTON'S LECTURE.

ADVERTISEMENT.

The author of the following lecture, yielded with reluctance to the request of the Censors, that he would furnish a copy for the press. The subjoined letter will show that it was only his own feeling of the inadequacy of what he has said in this lecture, to express his views of the greatness and importance of classical studies, which prevented his consenting as cheerfully to its publication, as he had to delivering it before the Convention.

TO THE CENSORS OF THE AMERICAN INSTITUTE.

Gentlemen,

The lecture which I now submit to your disposal, was not written with any view to publication, and I have therefore hesitated to send it to the press. The subject of classical learning is one of immense importance, when considered in all its bearings upon the intellectual culture of our times. It is impossible to do it anything like justice within the short compass of a single discourse; and I have not attempted it. The preeminent merits of the great productions of antiquity, when considered merely as works of original and creative genius; the fine, graceful, airy, intellectual finishing they received from the hands of their unrivalled authors; the intimate union of the classical taste, with all the best literature of succeeding times—with many other details, into which the argument for classical learning, in the present state of the literary world, must necessarily run, demand a wider space and more minuteness of discussion, than would be compatible with the purpose of a public discourse. On this account, I indulged in a rapid grouping of topics, a superficial and hurried series of sketchings, with as much of 'special pleading' as the occasion permitted; intending to correct these faults in a more extended work, for which I have been some time past collecting materials. It was my purpose to mould these materials into a volume of moderate compass, and submit it, at some future period, to the American Institute. That purpose I still retain; on which account I ask the indulgence of my readers for the obvious imperfections of the present lecture. Meantime, I beg leave to recommend to all interested in the subject of classical learning, an admirable 'Introduction' to the classics, by Mr Coleridge, a gentleman of kindred genius to his great poetical namesake. His work does not pretend to a full and philosophical exhibition of the claims of classical learning, as a leading object in a system of liberal education. But it is a tasteful disquisition on the characteristics of some of the elder Grecian writers, and proves that its author possesses, in a liberal measure, the spirit of noble and generous scholarship.

I am, gentlemen, with sincere respect,

Your obedient servant,

CORNELIUS C. FELTON.

LECTURE XII.

ON
CLASSICAL LEARNING.

BY CORNELIUS C. FELTON,
TUTOR IN GREEK, IN HARVARD UNIVERSITY, CAMBRIDGE.

IN discussing the claims of classical learning, it is not my intention to revive the half-forgotten disputes in which the scholars of old arrayed themselves in contending parties, under the banners of ancient and of modern genius. The spirit which animated those violent times, is foreign from an occasion like the present. The fanaticism which taught men to abuse and scorn each other for differences in literary opinion, and woman, in the person of a fair votary of the Muses, the only one of her sex whom the French Academy has ever deigned to eulogize, to fix upon her opponent, Lamothe, because he ridiculed Homer's mythology, the gentle epithets 'cold, flat, ridiculous, impertinent, grossly ignorant, proud and senseless,' and to remind him that Alcibiades boxed the ears of a rhetorician, because he had not Homer's works; this absurd fanaticism, it is far from my purpose to evoke. Yet it might well be matter of surprise, that the great masters of antiquity, whose works have stood the test of two thousand years, should, at this late day, be summoned before the tribunal of public opinion, their merits closely scrutinized, questioned, doubted, and, in some cases, passionately disputed. It might, I say, be matter of surprise, had we not all observed and felt the revolutionary character of the present age. There has been, for years past, a strong tendency to overturn old systems, however hallowed; to dispute old opinions, however established by the lapse of ages; and to carry the work of revolution and reform from the halls of legislation to the halls of learning. These stirring movements of the awakened and excited mind, have doubtless swept away many systems and theories that had their origin in an age of darkness, and were unfit for an age of light. They have taught men to examine, compare, think, decide and act for themselves. But it becomes a momentous inquiry for us, who are in the very vortex of the troubled waters, whether there is not great danger, as well as advantage, in our present situation; whether we may not, in the giddy whirl, neglect too much the old land-marks, and make shipwreck on the ocean of change.

The adversaries of classical learning assert, that 'the main reason for giving such importance to the ancient masters, in a course of liberal education, was, in former times, the fact that they were the only teachers. The moderns had not yet begun that series of researches and discoveries, which have been so splendidly exhibited in these latter days. The physical, moral, intellectual sciences were unknown, save as the sages of the Academy and the Porch had taught them. The genius of modern poetry was voiceless, or breathed only harsh strains in the barbarous Latinity of the Monks. It was therefore correct and proper that recourse should be had to their instructions, for want of better. But now the case is widely different; the tables are turned. The ancients were not wiser than we are, but we are wiser than they. We have carried on and perfected what they only began. They might have been giants, we grant, and we may be pigmies; but then we have the advantage of being upon their shoulders, and of course see farther. Shall we then continue to look with their eyes?' Such is the reasoning of the more moderate and rational among the opposers of classical learning.

Others have entered into the controversy with a spirit of violence and denunciation, altogether unbecoming gentlemen and scholars. The advocates of classical learning have been held up to the ridicule of the public as the bigoted adherents to a useless and cumbrous system, because they are too idle and selfish to admit the lights of modern improvement. They have been charged with palming off upon the world a cheap and trifling stock of words, a parade of verbal niceties, for the genuine learning which is to prepare young men to act their parts well in the great drama of life. A tone of bitterness, a rancor like that of personal hostility and family quarrels, has assailed them, and the whole armory of sarcasm has been exhausted. But denunciation and anathema are not to be reasoned with,—'and who can refute a sneer?' It often happens, we well know, that the most violent are the most ignorant. Men have derided the wit and wisdom of antiquity, who are unable to explain a classical allusion, or interpret a Latin sentence. Smatterers have assailed the reputation and denounced the writings of the mightiest of Grecian philosophers, to whom the curious inquirers into the mysteries of the Greek alphabet, would turn in vain for light. And yet the opinions of such men, unworthy as they are of confidence, derive from their impudent assurance, an authority against which reason, and good sense, and sound learning, are for a time of little avail. But the calm and rational skeptics have stated their questions, and deserve a reply. An exposition of the claims that classical learning still maintains upon our attention and respect, will contain that reply. Few, I believe, who reflect upon the prospect of our country, can doubt the importance of the question being candidly asked and candidly answered. A nation, embracing more than twelve millions of men, irresponsible to any higher power than themselves, with their own destinies, whether for good or for evil, in their hands, each generation training up those who are to succeed them in the high and perilous trust, has a deep, and almost overwhelming stake in the chance of success or ruin, and the means of securing the one or averting the other.

Much wit has been expended in ridiculing the pursuits of the philologist. But true philosophy regards every manifestation of mind, whether in the forms of language, the creations of poetry, the abstractions of science, or the godlike gift of oratory, as worthy of its study. The mind, the essential and immortal part of man, is not to be contemned in any one of its thousand fold aspects and operations. Among the most curious and subtile of these operations, the process unfolded by the developement of speech may fairly be classed. This gift, so universal, so indispensable, like the air we breathe, is scarcely valued because its loss is rarely felt. But let us reflect a moment upon its infinite importance, and we cannot, with anything like the spirit of true philosophy, scorn its study, as a puerile and trifling object. That power by which all other powers are guided and fashioned, by which all emotions are described, by which all the playful efforts of fancy are made distinct to the perceptions of others, by which, more than by all our powers besides, the creations of genius are illustrated—and *language* the instrument of that power, the most ingenious and finished of all instruments—can it indeed be so small, so contemptible, as to fix justly upon those engaged in its study the scornful epithets of 'word-weighers,' and 'gerund-grinders?' Language opens a wide and curious field to the observation of those whose pursuits lead them to trace the intricate phenomena of intellect. The great difficulty in studying the philosophy of mind, arises from the impalpable nature of the objects to be scanned in that study. Language is one of the modes, and a most essential one, by which the operations of intellect are distinctly made visible. In studying language, therefore, we are in fact studying *mind*, through the agency of its most purely intellectual instrument. In mastering language, we not only attain the power of wielding this most efficient instrument, but we make ourselves familiar with the results, and we comprehend the compass of those gifts which make us feel that we are 'fearfully and wonderfully made.' Such pursuits can have no other tendency than to strengthen and elevate the mind, and prepare it, consequently, to act with energy, dignity and success, upon the various objects presented to it in life. But it is said, the student of language is employed about *words* to the neglect of *things*. I cannot help calling such reasoning, or rather such assertions, for it is not reasoning, poor, unmeaning cant. Wasting time upon *words* to the neglect of *things!* Are not words, realities? Have they not a separate, an independent existence? Nay, more; have they not a power to stir up the soul, to sway nations even, such as no other *things* ever possessed or ever can possess? Did not the words of Demosthenes carry more dread to the heart of Philip than the arms of Athens and the fortresses of her tributary cities? Have not the words of Homer touched the hearts and roused the imaginations of myriads, many centuries since the walls of Troy and the armaments of Greece perished from the face of the earth, and the site of Priam's capital was lost from the memories of men?—It is true that the trifling and quibbling of some philologists give a plausible air to the objections raised against these studies. But would you condemn the mathematics, because one votary of the science declared his contempt for Paradise Lost—a work which proved no truth by a chain of geometrical or algebraic reasoning? Would you reject geology, because an enthusiast values a stone, apparently worthless, more than a splendid product of imagination? Would you shut your mind against the beautiful science of botany, because you have seen one so absorbed in its study that he would expend more anxious care in rearing a puny hot-house plant, than in alleviating sorrow or saving life? Are you prepared to throw away the hopes of religion, because a few bigots, attaching an overstrained importance to trifles, make it appear absurd, and strip it of almost every attribute that can command your respect? Analogy, I am aware, is not argument; but the same kind of reasoning, which is aimed at philological studies, might be aimed with equal success against every science we value, every truth we hold sacred.

Such are some of the general considerations that recommend the study of language. But the classical languages, besides these, have other and peculiar claims upon our attention. No one will for a moment dispute the importance of understanding the full power of our vernacular tongue. I assume this as a fact beyond discussion and argument. I assert, moreover, the impossibility of doing this without the aid of Greek and Latin. This latter position may be, and has been, disputed. It has been assumed a thousand times as an argument in support of classical learning, and a thousand times its force and pertinency have been denied. The case may, however, be stated briefly, and, as I think, convincingly. The progress of language, at least as far back as *written* language extends, may be traced with no great difficulty. We know not of what elements the Hebrew tongue was formed. It is the earliest and simplest language that we have the means of examining in written records. But we can easily trace the radical signification of many Greek words, to Hebrew forms; and the influence of one of these languages upon its successor, is as clearly perceptible as any phenomenon in physical science. And though a general knowledge of Greek, and one sufficient for all ordinary purposes, may be obtained without going higher than itself into the antiquity of speech, yet it is perfectly obvious that a thoroughly critical acquaintance with it can be purchased only at the price of resorting to the subsidiary dialects. The Latin was formed chiefly from a modification of Greek. The Romans drew largely from Grecian fountains, both in language and literature; and vain would be his labors, who should essay to comprehend the efforts of Roman genius, without first listening to the instructions of Rome's literary masters.

In the division of the Roman empire and the formation of modern states, other languages arose from the ruins of the Latin. Four of the principal dialects of modern Europe bear so strong a resemblance to the parent tongue, that a knowledge of the latter makes the attainment of the former an affair of trifling labor. Other languages of Europe, and our own among the rest, are derived but in part from the Latin; and I assert that so far as that part goes, a knowledge of Latin is essential to one who would understand it fully, and wield it with certainty and effect. Nearly all our words of Roman origin retain the radical meaning of their primitives. Their general import may, it is true, be gathered from English usage; but the peculiar, the nicely critical propriety of their application, is unknown, save to the classical scholar; and all others, who attempt to write their own mother tongue, especially in the discussion of literary subjects, are liable to mar their pages by slight inaccuracies of style, and inaccuracies in the use of single words, which destroy their claim to the honor of being classical models of composition. Such is the inevitable result of the natural progress of the human mind. Had we lived in the times of the ancients, and they in ours, the case would have been reversed. They would have drawn instruction from our writings; their languages would have received an infusion from ours; and to learn the exact quality of that infusion, they must have traced it to its fountain head with us. We do not compromise one particle of our claim to originality, by admitting the necessity of resorting to ancient tongues, in order to learn our own. It is only admitting, in the spirit of philosophy, what the natural course of human thought, and our relative position to the great civilized nations who have gone before us, make it incumbent on us, as reasoning men to admit. Perhaps the exceptions may be urged of such men as Franklin, who have written our language in great purity and elegance, without having been trained in the discipline of classical schools. If I grant that these apparent exceptions are exceptions in fact, I might defend my position by the plea, that a few exceptions never invalidate a general rule; and I might array in reply to every single exception, five hundred examples in which the rule holds good. But there is little argument to be drawn from the literary powers of Dr Franklin, against the utility of classical learning. According to his own statements, his style was formed by closely imitating the best models of English composition—the papers of the Spectator—which, we all know, are from the pens of the most accomplished classical scholars England has ever produced. The purity, simplicity and beauty of Dr Franklin's style, therefore, is, after all, the consequence of an exquisite taste in ancient literature; although with him, it comes at second hand. Is any one prepared to say that the language of Franklin would not have been more bold, more stirring, more eloquent, had his mind, after having been cultivated and refined in the study of antiquity, given free scope to its acknowledged powers, and acted by its own resistless impulses, untrammelled by the fetters of imitation?

Not only our language, but our literature, is closely dependent on the classical. The fine conceptions, the productions of the beautiful fancy of the ancients, have exerted so strong an influence upon the tone and genius of the elder English literature, that one half of the beauties of the latter are lost sight of without a knowledge of the former. The great writers of England have been filled to overflowing with classic lore. The history, and poetry, and oratory of Greece and Rome, have lent them their tributary aids; the sages of antiquity have poured out their richest treasures to illustrate, adorn, and enforce the glorious conceptions of English intellect. Classical allusions and illustrations, tastefully employed, are enchanting to a cultivated mind. In English literature they are used with a skill and beauty that form one of its most delightful traits. This does not arise from, nor does it argue, a want of originality. It would be impossible to prevent such influences of the literature of one age upon that of another, except by entire ignorance of everything that does not come within our own experience. We may complain of it, if we please, but we cannot change the order of time, and place ourselves at the beginning of the history of our race. The ancients were before us, and we have studied them, and cannot help it. We cannot read our own writers, without being constantly reminded of those great men. The law of progress requires that it should be so. As well might you attempt to throw up a dyke against the fountain-heads of a mighty river, and expect it to flow uninterruptedly on to the ocean, as to dam up the channels of thought, and hope to force the mind onward in the career of improvement.

Fortunate, indeed, is it for us, that the creations of Grecian genius were guided by such unerring taste. The intellectual character of that gifted nation was formed under the happiest auspices. Nature was lavish of her beauties upon her favored land; but she did not convert it into a region of oriental softness. Every influence that tended to give refinement and elegance to the mind, was there felt; but refinement and elegance were made to stop at the proper limits, and never allowed to become degenerate and effeminate. Her free and ofttimes tumultuous politics gave energy, her matchless climate infused vivacity and cheerfulness, her scenery inspired a pure taste and an exquisite perception of beauty. The human form was developed in its fairest proportions. The majestic and intellectual head, the finely expanded frame, the active and airy and graceful motion, gave to artists the prototypes of their chiselled gods. Add to this their beautiful modes of instruction; music and science uniting to give at once a humanized and manly tone to the character, in the groves of the Academy, on the places of public resort, by the wisest, best, and most eloquent from among them, with the noblest specimens of art all around them, the marble almost waking into life, the canvass glowing with the hues of heaven—and we cannot wonder at the perfection of Grecian taste;—we cannot but congratulate ourselves, that a race so favored, so gifted, were called to preside over the beginnings and direct the destinies of intellectual Europe,—that the Genius of Greece yet lives, as fresh, as bright, as beautiful, as her own blue hills, sunny skies, and green isles.

Another additional consideration in favor of the study of ancient languages, is the fact that they are more finished than any others. The perfection of the Greek tongue has always been the admiration of scholars. Its flexibility, its exhaustless vocabulary, its power of increasing that vocabulary at will by the use of compounds, make it an admirable vehicle for the communication of thought, even to the nicest shades; while its unrivalled harmony imparts to poetry a richness and beauty beyond the capacity of any modern tongue. The principles and power of language are here more fully unfolded; the philosophy of rhetoric is more thoroughly displayed. Add to this, the Greek grammar is now fixed and settled. There it is, beyond the reach of change, an object of study, to be resorted to at any time—ever perfect, ever beautiful. But beyond and above the study of mere language, I know of no better intellectual discipline than to determine the meaning of an ancient author. The principles of grammar are to be applied by the reason and the judgment; the situation of the author must be vividly presented to the mind by the memory and the imagination; the connexion of the passage in question with the context, is to be closely scrutinized; the style of ancient thought to be taken into consideration, and, after thus exercising the most important of our powers, the purport of a difficult passage may be settled. This is precisely the course of reflection and reasoning which men must follow, in determining the proper conduct for many difficult conjunctures in life;—it is acting upon probabilities.

Such is the process, and such the discipline, of determining single passages. Of a similar and more elevated kind, is the intellectual effort of comprehending the entire worth of an author. It is not enough barely to give his works a hasty perusal, or even a careful perusal, with a knowledge of the language simply. The student who would enter fully into the merits of a classical author, must take himself out of the influences immediately around him; must transport himself back to a remote age; must lay aside the associations most familiar to him; must forget his country, his prejudices, his superior light, and place himself upon a level with the intellect whose labors he essays to comprehend. Few are the minds that would not be benefited by such a process. We are disposed to permit our thoughts and feelings to repose too much upon the objects nearest us; and thus a constant reference to self becomes the habitual direction of our thoughts. What was the character of the age in which he lived? what was the religion? how far did it gain a hold upon the minds of cultivated men? to what extent did it influence the tone of poetry? what were the philosophical theories, and how far were they true, and how extensively were they believed? what was the character of the nation, and what had been its historical career? what was the state of political parties and what was the government? what were the doctrines held by each, and wherein did they differ—and how far was the individual mind of the author in question wrought upon by all these influences? are questions which should be asked, and, as far as possible, answered, by the scholar who would do himself and literature full justice, by the mode in which he pursues his classical studies. I am aware that such is not often the path followed by the scholars of our country; but I do sincerely believe that the worth of classical learning will never be realized until some such method is adopted. I know, too, it involves a depth of thought and a wide range of studies, from which we are apt to shrink in alarm, and ask ourselves if there is not some shorter way to attain the object; but reason, as I think, decides without appeal, that such is the price of genuine classical erudition.

Knowledge of the sort I have described, may not lead to the invention of a single new mechanical agent; it may not be the direct means of increasing our fortunes a single dollar. But it will give us an enlarged view of our nature; it will disclose the workings of our common powers under influences widely differing from any that have acted upon ourselves; it will teach us to judge charitably of others' minds and hearts; it will teach us that intellect, and sensibility, and genius, have existed beyond the narrow circle in which we have moved—

beyond the limits of our country—centuries before our age. Such lessons are needed in the every day concerns of life. Those who say that the classics are of no practical use—those even who say that they are merely ornamental in a liberal education, show an entire forgetfulness of their most striking and obvious effects. They are eminently practical. They require the most practical modes of reasoning to comprehend them; they give the most practical views of our nature; they prepare the professional man for his labors, by presenting a field of practically similar labor, before he enters upon its special duties. I have no hesitation in asserting, that a mind long trained in unfolding the meaning and worth of classical authors, by the course of inquiries I have described, will be eminently prepared for the intricate investigations of the profession of law.

I repeat again the qualification which must be made to these remarks, when applied to the classical studies common in our own country. We take them up, with little knowledge of ancient history, and none of mythology; we hurry through them, with or without a grammatical knowledge of the languages, as chance or caprice may direct; we bring them to the standard of modern tastes, and refer them to our own tribunals. Instead of transporting ourselves back to the time when they lived, we summon their Shades to appear before us,—differing in every respect from them, differing in religion, differing in morality, differing in prejudices—to answer for opinions and systems, put forth ages and ages before our own opinions and systems were thought of. Such is not doing the justice we owe them.

But apart from all other considerations, the merits of ancient lierature, as judged by *any* standard, entitle it to a high place in every system of education. My remarks apply chiefly to Greek literature, because it is not only the most exquisitely finished, but the fountain-head of the Roman and of all successive literature. I have already spoken in general terms of the circumstances which tended to give the Genius of Greece its unrivalled taste. If that high culture is more fully displayed in any one portion of Greek literature than in the rest, that portion is their poetry. From the first book of Homer to the last play of Euripides, the train of noble conceptions, exquisite expression, and matchless imagery, betrays the peculiar and unrivalled intellect of the finest masters in the art. It would be too much like the hundredth repetition of commonplaces to enlarge upon the noble character of Homer's poems;—

> Qui, quid sit pulchrum, quid turpe, quid utile, quid non,
> Planius ac melius, Chrysippo et Crantore dicit.

But I cannot forbear quoting the opinions of an illustrious German critic. 'The influence which the works and the genius of Homer have of themselves produced on after ages, or rather, indeed, on the general character and improvement of the human race, has alone been far more durable, and far more extensive, than the combined efforts of all the institutions of the Athenian, and all the heroic deeds and transcendent victories of the Macedonian. In truth, if Solon and Alexander still continue to be glorious and immortal names, their glory and immortality are to be traced rather to the influence which, by certain accidents, their genius has exerted on the intellectual character and progress of the species, than to the intrinsic value of a system of municipal laws, altogether discrepant from our own, or to the establishment of a few dynasties, which have long since passed away.'

Greek poetry is abundant in every department of the art. But if I were to select a part more worthy than the rest to be cultivated by an intellectual man, that would be the drama. This most singular and beautiful manifestation of Grecian genius, was favored by every circumstance that could make it purely and intensely national. The vivacity and inquisitiveness of the Athenians, their enthusiastic love of the arts and of poetry, rendered the drama an object in which the proudest spirits aspired for distinction. The Greek tragedies have, accordingly, been esteemed among literary men as the most interesting and valuable remains of ancient poetry; and this feeling of admiration has, among some modern nations, been carried to such a pitch of extravagance, that the expression of true, genuine, rational and modern feeling has been made to give place in literature, to a cold and heartless imitation, both of the classical style in language, and of the classical style in thought. But it may easily be shown, that the same principles of good taste which guided the ancients, should also teach modern nations to comply with the genius of the age.

To understand the Greek drama fully, we must not only ascertain the spirit of the people and the light in which they regarded it, but a minute acquaintance with the architectural construction of the theatre, and the scenic details, is absolutely necessary. It is impossible to gain from ancient authors all on this subject which may be desired; but a careful perusal of Vitruvius, with the proper explanations, will throw much light on this part of Grecian learning. The beauty of their climate enabled the Greeks to enjoy theatrical amusements with no roof above them but the sky. It seemed singularly appropriate, that representations in which the gods and heroes of their mythology bore so distinguished a part, should be held beneath the broad canopy of the heavens. The great interest felt in dramatic exhibitions, and the grave importance they attached to them, called the whole people, or as large a portion of the people as attended any public occasion, into the theatres; which therefore must have been of prodigious size. Indeed, it was to a certain extent a religious ceremony—an exhibition in honor of the divinities to whom, in a half poetical, half religious sense, they paid their adoration.

The character of the Greek tragedy is elevated high above the common, even the great characters of actual life. The traditions of an heroic age were gathered up and embodied—an age in which gigantic vices were united to heroic and noble qualities in the same individuals. The ancient kings, that ruled before the republican principle was introduced, are brought forward, in scenic grandeur—the terribly tragic events, half of human and half of divine agency, the memory of which was borne along in mythological tale, were woven into these sublime productions for the entertainment of an Athenian audience. Thus the drama became national from the heroic recollections it served to perpetuate, and the peculiarly religious air thrown over it. It was national also from the great public interest it excited, and the throngs it drew together. In tragedy, therefore, we may find the highest developement of Grecian character and genius; and he who is willing to expend the labor necessary to comprehend it, will find himself richly repaid. In the Prometheus, for instance, of Æschylus, one of the earliest dramatic performances which have come down to us—some of the most remarkable characteristics of tragedy, as well as of its author's astonishing genius, are singularly manifested.

The tone of Æschylus was stern and austere. He had fought in the battles of his country's liberties; and in one of his poems, 'The Persians,' had described the humiliation of Persia, and the ignominious retreat of her monarch from the Grecian shores. The martial spirit of the poet utters its trumpet-tones in the 'Seven before Thebes'—but, as I have remarked, the peculiar scope of Grecian tragedy is more traceable in the Prometheus—I mean the terrible power of Fate, subjecting gods and man to its inexorable dominion. It is supposed by critics that 'Prometheus' was the subject of a whole Trilogy, like that formed by the three connected dramas, 'Agamemnon, the Choephoræ, and the Eumenides.' The 'Fire-bringing,' the 'Chained,' and the 'Freed Prometheus,' form the subjects of the Trilogy—and these exhaust the mythus. The 'Chained Prometheus' is alone preserved, with the exception of a portion of the 'Freed Prometheus,' which has come down to us in a Latin translation. The disobedient act of bringing fire from heaven, had drawn upon the head of this great benefactor of man, the vengeance of the gods. He is condemned to be chained on a rock surrounded by the ocean. Strength and Force, two symbolical personages, compel Vulcan to carry their commands and threats into execution; but he remon strates with them on the inexorable decree, of which he is forced unhappily to be the agent. Prometheus then begins his solitary complaints. 'O divine sky, and ye swift-winged breezes, ye founts of rivers, ye countless ripples of the ocean-waves, thou universal mother earth, and thou all-seeing circle of the sun, I call on you to witness what I suffer at the hands of the gods.' A Chorus of the ocean nymphs appears and attempts to soothe him by their tender sympathy. Prometheus had closed his complaint by saying, 'The air resounds with the hurried flapping of birds' wings. Everything that approaches me is terrible.' The Chorus replies—'Fear not; this winged throng hath approached this place, in hurrying rivalry, but as thy friend—having with difficulty persuaded the mind of our father. The swift breezes brought us hither; for the sound of the clashing of brass hath penetrated the recess of our caverns, and startled us from our silent retirement—and we have rushed hither, unsandalled, with our winged chariot.'—*Prometheus.* 'Alas! alas! offspring of the prolific Tethys, children of Ocean, earth-encircling with his sleepless wave—behold! look! with what chains I am bound, and on the rocky summit of this steep, must ever keep a dreadful vigil.'—*Chorus.* 'We see, Prometheus, a sad and tearful cloud hath spread itself before our eyes, while looking upon thy body, exposed on these rocks, and held by adamantine chains; for new rulers govern Olympus —and with new laws Jupiter hath unjustly subjected it—and the powers of old he hath obliterated.' This, it is thought, alludes to the ancient warfare between the Titans, who symbolically represent the primeval powers of nature and the gods, which ended in the subjection of the former to the latter—or the changing of the universe from a state of chaos to a state of order and harmony. Prometheus then narrates the causes of his fall, and reveals a portion of the future. Oceanus, one of the ancient race of Titans, advises him to yield to the power of Jove, but is dismissed with deep contempt. Io appears, who is driven to wander from place to place, by the same resistless power, and listens to his prophetic revelation of her future sufferings. Mercury, the messenger of the gods, arrives, commanding him, in the name of Jupiter, to reveal the secret by which the power of Fate may be averted; but in vain. The overwhelming effects of the wrath of the King of Heaven, upon the unconquered and unconquerable victim of his power, are briefly described in a soliloquy of Prometheus, which concludes the poem. 'Now in deed, and not in word, the earth is shaken to its centre. The echo of the thunder bellows around me, and the fiery-forked lightnings gleam, and the whirlwinds roll the dust; the blasts of all the winds leap forth, rushing against each other in tempestuous uproar; and the sky is commingled with the sea; so great, so terrible a tumult, is visibly come upon me. O my worshipped Mother, and thou, Heaven, that circlest the common light of all; behold how unjustly I suffer.'

'The triumph of subjection,' says a deep classical scholar, 'was never celebrated in more glorious strains; and we have difficulty in conceiving how the poet, in the Freed Prometheus, could sustain himself on such an elevation.' This sublime poem, is, indeed, a magnificent developement of an unconquerable will, bearing up against a higher power, which had chosen, in the plenitude of its greatness, to lay upon Prometheus a tyrannical hand. Chained to a rock, amidst the most terrible and appalling array of power; threatened by the messenger of the gods; disheartened by the melancholy sympathy of the ocean nymphs, and counselled to submit by Oceanus himself; surrounded by storms, and thunder, and lightning, and earthquakes—he still maintains his determined purpose, sustained by an inward energy, which knows not submission—and boldly looking to a dim and distant future for deliverance from his present woes. These noble creations of Grecian genius, need, I trust, no arguments to present, in a striking light, the advantages of their study; they need to be understood only, and they will surely be ranked among the priceless treasures of the human intellect.

Such are the materials for reflection presented in the Grecian drama, the most perfect display, as I believe, of genius and taste that the world has ever witnessed. To set forth its claims adequately, a critical and philosophical examination of each piece would be required. I have barely given a simple and very imperfect sketch of one of the earliest—illustrated by a few brief quotations, which I have rendered in literal prose. To the drama itself I would urge you to resort, for the best exposition of its preeminent claims—for that ingenious and beautiful intermixture of ancient mythology, religion, deep philosophy, and lofty poetry, with the actual and genuine character of the Grecian intellect in its highest and purest form, which defies all rivalry and surpasses all description.

Another form in which the intellect of Greece was beautifully manifested, is to be found in her philosophy. We are too much given to hasty decisions on this interesting subject. In the pride of modern superiority, sweeping sentences of condemnation have been passed upon the whole circle of ancient labors in this curious and important department. Lord Bacon pointed out the proper mode of physical inquiry; and this mode has been adopted in mental investigation. The absurd quibbles of the schoolmen were detected, when the light of common sense shed upon them the strong illumination of truth; and the ridicule which they merited, went back and rested upon the head of Aristotle, whose principles they had so ignorantly abused. In the popular language of the last half century, absurdity, sophistry, and unmeaning jargon, have been almost synonymous with the logic and metaphysics of the Greeks. But literary justice requires that the earnest efforts of great minds, in whatever line of exertion, should be studied and appreciated in a spirit of candor.

When I contemplate the noble doctrines of Plato, and his noble manner of maintaining them; when I reflect that he taught the immortality of the soul, the corrupting power of vice, the stain which sin fixes upon the heart; that he supported his tenets by arguments which still serve as a basis to the best reasoning of the moderns; that he showed an unrivalled acuteness of intellect in his dialogues, as in the 'Sophist;' and joined to this a high-toned and uncompromising morality, inculcating adherence to duty, at the cost of life itself, pointing out the path of honor and virtue in the most trying situations, where fear and friendship and attachment to the world, and a sense of injustice powerfully aided the solicitations of friends, the arguments of beloved disciples, and the moving spectacle of an agonized family—exhibited in the delineation of Socrates, in the 'Phaedon'—that he portrayed the same great sage, in the character of a benevolent instructer, a kind friend, taking by the hand a youthful pupil, and leading him into the paths of true knowledge—in 'Theages'—that he himself performed the part of a devoted and affectionate disciple, in his beautiful and eloquent 'Apology'—I cannot but think it is much more fashionable to condemn, than it is to study, the philosophy of Athens. I am aware that Plato's imaginative mind led him into many fantastical theories. But it argues, I think, a feeble sense of justice, to scorn his noble views of God, of duty, and of immortality, because we may safely ridicule his 'Pyramid of Fire' and his theory of metempsychosis. We must admire and approve his belief in the divine origin and immutable essence of the soul, though we may neither admire nor approve his Utopian scheme of a republic, founded upon an unqualified extension of this system of psychology. It is but just to the writers of any country and of any age, to separate the great leading truths which they attempt to illustrate and enforce, from the particular forms, in the shape of theories and hypotheses in which those truths are folded; for theories and hypotheses may be false or visionary, but they may serve as vehicles for that sentiment of truth, which, so long as yon broad sky is above us, and this fair earth beneath us, and this mysteriously mingled union of physical and immortal powers is within us—will be an inmate of the human soul.

When I reflect that Aristotle listened twenty years to the instructions of his master; that he compassed the whole extent of human learning; that, in natural history and philosophy, he stood unrivalled and alone; that he drew up a system of logic, which, more than any system ever devised by man, has received the applause and guided the researches of past ages; that to his instruction the greatest general of antiquity confessedly was more indebted than to all besides, for his commanding preeminence; that Cicero, the best judge in literary and philosophical matters that the ancient world produced, said of him, *Excepto Platone, haud scio an recte dixerim principem philosophorum;*—I must still believe it more fashionable to utter fluent and flippant contempt against the quibbles of the Stagyrite, than to study the hard, severe, the iron reasoning of 'the Prince of Philosophers.'

When I contemplate the character of Socrates, as portrayed by Plato and Xenophon, his pure, precise, and philosophical ethics, his almost christian temper, his high moral firmness, his confidence in a future existence, his belief in the rewards of virtue—when I contemplate this character, formed by self-discipline, from natural propensities to licentiousness and depravity—when I read that from his instruction went forth a school of sages to whom Greece owed, in great part, that splendid reputation for wit, genius, and philosophy over which 'decay's effacing fingers' pass but lightly—my belief is yet stronger, that it is much more fashionable to descant upon the worthlessness of Grecian philosophy and Grecian morality, than to study the noble characters which that philosophy and morality produced.

The most practically useful portion of Greek literature, to an American student destined for public life, would perhaps be considered its oratory. The publicity with which great national questions were discussed in Greece, gave rise, particularly in Athens, to the strenuous study of this art. All public men were public speakers. It was by direct action upon the popular mind, that commanding influence was won and retained. The example and history of the first of orators, are most worthy models for the imitation of all in every age, who aspire to the glory of oratorical renown. The style and power of the eloquence of Demosthenes have been two long celebrated for me to urge them upon your consideration now. But there is one portion of that great man's history, to which I cannot forbear alluding, as a most thrilling passage. I mean the 'Contest for the Crown.' The Athenian people had resolved to reward the public services of Demosthenes, by presenting him with a golden crown. Ctesiphon had taken the lead in this act of popular recognition of the orator's merit, and became, in consequence, odious to his enemies. Æschines, whose jealousy and enmity to Demosthenes had been manifested on several previous occasions, instituted an impeachment, and had Ctesiphon prosecuted before the public assembly. This was a great, an intensely interesting occasion. Public curiosity was awake; expectation was excited; the two greatest orators were to appear, in the desperate attempt to measure strength with each other. Never was an occasion more exactly calculated to arouse Athenian inquisitiveness than this. On the one side was jealousy, vindictiveness, and envy, supported by powers acknowledged to be second to none but those of the man of the nation. On the other, the popular enthusiasm to bear onward, unrivalled reputation to sustain, the consciousness of resistless power, and the tremendous consequences of defeat. Every motive that could be impressed upon the mind in that age, was present before them. The day came on. The crowd was assembled. The orators successivly arose, and the listening multitudes hung, hour after hour, upon the speakers' lips. But the matchless eloquence of Demosthenes prevailed, and his enemy was banished. Fortunately we have these celebrated orations preserved, and can therefore appreciate those gifts, which, at Athens, were ranked so high. The eagerness with which the Greeks listened to these magnificent efforts of intellect, and read them from year to year, may be estimated by the eagerness with which we lately rushed to the pages of our own Demosthenes, after he had won his splendid victory on the Senate-floor of our country.

1. The orations of Demosthenes afford an admirable study, both to discipline and arouse the mind. It requires no little

labor to acquire the power of entering into their spirit fully. They must be studied until the train of thought, the peculiar expressions, and the general character of the whole are perfectly familiar; and then it is impossible for any one, who feels the power of eloquence, not to be borne irresistibly along by their impetuous torrents of thought, argument, and illustration. The effects of this thorough and reiterated study of Demosthenes, are well described by Wyttenbach, one of the most distinguished classical scholars the continent of Europe has lately produced. 'O salutare repetitionis consilium nec unquam satis prædicandum! ecce denuo religens, novus plane et incognitus ad animum meum accidit sensus. Adhuc in aliis auctoribus, intelligentia non nisi delectationis mihi voluptatem attulerat, cum ex rerum verborumque perceptione, tum ex progressuum meorum animadversione: nunc inusitatus et plus quam humanus affectus mentem permeat, et quâvis lectione invalescit. Video oratorem ardere, dolere, impetu ferri; incendor et ipse, eodemque motu auferor: altior fio nec sum qui fueram; videor mihi Demosthenes ipse esse, stans in tribunali hanc orationem habere, Atheniensium concionem ad majorum virtutem et gloriam hortari; nec tacitus lego, ut inceperam, sed altâ voce; ad quam tollendam imprudens inducor, cum sententiarum evidentiâ et fervore, tum numeri oratorii efficaciâ.'*

---

* 'O excellent plan of reviewing! never sufficiently to be inculcated! Lo! as I re-peruse the orator's pages, a new and before unknown feeling penetrates my mind. Before this time, in reading other authors, I had derived, from understanding them, gratification and delight, both in comprehending the train of thought and language, and in observing my own advancement. Now, an unusual, a more than human excitement rushes upon me, and grows stronger by every repeated reading. I see the orator ardent, indignant, hurried by the flow of his eloquence. I am enkindled myself, and borne along by the same mighty impulse. I become loftier, and am no longer the man I was: I seem to myself to be Demosthenes, standing upon the tribunal, pronouncing that same oration, exhorting the assembled Athenians to imitate the valor and win the glory of their ancestors. I read no longer silently, as I had begun, but aloud. I am led unconsciously to raise my voice, by the clearness and fervor of his sentiments, and the power of his rhetorical harmony.'

2. It would be useless for me to attempt a full and just exposition of the claims of Grecian genius upon our studious attention. As I have before remarked, a detailed and philosophical history would alone unfold all the relations, in which a familiar acquaintance with its masterly excellences would benefit the mind, and prepare it for future usefulness in the actual world around it. But I cannot help adverting to the high moral effects of a classical course of study, upon the heart and character.

I am aware that wise and good men have objected to ancient literature, on the ground, that the deities of Greece and Rome are represented as indulging in human vices and passions. But it does not seem to me possible that a poetical description of the pagan gods—understood to be merely poetical—can have any bad tendency. At least, the mind capable of being injured by an influence so indirect and distant, would be injured in a tenfold greater degree by the most ordinary temptations of daily life. In all other respects, the moral influence of classical learning, is certainly excellent; and this excellence appears most conspicuous on comparing it with the miscellaneous reading so common among students of the present day. The severe intellectual discipline of former times, has, I fear, become too nearly obsolete. The great passion of our age, is to acquire knowledge without labor. This I think is to be deprecated. Labor is the unavoidable condition of all excellence whatever. He who attempts to reverse this first law of our being, attempts the greatest of impossibilities. We read the periodicals and other popular works, and dream that we are winning knowledge with infinitely greater rapidity than our predecessors; and congratulate ourselves, that the studious days and watchful vigils of the gigantic scholars of old, are now no more. Besides that portion of our popular reading, which is merely light, there is much positively pernicious. The dangerous and seducing sentiment of many works which the press in its abundance pours out upon us, weakens the character and corrupts the heart. It steals in, like a subtle poison, with the beauties of imagery and the fascinations of style, softens the firmness of moral feeling, and destroys the sternness of virtue. The elegant vices of fashionable life come to us adorned with the charms of perverted genius, and fasten themselves, with their taint and their blight, upon the young and excitable spirit. Even when these vices are described but to be satirized, they are held up in such a light, as to tempt imitation. Who has not seen the influence of 'Pelham' in the affected, effeminate, absurd manners of many young men of the present day? Who has not seen the moody melancholy of Byron transferred from his pages to the brows of many a conceited misanthrope, whose only resemblance to the poet was his bared neck and his down-turned collar? It is this pernicious influence of our present light reading, upon the character, the manners, and the heart, which most needs correction. Such a work as Mr Moore's Life of Byron is calculated to effect more injury, by smoothing over a life filled up with the most degrading vices, and by representing utterly abandoned profligacy as the venial and even necessary foible of splendid genius, than the whole circle of heathen gods and goddesses, were they ten times as bad as they are represented in Homer's Olympus.

The tone of ancient literature is everywhere high. A clear and severe study of it, does, I am convinced, contribute more to the formation of a truly manly character, than any other study whatever. The strong patriotism, which is one of its leading traits, when modified by the superior light of modern times, is, to my mind, a strong recommendation. There is not the slightest danger, that we shall fall into ancient excesses, and stigmatize all who are not born on our American soil, with the epithet of barbarians. We look with too much reverence every opinion imported from beyond the Atlantic, and with too much distrust upon our own, for the just apprehension of such a danger. The patriotic spirit of ancient literature, strong as it is, may safely be met, in the education of our young men. They will find nothing of that vitiating sentiment, which taints so large a portion of the common literature of the day, in the pages of Grecian and Roman classics. The fine minds of antiquity were filled and glowing with visions of the greatness and happiness of mental excellence—the *aliquid immensum infinitumque* of Cicero, was aspired after, in the longings of those noble spirits, in other regions of intellect no less than in oratory. Believing as I do of those studies, I cannot but regret the comparative indifference, with which, in these days of utility and reform, we have seen them treated. I trust the prejudice against them is one of those popular prejudices, which, after a temporary triumph, sink to an everlasting oblivion. I trust the cavils of men who never read an ancient author in the comprehensive spirit of philosophical research will not, in many minds, be permitted to outweigh the united testimonies of the greatest men the world has ever seen. The long array of scholars, and poets, and orators, and statesmen, who formed their tastes in the school of antiquity, form a cloud of witnesses, whose testimony goes as far as testimony can.

But I do not think we are able to judge, from the course of classical learning common among us, of its legitimate effects. A few volumes of extracts, some of them containing but poor specimens of the rich literature of the Greeks, constitute the whole mass of reading, by virtue of which we call ourselves classical scholars. Not one graduate in a hundred, probably, from our best colleges, has ever read the entire works of a single Greek author—and yet we do not blush to talk loudly of the uselessness of classical learning. That this department of education ought to be placed on a widely different footing, I have no hesitation in asserting. Instead of confining our courses of what we call a liberal education, to Professor Dalzell's Minora and Majora, or other books of a similar nature, which would answer well enough for elementary works in schools, we must take up the general study of antiquity—read the authors connectedly and entirely—illustrate them by philosophy, politics, geography, history, customs and manners, mythology and religion—and then we may decry, if we will, the advantages of classical learning. In the present day, we not only confine ourselves to the shreds and patches of ancient literature, but are devising new modes to shorten the labor of acquiring this poor supply of 'beggarly elements.' Almost every day presents some wonderful apparatus for attaining, in a few months, a thorough knowledge of Latin or Greek or Hebrew, which, when men could talk Greek, as Cotton Mather says, by the hour, and write Hebrew as fast as their mother tongue, would have entitled them to the penalties attached in those days to the forbidden exercise of unholy powers.

I am no advocate for the old scholastic systems of teaching. I have no wish to see young scholars forced to spend tedious days and months and years, in conning, page after page of barbarous Latinity, before they understand the meaning of a single word. But I do believe, and I think my opinion is borne out by literary history, that the old-fashioned systems, bad, absurd, oppressive, as many of them were, produced better scholars, riper intellects, cooler heads, than any of the labor-saving machines, which have in such multitudes been the playthings of this self-indulging age. I doubt not they have apparently promoted the rapid and easy attainment of learning; but, if they have been successful in the final issue, it has been only through the skill of the teacher and the genius of the learner, which gained the object in spite of them.

If, then, it be a desirable thing that our young scholars should be trained up in classical pursuits, and in such a manner as best to fit them for the duties of life, it is evident a general change must be made, and that change must begin somewhere. Those who are devoted to the business of instruction, must enter more deeply, more philosophically, into the spirit of the classics, than has been common among us in these latter times. We must put forth our best energies to master the treasures of learning, and awaken in our pupils an enthusiasm for similar pursuits. No great object has ever been achieved, no glorious enterprise has ever been accomplished, without the inspiration of an enthusiastic soul to lead onward—to conquer difficulties—to fulfil miracles. No halfway devotion of the powers will win that success which a man of genius may be proud of, in this laborious career. It is no theatre for the labors of him who aims at another and a different profession—it is no stepping-stone to a more elevated position in society. If it were, no man, conscious that he has within him the elements of distinction, would stoop his eagle faculties to an employment, fit only to exercise the genius of a plodder. In the whole circle of the learned professions, I know of none which presents nobler topics of eloquence, more exciting and elevating subjects of reflection—and, I may add, more useful fields of labor, than that of a man of letters. Indolence and stupidity have no part nor lot here—every power is called upon—every moral feeling is confirmed—and every honorable aspiration may be gratified. It is not my purpose to eulogize the profession of a teacher; but when I see many engaging in it with dread, and leaving it with pleasure—when I hear it spoken of as a fit resort for the drudge and the blockhead—I cannot but ask, if the explanation of the great authors of the ancient world—embracing, as it does, such a depth and variety of learning—admitting, as it does, the highest flights of imagination and eloquence—employing, as it does, thousands of the first intellects of the first intellectual country on earth—I cannot but ask, if it *is* a fit resort for a drudge or a blockhead,—if it *is* a pursuit to be adopted with dread, and relinquished with pleasure. My answer to these questions would be one and decided.

It seems to me, that American intellect enjoys peculiar advantages for its developement. We feel immediately every movement of the spirit of the age; our plastic institutions adapt themselves at once to every improvement: but the danger is lest we mistake empiricism for improvement. If we are careful to adopt the good and avert the evil of our singularly happy situation, our intellectual destiny is fixed. Aloof from the corruptions and quarrels of the old world, we enjoy, as soon as wind and wave can waft them to our shores, the science and the literature, so profusely nurtured in those, their ancient abodes. With ourselves it must remain, to cultivate the manly spirit which is so preeminently the tone of the literature of antiquity.

August 14, 1830.

MR ADAMS' LECTURE.

LECTURE XIII.

ON THE CONSTRUCTION AND FURNISHING OF SCHOOL ROOMS; AND ON SCHOOL APPARATUS.

BY WILLIAM J. ADAMS.

Among the means of instruction hitherto deemed but secondary, or overlooked as insignificant, may be mentioned the construction, furniture, and apparatus of school-houses. To many, even at this moment, the whole subject appears unprofitable and barren. 'Why waste time,' says one, 'in a grave disquisition upon black-boards and birch rods? The pegs for the hats, and the semicircles for the toes, are they not described in the books of Bell and Lancaster?'—'What matter,' demands another, '*where* the child gets learning, provided he actually gets it? The Athenian sage gave lessons in the fields;—and in this very city, the Athens of New England, the best of schools is found in the worst of buildings.'—'Observe,' says a third, 'the spirit of the age! In these mechanical, labor-saving times, we must have a *mill*, in which to *grind* scholars;—something in which the moving power is no longer the unfailing stream of patient, sound instruction,—a *machine*, in fact, which steam may turn, and a child direct.'

Such levity, let us pardon and dismiss. It is not my design to give an undue consequence to trifles. In the great cause, which it is the object of this convention to advance, a deep and unusual interest begins to pervade our land; and the improved vision, which magnifies and more highly appreciates the end, discerns more clearly the importance of the means. I call my brethren to witness, whether the embarrassment arising from an ill-constructed school-room deserves to be called a *trifle*. Is there nothing desirable in a quiet location—in pure air, agreeable temperature, ample space, and sufficient light?—in seats and desks adapted to the comfort and health of the pupils, and to the best modes of preserving order, and communicating knowledge?

Absolutely, therefore, as well as relatively, the subject is one of high importance, and deserving of more respectful attention than it has yet received in New-England. *School architecture*, among us, is an art, of which one man knows as much, or rather as little, as another. A school-house is to be erected. Observe the process. The affair is entrusted to a building committee;—patrons of learning, indeed, but wholly unpractised in the routine of schools. These worthy men, faithful economists of the public money, proceed to calculate the greatest number of children that can exist in a given space. Each has his own favorite plan, in the very novelty of which he has found amusement, yet is courteous enough to yield something to the rest;—and thus, an edifice, monstrously inconvenient, and without unity of design, is the harmonious result.

The want of certain rules and fixed principles in the construction of school-houses, is at length beginning to be felt. School-rooms have been remodelled, new ones are visited, and plans are in demand. It is my present purpose rather to introduce the subject to the notice of the convention, and to commend it to the consideration of every member, than to afford any valuable information upon it. It must remain for future lecturers, to lay before you opinions longer agitated, better sanctioned, and more profitable, of course, than the crude hints of an individual.

In the construction of school-houses, it were vain to expect a perfect uniformity. The arrangement of rooms must vary, not only with the mode of instruction, but with the number, age, sex, studies, and classification of the pupils. Arrangements widely different from each other may, indeed, sometimes prove equally good. There are, nevertheless, several established principles which apply to every case.*

In erecting a school-house, the first object is its *location*. This should, if possible, be quiet and retired. The ground should be dry, the air pure, and surrounding objects agreeable. For the same reasons that it is desirable to procure a teacher of pleasing address and happy temper, all other means of endearing the spot, and investing it with pleasant associations, should be diligently sought. This consideration is often overruled by the absurd demand for a situation precisely *central*; and thus the school-house, instead of being placed on a quiet hill-side, where oaks wave and birds sing, stands far down the valley, echoing forever the din of the blacksmith, and the roar of the factory. In cities, retirement is generally out of the question. Yet even here, it were desirable that the access should be through an arched way or alley, to a spacious court within. Such retirement would be worth more than the most advantageous display that could be made of the building as a public edifice. To spare the student the annoyance of stages passing every hour, and '*hourlies*' every fifteen minutes, it would be well if that part of the street against which the school-house stands, were *macadamized*. Some protection might be found in placing the building, if oblong, with an end, rather than a side, towards the street.

Every school-house should have its *play-ground*. This should not lie in front of the building, especially in cities, un-

---

* Some of these may be found in the School Manuals. There is a valuable article upon the subject in the School Magazine, No. 1, published as an appendage to the Journal of Education in April, 1829.—Wilson's Manual has lately been republished in New York, with improvements adapted to the Infant Schools of the United States, and contains an excellent plan for the construction of a building for this class of schools.

less screened from the street by a high wall, or fence. A large space should if possible be planked, or paved with bricks, and a portion sheltered by a roof. Here should be a pump, with good water, and some of the cheapest and least perilous articles of gymnastic apparatus.

In considering the interior of the 'noisy mansion,' we have to solve a variety of problems. Is it an infant school, or a high school?—for males, or females?—in town, or country?—Is the course of study limited or extensive?—the instruction given by several professors, each engaged in a separate field, and requiring his separate recitation-room?—or is the whole business conducted, as in mutual instruction, in a spacious hall, and under a single head?

Under all varieties, there is one point which should never be neglected; viz. *ventilation*. In the pressure of recitations, and the ardor of business, teachers are apt to overlook several of these minor points, less momentous, indeed, than the sciences they teach and yet perfectly indispensable. It is not my present business to treat of physical education, and I shall only notice two valuable modes of ventilation that are getting much into use; 1st. that of making the windows so as to be easily let down at top, and, 2dly. that of having oval apertures in the ceiling, for the escape of impure or heated air.

In this connexion, may be mentioned the *warming* of school-rooms. Fire-places are in general preferable to stoves, and open stoves to close ones. In sea-ports, however, there is less expense, if not less trouble, in the use of coal, than in that of wood. When a close stove is used, it should be placed in a corner of the room, against a fire-proofed wall, and very near the door, through which, when opened, the current of air shall pass between the stove and the pupils. This is admirably arranged in the Boylston School of this city. When a fire-place, or open stove is used, there should be behind the chimney, a space, or chamber of brick, communicating with the external atmosphere. Into this, according to well-known principles, the cold air rushes from without, becomes heated, and sends into the room, through orifices in the jambs, an agreeable and wholesome warmth. In the English High School of Boston, this is the only heat obtained, the furnace being in the cellar, and the warm and rarefied air ascending into the different rooms through flues built into the walls.

To regulate the temperature, whether in summer or winter, every school-room should be furnished with a thermometer.

A great error in the construction of the school-houses of Boston, and with which, it is believed, those of New York and Philadelphia are much less chargeable, is the want of *sufficient space*. More pupils are crowded into one room than is consistent either with comfort or health. Ample room is important from other considerations besides that of mere ventilation. Beyond a certain limit of numbers, or rather a certain proportion of numbers to the whole area of the floor, all the school evolutions become embarrassed. If possible, the number of seats should be such as to leave space for the whole school to come out, if required, and stand in straight lines, or in semicircles, to recite. I would not here be understood to prescribe the mode of conducting recitations, but only to recommend the amount of space to be reserved. In large buildings, one end should be partitioned off, making one or more class-rooms, without desks, and merely for the purpose of conducting a recitation in greater retirement. This point is very conspicuous in the High Schools of New York. Judging from my own observation, those schools are conducted with peculiar ease, and wear the most cheerful aspect, where there is a wide passage between the body of desks and the wall, quite round the room. In monitorial instruction, this allowance of space is indispensable, and, under any system, it is desirable, both on account of the increased airiness of the room, and as furnishing an agreeable promenade for the pupils in inclement weather. The space thus reserved is also valuable for the convenience of public exhibitions, for which the schools of Boston appear to make no provision.

To exhibit the comparative liberality of different cities in their allowance of space to schools, I have collected the following facts.

The Bowdoin School, Boston, 66 ft. by 33, receives 300 pupils on a floor.
" Franklin School, Boston, 60 ft. by 40, " 300 "
" Locust St. School, Philad. 80 ft. by 50, " 320 "
" Providence High School, 98 ft. by 40, " 250 "
" N. York Male High School, 72 ft. by 47 " 200 "

Dividing the space among the pupils who occupy it, gives to each pupil in the Bowdoin School 7¼ square feet.*
" Franklin, " 8 " "
" Locust St. " 12 " "
" Providence High, " 12 " "
" New York High, " 16 " "

Of these,* the minimum is *seven and a quarter* feet; the maximum, *sixteen*. Joseph Lancaster, the greatest of school economists, in his arrangements for cheap and extensive charity-schools, allows to each pupil *nine* feet.

It is often found inconvenient to occupy a considerable portion of the floor, owing to its proximity to the windows. It may here be recommended as an improvement, to place the windows at a greater height than has been customary. A space of wall under the windows, is thus furnished for hanging maps, pictures, printed lessons, black-boards, or, if necessary, hats and coats. Another advantage is, that the windows may be opened, if thus placed, with less danger from cold air; and a third, that the attention of the children is less liable to be diverted by objects out of doors. The height of the window-sill from the floor, should be at least five feet.

It is a custom of long standing, to place the seats and desks upon an *inclined floor*, or a series of gradually ascending platforms, for the purpose of giving the teacher a facility of seeing all his pupils at one view. This I deem unnecessary, except when the floor is of very great extent. It is more convenient, and far less expensive, to increase the elevation of the master's desk. It is surprising how small an elevation of the platform will suffice to give him a free inspection of the whole school.

* In obtaining these results, the space used for entries has been uniformly deducted.

Eighteen inches is generally sufficient, though in some schools I have found it three feet. A level floor affords the most space for air, and with it, the advantage of high windows, just mentioned, is the more easily secured.

There is still another evil attending the inclined plane. As heated air rises to the highest level, it has been observed in rooms warmed by a current of such air received from furnaces, that children suffer from cold in the lowest seats, and from heat in the highest, at the same moment.

There is, however, one case in which the inclined plane offers an important advantage. In producing the desired inclination, the beams of the floor may be so framed as to afford the advantage of an arch, and thus, in a building of more than one story, to prevent the necessity of disfiguring any of the rooms by pillars. Diagram, No. 1, represents a construction of

No. 1.

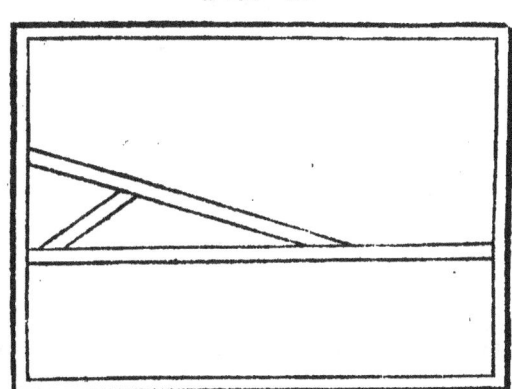

this kind. The sleepers, together with their braces being mortised into the beams, the floor is rendered perfectly firm and inflexible. Where the height of the several stories will permit, plan No. 2, is much to be preferred. A level floor is here

No. 2.

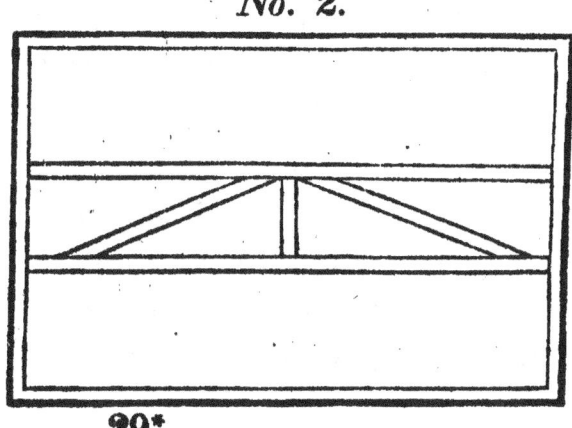

retained, at the same time that its strength is greatly increased, and the walls are secured from lateral pressure. The loss of the space left between the upper floor and lower ceiling, is still further compensated by a construction which renders the noise of feet above, imperceptible below. This space, in ordinary cases, needs not exceed two feet.

The next point to be considered is the construction of *seats* and *desks*. The most economical, not only of room, but of the quantity and expense of material, is, doubtless, that ancient form, in which the seat occupied by a row of pupils is attached to a desk of the same length immediately behind,—which supports the back. The inconveniences of this arrangement are obvious. As there is no precise length of seat appropriated to each individual, much crowding must occur. Most of the pupils, in order to leave their seats, must interrupt their neighbours by climbing up behind them. There must necessarily be many, whom the teacher cannot approach near enough, either to inspect their work, or to render them assistance. There is, however, one case, in which this form is preferable to any other; viz. in mere *recitation-rooms*, or those in which large numbers assemble to hear a lecture, or a declamation.

The most modern construction appears to be that of detaching the seat occupied by each pupil both from the desk behind, and from the other seats;—the desks themselves remaining continuous, as before. The seats are made without backs, and behind them is a passage for walking. In this way each child is *insulated*, is perfectly accessible, and can leave his place at any time without interrupting his class-mates. This arrangement is favorable to the coolness and general comfort of the pupils, as well as to the preservation of order. Each seat should be about eight inches distant from the next in the same row, and the passage behind should be twelve inches wide. The seat itself is either a piece of plank, nine inches by twelve, with the corners rounded off, nailed upon a firm pedestal; or, it may be simply a *box* without a cover, made to stand upon one end, and fastened to the floor. The open side is in front, and within is a hook for hanging a hat.

To the plan just described there is still one objection; viz. the want of some support for the back. This want may be supplied by the upward continuation of the board which forms the rear of the box,—perpendicularly, so as not to encroach upon the passage behind, and so low as to reach only the hollow of the back of the child, without touching the shoulder-blade.

If, after all, we regard cheapness, and the facility of sweeping the floor,—matters of some importance in a large school, and in a great degree sacrificed in the construction last mentioned,—there is still a modification of the old plan, which may be sometimes found preferable to all others. It is that in which the length of each desk with its seat, is made sufficient for only two pupils. By means of the *transverse* passages thus formed, and without passages in the rear, the teacher may readily place himself at the side of any individual, and the pupil is at the same time exempt from the painful durance of the old form. If, therefore, instead of passages of twelve inches behind the seats, we suppose these transverse passages of sixteen inches, the area gained will be equivalent to a space twelve inches long by four inches in width, for every pupil. This construction may sometimes be still further improved, by leaving the front row of desks without transverse intersections, and allowing it the rear passage. A recitation bench is in front of all, upon which a class may sit, free from the interruption of other boys, who, in coming in or going out, might be obliged to pass between the master and his class.

A convenient rule for regulating the height of seats and desks, is, to suppose the former of such a height that the knee shall be bent at a right angle, the foot resting firmly on the floor. If, then, the pupil sit perfectly upright, the place of the elbow will indicate the true level for the *edge* of the desk. Each desk should have a slope, but so slight that books and slates may not slide off.

The inkstands need be nothing more than a small cup, fitted into a hole bored through the wood, but so loosely as to be easily taken out for the purpose of filling. They may be covered, as in Mr G. F. Thayer's School, with wooden slides, or, as in the Boylston School, with a metallic lid resembling a common butt hinge.

The desk may either have a shelf beneath, or it may be a box, of which the lid is the cover. By the former modes much noise is prevented, while the latter is more favorable to neatness and good order in depositing the books. Locks and keys are unnecessary, and the frequent losing of keys is found to cause much trouble. The noise of desk-lids may be diminished by nailing list under the edges. Through the highest level of each desk a groove should be cut, forming a deposit for the slate, which, when thus placed, is always at hand, yet takes up little space, and is out of the way.

It remains to add some remarks upon School Apparatus.

For many a generation, this was simply the *book* and the *ferule*. Wisdom has at length listened to Philosophy, and borrowed from her various other implements, which she now substitutes occasionally for both. Sensible objects, judiciously selected, and properly exhibited to the young student, are found to contribute wonderfully to his advancement in all good learning. In fact, books and lectures, without these means of illustration, are precept without example; theory without practice; uninteresting, hard to be understood, and soon forgotten. The ruinous practice of requiring the assent of children to abstract truths before they have been made acquainted with particular facts, is happily going into disuse. Children are now permitted, to some extent, to gather knowledge as men do. Let us encourage this reasonable revolution. Let children have opportunity to see, think, and judge for themselves, and their increased vigor of mind, and early force of character, will doubtless raise them, under judicious guidance, to the rank designed for them by their Creator. The world is full of apparatus;—but the teacher, in times past, has been too slothful, or too dogmatical, even to point to it. If unprovided with an artificial globe, he could not think even to buy an orange, and draw upon it with his pen an outline of the continents;—much less, besides this, to take off the rind, and illustrate the projection of maps. If the boy had to learn geographical definitions, he could not guess their meaning, or perhaps he entirely misapprehended it. 'The earth is *spherical*,' said the pupil, 'i. e. *round*,' said the master,—(if he said anything at all,)— and the child readily assented, all the time understanding by this globe, a circular plane,—or, to mention the writer's own early experience, a hollow ball,—half filled with earth, upon the level surface of which, he himself was standing, while the shell above him formed the sky!

Infant schools, particularly, require much apparatus. The room should abound in specimens and pictures,—exhibiting the various trades of men, the costumes of nations, the habits of animals,—and illustrating all the simpler laws of the universe.

To proceed to schools of a higher grade, still keeping within the range of things practicable in what are called common schools, I shall conclude with mentioning the most essential articles:

1st. A *Time-piece*,—placed so as to be easily seen by the whole school. The advantage thus gained consists in the tendency to produce habits of punctuality and dispatch.

2d. *Maps* and *Globes*,—and in general, any other apparatus, provided it be simple and cheap, which helps to explain the great phenomena of the earth. Many valuable articles of this kind, designed for common schools, have been made under the direction of Mr Holbrook, and are for sale in this city.

3d. *The Black-board.*—One or more of these should be found in every school. For the facility it affords the teacher in making illustrations and in exhibiting the proficiency of pupils, this piece of school-furniture is almost invaluable. In some schools, it has been deemed so important as to form part of the *wall*, all round the room. Its uses are not confined to arithmetic and algebra, but are important in geography, astronomy, grammar, translation, drawing, penmanship, and almost every other branch.

4th. The *Abacus*, or *Numeral Frame*.—This 'consists of a square frame, divided by ten strong wires, each of which passes through ten painted wooden balls, easily moveable from one end to the other.' This instrument is highly useful in illustrating the various combinations of numbers. Its use is, nevertheless, found injurious, if continued beyond a certain period,—and should be occasionally dispensed with, from the first.

It is not my business to speak of all the conveniences desirable in schools conducted in peculiar modes. Infant schools, and monitorial instruction, require their appropriate apparatus; and are topics so extensive, as justly, in the opinion of our Committee, to demand a distinct consideration. Neither is it within the limits of this lecture to mention all the apparatus proper for schools of the highest grade. It is not our colleges, so much as the common schools of our country, that claim the earliest care of this association. I feel justified, therefore, in having solicited your undivided attention, for the present, to this latter and far wider field. Beyond this I shall go no farther than to call your attention to the *optical instruments* manufactured by Pike, of New York; the *air-pumps*, by Mason of Philadelphia, and to the originality and surprising simplicity exhibited in the *pneumatic apparatus* and *steam engine*, made by Messrs Codman and Claxton of this city.

In laying these suggestions before the association, I feel much diffidence, when I consider that many who have heard them, are quite as familiar with the subject as myself. Yet I offer no apology,—feeling assured that Science will not frown on the humblest attempt to enlarge and beautify her temples.

CONSTITUTION

OF THE

AMERICAN INSTITUTE

OF

INSTRUCTION.

PREAMBLE.

WE, whose names are hereunto subjoined, pledging our zealous efforts to promote the cause of popular education, agree to adopt the following Constitution, and to obey the By-Laws made in conformity thereto.

ART. I.—NAME AND OBJECT.

THE Society shall be known by the title of the AMERICAN INSTITUTE OF INSTRUCTION. Its object shall be the diffusion of useful knowledge in regard to education.

ART. II.—MEMBERS.

1. Any gentleman of good moral character, interested in the subject of Education, may become a member of this Institute, by signing this Constitution, and paying, at the time of his admission, a fee of one dollar.

2. An annual assessment of one dollar, shall be laid upon each member; by neglecting to pay which, for more than one year after due notice from the Treasurer, he shall cease to be a member of the Society.

3. Any gentleman, by paying at one time the sum of twenty dollars, shall become a member of the Institute for life, and be exempted from all future assessments.

4. Honorary members may be elected by the Institute, at the recommendation of two thirds of the Directors present at any stated meeting of that Board.

5. For dishonorable or immoral conduct, a member may be dismissed from the society, by a vote of two thirds of the members present, at any regular meeting.

6. Ladies, engaged in the business of instruction, shall be invited to hear the annual address, lectures, and reports of committees on subjects of Education.

Art. III.—MEETINGS.

1. The annual meeting of the Institute shall be held at Boston, on the Thursday next preceding the last Wednesday in August, at such place and hour as the Board of Directors shall order.

2. Special meetings may be called by the Directors.

3. Due notice of the meetings of the Society shall be given in the public journals.

Art. IV.—OFFICERS.

1. The officers of the Society shall be a President, Vice Presidents, a Recording Secretary, two Corresponding Secretaries, a Treasurer, three Curators, three Censors, and twelve Counsellors, who shall constitute a Board of Directors.

2. The officers shall be elected annually, in August, by ballot.

Art. V.—DUTIES OF OFFICERS.

1. The President, or, in his absence, one of the Vice Presidents, or, in their absence, a President *pro tempore*, shall preside at the meetings of the Institute.

2. The Recording Secretary shall notify all meetings of the Society, and of the Board of Directors; and he shall keep a record of their transactions.

3. The Corresponding Secretaries, subject to the order of the Board of Directors, shall be the organs of communication with other Societies, and with individuals.

4. The Treasurer shall collect and receive all moneys of the Institute, and shall render an accurate statement of all his receipts and payments, annually, and whenever called upon by the Board of Directors; to whom he shall give such bonds for the faithful performance of his duty, as they shall require. He shall make no payment except by their order.

5. To the Board of Directors shall be entrusted the general interests of the Society, with authority to devise and carry into execution such measures as may promote its objects. It shall be their duty to appoint some suitable person to deliver an address before the Institute, at their annual meeting; to select competent persons to serve on Standing Committees, or to deliver lectures on such subjects relating to education as they may deem expedient and useful; to collect such facts, as may promote the general objects of the Society; and to provide convenient accommodations for the meetings. They shall, at the annual meeting, exhibit their records, and report to the Institute. They shall have power to fill all vacancies in their Board, from members of the Society, and make By-Laws for its government.

6. It shall be the particular duty of the Curators to select books, and to take charge of the library of the Institute.

7. The Censors shall have authority to procure for publication the annual address and lectures. It shall be their duty to examine the annual reports of the Standing Committees, and all other communications made to the Society; and to publish such of them, as, in their estimation, may tend to throw light on the subject of Education, and aid the faithful instructer in the discharge of his duty.

8. It shall be the duty of the President, the Vice Presidents, and Counsellors, severally, to recommend to the consideration of the Board of Directors, such subjects of inquiry, as, in their opinion, may best advance the great objects of the Institute.

9. Stated meetings of the Board of Directors shall be held at Boston, on the first Wednesday in January; on the last Wednesday in May; and on the day next preceding that of the annual meeting of the Institute, in August.

Art. VI.—BY-LAWS AND AMENDMENTS.

1. By-Laws, not repugnant to this Constitution, may be adopted at any regular meeting.

2. This Constitution may be altered or amended, by a vote of two thirds of the members present at the annual meeting, provided two thirds of the Directors, present at a stated meeting, shall agree to recommend the proposed alteration or amendment.

BY-LAWS.*

1. ON A QUORUM.

At all meetings of the Board of Directors, seven members shall be necessary to constitute a quorum for the transaction of business.

2. COMMITTEE OF FINANCE.

The Board of Directors shall annually choose a Committee of Finance, whose duty it shall be to audit the accounts of the Treasurer, and, under control of the Board of Directors, to draw orders on the Treasurer for the payment of charges against the Institute.

3. SPECIAL MEETINGS.

It shall be the duty of the Recording Secretary, on application of any two members of the Board, to call special meetings of the Board of Directors.

* Adopted August 24, 1830.

OFFICERS

OF THE

AMERICAN INSTITUTE OF INSTRUCTION,

FOR THE YEAR 1830—1831.

PRESIDENT.

FRANCIS WAYLAND, jr. President of Brown University, Providence, Rhode Island.

VICE PRESIDENTS.

WILLIAM B. CALHOUN, Springfield, Massachusetts.
WILLIAM SULLIVAN, Boston, Massachusetts.
JOHN ADAMS, Andover, Massachusetts.
JOHN PARK, Boston, Massachusetts.
NATHAN LORD, President of Dartmouth College, Hanover, New Hampshire.
THOMAS H. GALLAUDET, Hartford, Connecticut.
ANDREW YATES, Chittenengo, New York.
THEODORE FRELINGHUYSEN, Newark, New Jersey.
ROBERTS VAUX, Philadelphia, Pennsylvania.
WILLIAM C. FOWLER, Middlebury, Vermont.
REUBEN HAINES, Germantown, Pennsylvania.
BENJAMIN O. PEERS, Lexington, Kentucky.
NATHAN GUILFORD, Cincinnati, Ohio.

RECORDING SECRETARY.

GIDEON F. THAYER, Boston, Massachusetts.

CORRESPONDING SECRETARIES.

Solomon P. Miles, Boston, Massachusetts.
William C. Woodbridge, Hartford, Connecticut.

TREASURER.

Benjamin D. Emerson, Boston, Massachusetts.

CURATORS.

Abraham Andrews, Boston, Massachusetts.
Josiah Holbrook, Boston, Massachusetts.
William Russell, Milton, Massachusetts.

CENSORS.

Ebenezer Bailey, Boston, Massachusetts.
Jacob Abbot, Boston, Massachusetts.
George B. Emerson, Boston, Massachusetts.

COUNSELLORS.

William J. Adams, New York, New York.
James G. Carter, Lancaster, Massachusetts.
Joseph Emerson, Weathersfield, Connecticut.
Cornelius C. Felton, Cambridge, Massachusetts.
William Forrest, New York, New York.
Walter R. Johnson, Philadelphia, Pennsylvania.
J. Kingsbury, Providence, Rhode Island.
Samuel P. Newman, Professor in Bowdoin College, Brunswick, Maine.
Henry K. Oliver, Salem, Massachusetts.
Asa Rand, Boston, Massachusetts.
O. A. Shaw, Richmond, Virginia.
Elipha White, John's Island, South Carolina.

NEW WORKS IN PRESS,

AND

BOOKS PUBLISHED AND FOR SALE,

BY

HILLIARD, GRAY & CO.

BOSTON.

 Retail price.

Abbott on Shipping, a new and much improved edition. By Judge Story	sheep	$7 50
Abbott's Letters from Cuba,	boards	2 00
A Year in Spain, a new edition, 2 vols.	boards	2 00
American First Class Book, by Pierpont,	sheep	1 00
American Popular Lessons,	half bound	50
Allen's Easy Lessons in Geography,	paper	18¾
Adams' Lectures, 2 vols.	sheep	5 00
A System of Artillery Tactics,	sheep	1 00
Abstract of Infantry Tactics,	sheep	75

☞ *These works are the same as those furnished the United States by contract for the use of the militia.*

Angell on Tide Waters,	sheep	3 00
Do. on Adverse Enjoyment,	sheep	1 50
Do. Essay on the Right of States to Tax a Body Corporate,	paper	37½
Do. on Limitations,	sheep	5 00
Do. on Corporations, in press,		
Buttman's Greek Grammar, 8vo.	sheep	2 00
Do. do. do. 12mo. abridged,	sheep	62½
Bigelow's Plants of Boston,	boards	2 75
Bible, 8vo. fine Boston edition, with Apocrypha,	sheep	3 50
Do. 8vo. without Apocrypha,	sheep	3 25
Burlamaqui's Law, 2 vols.	sheep	4 50
Brown's Philosophy, by Hedge, 2 vols.	boards	4 50
Botta's History of the American Revolution, translated by G. A. Otis, 2 vols. second edition,	boards	6 00
Boyer's French and English Dictionary,	sheep	5 00
Book for Massachusetts' Children,	half bound	62½
Bayley on Bills, with Phillips' and Sewall's notes,	sheep	4 00
Bishop Butler's Works, 2 vols.	boards	3 00
Baylie's History of Plymouth, 2 vols.	boards	5 00
Bigelow's Digest of Mass. Reports,	calf	9 00

HILLIARD, GRAY & CO.'S PUBLICATIONS.

Retail price.

Title	Binding	Price
Bigelow's Supplement or Digest of Pickering's Reports,	sheep	3 50
Bourdon's Algebra, by Prof. Farrar, in press,		
Brunton's Mechanic's Text Book,	sheep	75
Blair's Probate Digest,	sheep	2 75
Cubi's Traducteur François,	sheep	1 50
Do. do. Espanole,	sheep	1 50
Do. Latin Translator,	sheep	1 25
Cleveland's Grecian Antiquities, new edition, in press,		
Cummings' Geography and Atlas,	half bound	1 37½
Do. Spelling Book,	half bound	25
Do. First Lessons,	paper	25
Do. Testament, fine,	calf	1 25
Do. do. coarse,	sheep	75
Do. Questions on New Testament,	paper	37½
Do. Ancient Atlas,	paper	87½
Colburn's Arithmetic,	half bound	37½
Do. Plates to do.	paper	12½
Do. Sequel,	sheep	1 00
Do. Key to Sequel,	half bound	75
Do. Algebra,	sheep	1 25
Do. Key to Algebra,	half bound	75
Do. First Lessons in Reading and Grammar, in press,		
Do. Second, do. do. do.		
Do. Third, do. do. do.		
Cornelius Nepos, a new edition,	sheep	75
Cleaveland's Mineralogy, 2 vols. new edition, in press,		
Calculus,	boards	1 50
Cambridge Mathematics, 2 vols. by Prof. Farrar,	sheep	7 00
Channing's Catechism,	paper	06¼
Cæsar's Commentaries, with English notes,	sheep	1 37½
Child's Companion, new edition,	half bound	12½
Cicero's Orations, stereotype edition,	sheep	1 50
Catechism on the Constitution of the U. S.	hlf. bd.	37½
Carter's Geography of Massachusetts with a Map,	half bound	75
Children's Robinson Crusoe,	cloth	1 25
Disorders of Literary Men,	boards	62½
Dana's Questions to Gould's Latin Grammar,	paper	31
Davis's Criminal and Civil Justice, new edition,	sheep	4 50
Dane's Abridgement of American Law, 9 vols.	sheep	56 50
English and Italian Phrase Book, by Bossut,	half bound	37½
Elements of Technology, by Dr. Bigelow,	cloth	4 00
Enfield's Philosophy,	sheep	7 50
Electricity and Magnetism, by Prof. Farrar,	boards	3 50
Euler's Algebra, by Prof. Farrar,	boards	1 50
Engineering, translated from the French of Sganzin,	boards	2 00
Easy Lessons in Perspective,	cloth	62
Flint's Travels,	boards	2 25
Do. Geog. and Hist. of West. States, 2 vols. 8vo.	boards	6 00

HILLIARD, GRAY & CO.'S PUBLICATIONS.

		Retail price.
French Phrase Book, by Bossut,	half bound	37½
Fowle's French Accidence,	cloth	37½
Do. French Writing Exercises, adapted to the above,	cloth	37½
Francis Berrian, 2 vols.	boards	2 00
Filial Affection,	half bound	75
Fisk's Greek Grammar.	sheep	1 25
Do. Greek Exercises, in press,		
Do. Key to Greek Exercises, in press,		
Fowle's New English Grammar, 2d part,	hf. bd.	37½
Four Gospels and Lexicon, Greek,	sheep	2 25
Farrar's Astronomy,	boards	3 75
Fischer's Elements of Nat. Philos. by Prof. Farrar,	boards	3 00
Greenwood's Lives of the Apostles,	boards	75
Grove's Greek and English Dictionary,	sheep	3 75
Do. Greek and English Dictionary, fine paper,	sheep	4 50
Geneva Catechism, Part 1.	paper	10
Greek Reader, by F. Jacobs, a new edition,	sheep	2 25
German Grammar, by Dr Follen, 2d edition,	boards	1 50
German Reader, by Dr Follen 2d edition,	boards	1 25
German and English Phrase Book, in press,		
Gould's Latin Grammar,	sheep	1 00
Do. Virgil, with English notes, 8vo.	sheep	3 50
Do. Virgil, with English notes, 12mo	sheep	2 25
Do. Ovid, with English notes,	sheep	1 25
Do Horace, with English notes,	sheep	1 75
Graglia's Italian and English Dictionary improved,	sheep	2 25
Græca Minora,	sheep	2 25
Græca Majora, 2 vols.	sheep	7 00
Gerard's Institutes,	boards	2 25
German Popular Stories,	boards	75
Hobomok,	boards	75
Homer's Iliad, 2 vols. with English notes, in press,		
Hedge's Logic, a new stereotype edition,	sheep	87½
Do. Questions to Logic,	paper	12½
Heeren's Greece,	boards	2 25
Hemans' Poems, 8vo. vol. 1.	boards	2 50
Do. do. 8vo. vol. 2, Part I.	boards	1 25
Do. do. 8vo. vol. 2, Part II.	boards	1 25
Do. do. 18mo. 2 vols.	boards	1 75
Do. Earlier Poems, 2 vols. 18mo.	boards	1 75
Do. Hymns,	paper	12½
Haven's Remains, 12mo.	boards	1 50
Haven's Sunday School Address,	paper	12
Hobart's Reports, by Judge Williams,	sheep	7 50
Irving's Elements of English Composition,	sheep	1 25
Improved Guide, by William B. Fowle,	half bound	25
Italian Grammar, by Bachi,	boards	1 75
Inductive Grammar,	half bound	12½
Judith and Esther,	boards	62½
Junius Unmasked,	boards	1 00
Juvenal with English notes,	sheep	1 00
Last Judgment,	boards	62
Linear Drawing, third edition, enlarged,	sheep	87½

HILLIARD, GRAY & CO.'S PUBLICATIONS.

		Retail price.
Latin Reader, Part 1, with English notes,	sheep	87½
Latin Reader, Part 2,	sheep	75
Latin Tutor, new and improved edition,	sheep	1 25
Key to Latin Tutor,	bound	1 00
Lacroix's Arithmetic, by Prof. Farrar,	boards	1 00
Lacroix's and Euler's Algebra, bound together,	sheep	2 50
Lacroix's Algebra, by Prof. Farrar, third edition,	boards	1 50
Laplace's Mécanique Céleste, by Dr Bowditch, vol. 1,	cloth	8 00

☞ *Those who take this vol. must agree to take four more volumes of the same work, if published.*

Letters on the Gospels, by H. Adams,	half bound	50
Long on Sales of Personal Property,	sheep	3 50
Laws of Massachusetts, 2 vols.	sheep	10 00
Do. do. vol. 3,	boards	2 00
Lawyer's Common Place Book,	half bound	3 50
Locke's do. do.	half bound	3 50
Legendre's Geometry, by Professor Farrar, new stereotype edition, with improvements and additions,	boards	2 00
Lectures before American Institute of Instruction 1830,		2 50
Merchant's Memorandum and Price Book,	half bound	75
Do. do. abridged.	half bound	50
Massachusetts Reports, 17 vols.	sheep	100 00
Mason's Reports, vols. 3, 4, and 5,	sheep pr vol.	6 00
Memoirs of Josiah Quincy, Jr.	boards	2 50
Mechanics, by Prof. Farrar,	boards	4 00
Murray's Grammar, improved by Putnam, st. ed.	hlf. bd.	18¾
Do. Introduction, with Definitions,	half bound	37½
Mitford's Pleadings,	sheep	2 50
More's (Hannah) Spirit of Prayer,	boards	62½
New Speaker, by W. B. Fowle,	sheep	1 00
Negris' Modern Greek Grammar,	cloth	75
Do. Edition of Aspasia, a modern Greek Tragedy,	pap.	50
Neuman's Spanish Dictionary, 2 vols. 8vo.	sheep	9 00
Nuttall's Botany,	boards	2 00
National Reader, by Rev. John Pierpont,	sheep	75
Oliver's Am. Precedents of Declarations, new ed.	sheep	6 00
Orations of Æschines and Demosthenes, for the Crown, with English notes for schools and colleges,	sheep	2 25
Optics, 8vo. by Prof. Farrar,	boards	3 00
Orfila on Poisons,	boards	1 25
Phillips' Political Economy,	boards	1 75
Pickering's Greek and English Lexicon, 2d ed.	boards	5 50
Phædrus' Fables, with English notes,	sheep	62½
Parsing Lessons, by John Frost, 2d edition,	paper	12½
Pickering's Reports, 8 vols. 9th vol. in press,	sheep. p.vol.	4 50
Phillips on Insurance,	sheep	6 00
Robinson's Sermons,	boards	1 25
Rational Guide, by W. B. Fowle,	half bound	25
Rhetorical Grammar,	sheep	2 25
Revised Testament,	sheep	50
Robinson's Elementary Lessons in Arithmetic,	hlf. bd.	12½
Sunday Evening Lectures,	boards	31
Saratoga, 2 vols.	boards	2 00
Selections from Fenelon, 2d edition,	boards	1 00
Sugden on Vendors,	sheep	7 50

HILLIARD, GRAY & CO.'S PUBLICATIONS.

		Retail price
Smellie's Philosophy, by Dr Ware,	boards	2 25
Shaler's Algiers, edited by Mr Sparks,	boards	1 75
Starkie's Nisi Prius Reports, 2 vols.	sheep	12 00
Sampson on Common Law,	boards	1 25
Sequel to Frank, 2 vols.	boards	1 50
The Rebels,	boards	1 00
Thiersch's Greek Tables,	boards	75
The Hunter, (a Poem,)	boards	75
Third Class Book,	half bound	37½
Testament, 8vo large type without chapters or verse,	shp.	1 75
Trigonometry, by Prof. Farrar	boards	1 50
Trimmer's Natural History, 200 cuts,	half bound	62½
Topography, by Prof. Farrar,	boards	2 00
Todd's Johnson and Walker's Dictionary combined, medium 8vo.	sheep	5 00
Same work, fine royal 8vo.	calf	6 00
Tacitus, 2 vols. with English notes, in press,		
Tales of the North West,	cloth	1 00
Venice and Genoa, a new translation,	boards	75
Valpy's Greek Grammar,	sheep	1 00
Do. bo. Delectus,	sheep	62
Viri Romæ, with English notes,	sheep	87½
Wordsworth's Works, 4 vols.	boards	6 25
Wilkins' Astronomy,	half bound	87½
Wilbur's Text Book,	half bound	37½
Do. Reference Testament,	half bound	37½
Worcester's (Thomas) Sermons,	paper	37½
Worcester Catechism,	paper	12½
Worcester's Primer, stereotype edition,	paper	12½
Worcester's Geography and Atlas,	sheep	2 00
Do. History and Chart,	sheep	2 75
Do. Questions to Elements of History,	paper	18¾
Do. Sketches, 2 vols.	half bound	3 50
Do. Epitome of Geography and Atlas,	hlf. bd.	1 25
Do. Universal Gazetteer, 2 vols.	sheep	11 00
Do. Illustrations of History,	paper	12½
Do. Epitome of History and Chart,	half bound	1 00
Do. Scripture Geography and Atlas,	paper	37½
Do. School Dictionary,	sheep	1 00
Do. Ancient Atlas,	paper	87½
Do. Outline Atlas,	paper	1 00
Ware's Hints on Extemporaneous Preaching, 3d edition, enlarged,	boards	37½
Xenophon's Anabasis, with English notes,	sheep	1 50
Yelverton's Reports,	sheep	3 50

☞ The prices on the above list are those from which the discounts are made. To those persons who purchase only a few Books, the discount is small; to School Committees and Instructers it is larger, and the most liberal discounts are made to Booksellers, according to the amount taken at one time.

www.ingramcontent.com/pod-product-compliance
Lightning Source LLC
Chambersburg PA
CBHW080051190426

43201CB00035B/2167